City versus Countryside in Mao's China

The gap between those living in the city and those in the countryside remains one of China's most intractable problems. As this powerful work of grassroots history argues, the origins of China's rural-urban divide can be traced back to the Mao Zedong era. While Mao pledged to remove the gap between the city worker and the peasant, his revolutionary policies misfired and ended up provoking still greater discrepancies between town and country, usually to the disadvantage of villagers. Through archival sources, personal diaries, untapped government dossiers, and interviews with people from cities and villages in northern China, the book recounts their personal experiences, showing how they retaliated against the daily restrictions imposed on their activities while traversing between the city and the countryside. Vivid and harrowing accounts of forced and illicit migration, the staggering inequity of the Great Leap Famine, and political exile and deportation during the Cultural Revolution reveal how Chinese people fought back against policies that pitted city dwellers against villagers.

Jeremy Brown is Assistant Professor of Modern Chinese History at Simon Fraser University. He is coeditor, with Paul G. Pickowicz, of *Dilemmas of Victory: The Early Years of the People's Republic of China* (2007), and he has published articles in *Late Imperial China* and the *Copenhagen Journal of Asian Studies*.

City versus Countryside in Mao's China

Negotiating the Divide

JEREMY BROWN
Simon Fraser University

CAMBRIDGE
UNIVERSITY PRESS

32 Avenue of the Americas, New York NY 10013-2473, USA

Cambridge University Press is part of the University of Cambridge.

It furthers the University's mission by disseminating knowledge in the pursuit of education, learning and research at the highest international levels of excellence.

www.cambridge.org
Information on this title: www.cambridge.org/9781107424548

First published 2012
First paperback edition 2014

A catalogue record for this publication is available from the British Library

Library of Congress Cataloguing in Publication data
Brown, Jeremy, 1976–
City versus countryside in Mao's China : negotiating the divide / Jeremy Brown.
p. cm.
Includes bibliographical references and index.
ISBN 978-1-107-02404-5 (hardback)
1. China – Economic conditions – 1949–1976 – Regional disparities. 2. Rural-urban divide – China. 3. Rural-urban relations – China. 4. Tianjin (China) – Social conditions. I. Title
HC427.9.B73 2012
330.95105–DC23 2011045915

ISBN 978-1-107-02404-5 Hardback
ISBN 978-1-107-42454-8 Paperback

Contents

Maps

Tables

Acknowledgments

My first thanks go to Joseph Esherick and Paul Pickowicz, the best mentors a budding historian of modern China could hope for. They encouraged me to pursue post-1949 history, pushed me to become a better writer, demanded that I find unique sources and use them carefully, and were my most loyal advocates and toughest critics. Readers will see their influence on every page of this book.

Michael Schoenhals taught me how to find the sources necessary to write a grassroots history of the People's Republic of China (PRC). Thanks to his encouragement, I got my hands dirty every weekend sifting through files at Tianjin's used book markets. Michael also shared so many of the sources in his own collection that I cannot mention each one individually in the footnotes; instead I offer my appreciation here.

I offer heartfelt thanks to Sigrid Schmalzer, who became my role model the first day I met her, and whose detailed comments on the entire manuscript were incredibly helpful in the last phase of revision. I also very much appreciate extensive feedback from Takashi Fujitani, Joshua Goldstein, Richard Madsen, Nayan Shah, and Steve Smith, who read and commented on the chapters. Many others offered suggestions and pointed questions in classrooms and at conferences, symposia, and workshops over the years, and it is with deep gratitude that I acknowledge their help.

My fantastic colleagues in the history department at Simon Fraser University have been constant reminders of how fortunate I am to have ended up in Burnaby. Felicitas Becker, Andrea Geiger, Thomas Kuehn, Jennifer Spear, and Ilya Vinkovetsky provided valuable feedback on a draft introduction.

Liu Haiyan and Zhang Limin of the Tianjin Academy of Social Sciences' Institute of History opened many doors for me during my research in the city. Wang Hui provided many introductions and valuable knowledge from his time working in the Tianjin Municipal Party Committee. Zheng Wei helped me find my way around Nankai University, where Jiang Pei got me started on Xiaojinzhuang and provided influential advice along the way. I would also like to thank Huang Bo, Flower Zhao, Liu Bingxian, and Zhang Xiaoyan for research assistance.

I cannot name the many people who provided introductions and helped to navigate difficulties in Baodi, Shexian, Shijiazhuang, and the Tianjin suburbs. Their help was vital and I thank them here. I would also like to thank archivists and librarians at the Hebei Provincial Archive, Tianjin Municipal Archive, Hexi District Archive, Tianjin Municipal Library, the National Library in Beijing, and the Universities Service Centre at the Chinese University of Hong Kong.

Research and writing were supported by a Fulbright-Hays Doctoral Dissertation Research Award and a Social Science Research Council International Dissertation Field Research Fellowship with funds provided by the Andrew W. Mellon Foundation, a Doctoral Dissertation Fellowship from the Chiang Ching-kuo Foundation, a UCSD Center for the Humanities Award, and a Simon Fraser University President's Research Start-up Grant.

It has been a pleasure to work with Cambridge University Press. I am deeply thankful for Marigold Acland's energetic advocacy and support, and I very much appreciate Joy Mizan, Sarika Nakula, and Mark Fox's work in moving the book forward. Laura Lawrie has been a fantastic production editor and copy editor, and Enid Zafran worked her magic in creating the index. Funding for indexing was provided by Simon Fraser University's University Publications Fund.

Passages from earlier publications appear in this book, with permission from the original publishers: portions of Chapter 2 are from "The Village in the City: Rural Migrants in 1950s Tianjin," *Chungguksa yongu* [The Journal of Chinese Historical Researches, Taegu, Korea] 40 (February 2006): 383–428, © 2006 by *Chungguksa yongu*. Parts of Chapter 3 first appeared in "Great Leap City: Surviving the Famine in Tianjin," reprinted with permission of the publisher from *Eating Bitterness* edited by Kimberley Ens Manning and Felix Wemheuer © University of British Columbia Press 2010, all rights reserved by the publisher. Some material from Chapter 5 comes from "Burning the Grassroots: Chen Boda and the Four Cleanups in Suburban Tianjin," *Copenhagen Journal of*

Asian Studies 26.1 (2008): 50–69, © 2008 by *Copenhagen Journal of Asian Studies*. Chapter 8 is adapted from "Staging Xiaojinzhuang: The City in the Countryside, 1974–1976," in *The Chinese Cultural Revolution as History*, edited by Joseph W. Esherick, Paul G. Pickowicz, and Andrew Walder © 2006 by the Board of Trustees of the Leland Stanford Jr. University, all rights reserved, used with the permission of Stanford University Press, www.sup.org.

Not every writer is lucky enough to have a mother who also happens to be a professional editor. Carolyn Brown has shaped my writing since I first put crayon to paper, and she still edits everything I send her way, including e-mails about her grandsons. Thanks, Mom.

Laura Benson's influence on this project is deeper than she knows. Her activism taught me to take notice when injustice and inequality are staring me in the face. That's why I wrote this book.

Abbreviations

Frequently cited works are referred to in the notes by the following abbreviations. Whenever possible, I have indicated the repository or published collection. Documents, files, and manuscripts from my own collection are denoted by the abbreviation "AC," for "author's collection."

Citations referring to documents from the Hexi District Archive, Hebei Provincial Archive, and Tianjin Municipal Archive look like this: 1–6–33C. The numbers indicate the batch number (*quanzong hao*), catalog number (*mulu hao*), and file number (*juan hao*), respectively. The letter at the end of the entry refers to the time limit for storage (*baoguan qixian*): "Y" means perpetual (*yongjiu*), "C" means long-term (*changqi*), and "D" is short-term (*duanqi*).

AC	Author's collection
GJG:1	Gao Jianguo. "Xiaojinzhuang de chenfu" [The rise and fall of Xiaojinzhuang]. Pt. 1. *Sanyue feng* 15 (February 1986): 3–17.
GJG:2	Gao Jianguo. "Xiaojinzhuang de chenfu" [The rise and fall of Xiaojinzhuang]. Pt. 2. *Sanyue feng* 16 (March 1986): 6–20.
HDA	Hexi District Archive (Tianjin)
HPA	Hebei Provincial Archive (Shijiazhuang)
HZDSJ	Tianjin shi nongcun hezuo zhi fazhan shi bianji bangongshi, ed. *Tianjin shi nongcun hezuo zhi dashiji: 1949–1987* [Chronology of the Tianjin village cooperative system, 1949–1987]. Tianjin: Tianjin shi nongye hezuo zhi fazhan shi bianji bangongshi, 1988.
MWG	*Jianguo yilai Mao Zedong wengao* [Mao Zedong's manuscripts since the founding of the People's

Republic of China]. 13 vols. Beijing: Zhongyang wenxian chubanshe, 1987–1998.

NBCK *Neibu cankao* [Internal reference]

NCS Tianjin gongnong lianmeng nongmuchang shizhi bangongshi. *Gongnong lianmeng nongchang shi* [History of the worker-peasant alliance farm]. N.p.: Tianjin, 1992.

RMRB *Renmin ribao* [People's Daily]

TJJG Zhonggong Tianjin shiwei dangshi ziliao zhengji weiyuanhui, Tianjin shi dang'anguan, eds. *Tianjin jieguan shilu* [History of the takeover of Tianjin]. 2 vols. Beijing: Zhonggong dangshi chubanshe, 1991, 1994.

TJRB *Tianjin ribao* [Tianjin Daily]

TJWB *Tianjin wanbao* [Tianjin Evening News]

TMA Tianjin Municipal Archive

WDGW Song Yongyi, ed. *Zhongguo wenhua da geming wenku* [Chinese Cultural Revolution database]. Hong Kong: Xianggang Zhongwen daxue Zhongguo yanjiu fuwu zhongxin, 2002. CD-ROM.

ZGSX Zhonggong zhongyang dangxiao dangshi jiaoyan er shi. *Zhongguo gongchandang shehuizhuyi shiqi wenxian ziliao xuanbian* [Selected documentary materials from the Chinese Communist Party's socialist period]. N.p., 1987.

ZYWX Zhonggong zhongyang wenxian yanjiushi, ed. *Jianguo yilai zhongyao wenxian xuanbian* [Selected important documents since the founding of the People's Republic of China]. 20 vols. Beijing: Zhongyang wenxian chubanshe, 1992–1998.

Introduction

Over the summer of 2011, Beijing authorities demolished approximately thirty schools for the children of rural migrant workers, leaving thousands of young students in limbo. Only those children whose migrant parents were able to produce "five documents" (*wu zheng*) affirming their legal residence and proof of employment in the Chinese capital would be allowed to attend other Beijing schools. Few could do so. Of the more than fourteen hundred students at one demolished school, only seventy had parents who had the required papers. The rest were out of luck. They were effectively illegal immigrants in their own country. "I don't get it," the principal of one closed school said with tears in her eyes, "I've been working in schools for migrant children for more than ten years and I've always thought I was doing a good deed. But invariably, they get rid of us."[1]

The gap between city and countryside is one of contemporary China's most pressing social problems. The roots of today's rural-urban divide can be found in the Mao Zedong era (1949–1978). This is puzzling and ironic. Mao led the Chinese Communist Party to power on the strength of a peasant-backed revolution that promised to eliminate the "three great differences" between worker and peasant, city and countryside, and mental and manual labor.[2] But in spite of Maoist programs to redistribute

[1] Shi Minglei, Wang Jialin, and Du Ding, "Jin 30 dagong zidi xiao shoudao guanting tongzhi" [Around 30 schools for the children of migrant workers receive closure notices], *Xinjingbao*, August 16, 2011, A12, http://epaper.bjnews.com.cn/images/2011-08/16/A12/A12816C.pdf

[2] Some writers refuse to translate *nongmin* as "peasant" because the word can be pejorative. I follow Sigrid Schmalzer in using "peasant" because it was an "actors' category"

wealth, encourage rural industry, transfer urban youth to villages, train barefoot doctors, and educate villagers, the Communists ended up sharpening rural-urban difference rather than erasing it. Over the course of the 1950s, 1960s, and 1970s, cities became privileged spaces while villages became dumping grounds. City-dwellers enjoyed special perks while villagers endured bitter sacrifices. Contrary to the wishes of Mao and other top leaders, cities and villages became alienated from one another. This book seeks to explain this process of alienation by focusing on how people experienced it at the grassroots.

Given the challenges and constraints facing the Communists when they assumed power in 1949, the achievements of the Mao era appear all the more remarkable, and it is unfair and unrealistic to bash Mao for failing to completely eradicate inequality.[3] It is fair, however, to ask how the result of the revolution differed so starkly from its originally stated ideals. The answer begins with tension between the Communists' intertwined goals of revolution and modernization. On the one hand, Mao wanted to build a strong, prosperous, and modern nation that would no longer be humiliated by foreign powers. On the other hand, he sought to make China a more equal and fair society by eliminating class exploitation and redistributing property. Mao and his colleagues in party center never saw these goals as mutually exclusive – they thought China could simultaneously become richer and fairer through revolutionary modernization.[4] A widening rural-urban divide was one of the unintended consequences of this revolutionary modernization project.

during the Mao era, and precisely because the word had pejorative connotations during the modern period. To obscure this fact by using equally problematic words like "farmer" would mean sacrificing historicist authenticity. Sigrid Schmalzer, *The People's Peking Man: Popular Science and Human Identity in Twentieth-Century China* (Chicago: University of Chicago Press, 2008), xviii.

[3] By challenges and constraints I mean the effects of a century of war, hunger, instability, and poverty leading up to 1949, plus a massive war against the United States in Korea in the early 1950s. The achievements of the Mao period include increases in life expectancy and literacy, and also laying the foundation for rapid economic development after 1978. See Barry Naughton, *The Chinese Economy: Transitions and Growth* (Cambridge, MA: MIT Press, 2007), 82; and Chris Bramall, *In Praise of Maoist Economic Planning: Living Standards and Economic Development in Sichuan since 1931* (New York: Oxford University Press, 1993).

[4] Referring to the shared goals of "Mao and his colleagues" is, of course, an oversimplification that obscures heated policy debates among central leaders. Top officials during the Mao period, however, were consistently committed to revolutionary modernization. Their debates were about how to reach their goals and whether class struggle or careful state planning deserved more emphasis.

My use of the word "unintended" to describe the deepening rural-urban divide under Mao should not be read as an attempt to apologize for or defend the staggering human costs of the Great Leap famine and the Cultural Revolution. The evidence is clear: Mao and other leaders often displayed a callous disregard for human suffering, and were particularly cavalier about the lives of rural people. But condemning Mao as fundamentally evil or equating him with Hitler, as some scholars have done, actually hampers our understanding of modern Chinese history.[5] Debating whether Mao was a great leader or an evil dictator equivalent to Hitler sheds no light on how people in China experienced life during the period of his rule. Focusing instead on unintended consequences means that I take Mao's goals seriously, assess how his projects went so wrong, and focus on how people dealt with the fallout.

The pages that follow tell the story of how people in the Tianjin region of north China negotiated the rural-urban gap in their everyday lives. Rather than a case study of a single city or village, this is a book about interaction between the two realms. Examining rural-urban interaction during the Mao period shows how individuals created and contested a divided society of privileged urban citizens and second-class peasants. The most significant structural factors in creating the divide were the two-tiered household registration (*hukou*) system and grain rationing regime, which classified every individual in China according to rural or urban residence.[6] Household registration was gradually implemented during the 1950s, first as a way for police to monitor the population amid fears of counterrevolutionary sabotage, and later as a way to stem the influx of rural migrants seeking work in cities. It was not until the early 1960s that central leaders firmly institutionalized the *hukou* system in response to the starvation and massive population dislocation of the Great Leap famine. Planners in Beijing attributed the Great Leap crisis to a lack of centralized control over the labor force. Their solution was to attempt to fix everyone in place. An urban, or "non-agricultural"

[5] One of the most recent and influential demonizations of Mao is Jung Chang and Jon Halliday, *Mao: The Unknown Story* (New York: Knopf, 2005).

[6] Important works about the systemic dimensions of this two-tiered society include Martin King Whyte and William L. Parish, *Urban Life in Contemporary China* (Chicago: University of Chicago Press, 1984); R. J. R. Kirkby, *Urbanization in China: Town and Country in a Developing Economy, 1949–2000 A.D.* (New York: Columbia University Press, 1985); Andrew G. Walder, *Communist Neo-Traditionalism: Work and Authority in Chinese Industry* (Berkeley: University of California Press, 1986); and Sulamith Heins Potter and Jack M. Potter, *China's Peasants: The Anthropology of a Revolution* (New York: Cambridge University Press, 1990), especially 296–312.

(*fei nongye*) classification guaranteed food rations, housing, health care, and education to city residents. Families holding "agricultural" (*nongye*) *hukou* were expected to be self-reliant and were restricted from moving to cities.[7]

This systemic inequality was justified by the socialist planned economy's emphasis on heavy urban industry. Why stress city factories? In the face of national security threats, top leaders argued, China had to become stronger and more modern before it could eliminate the "three great differences." So China emulated the Soviet Union's path of expropriating grain from the countryside in order to develop heavy industry. Top-down planning put rural people at the bottom of the economic and political hierarchy, and had the practical effect of turning a diverse rural population into "peasants" tied to agricultural collectives that produced grain for the state.[8] As Jacob Eyferth writes, "In the view of Chinese state planners, modernity lay in the rational division of the economy into discrete, hierarchically ordered jurisdictions, arranged and interlinked in such a way that a person at the top could trace and direct the flow of resources through the system."[9] People "at the top" lived in cities and prioritized them over villages.

Top leaders in Beijing including Mao remained consistently committed to this Stalinist development model throughout the 1950s, 1960s, and 1970s. Mao periodically attempted to address the imbalances that had been caused by prioritizing heavy urban industry, most notably when launching the leap in 1958 and at the outset of the Cultural Revolution (1966–1968). And between 1949 and 1978, rural areas did see significant

7 Tiejun Cheng, "Dialectics of Control – The Household Registration (Hukou) System in Contemporary China" (PhD diss., State University of New York at Binghamton, 1991); Tiejun Cheng and Mark Selden, "The Origins and Consequences of China's Hukou System," *China Quarterly* 139 (1994): 644–68; Kam Wing Chan, *Cities with Invisible Walls* (New York: Oxford University Press, 1994); Fei-Ling Wang, *Organizing through Division and Exclusion: China's Hukou System* (Stanford: Stanford University Press, 2005); Ching Kwan Lee and Mark Selden, "Durable Inequality: The Legacies of China's Revolutions and the Pitfalls of Reform," in *Revolution in the Making of the Modern World: Social Identities, Globalization, and Modernity*, ed. John Foran, David Lane and Andreja Zivkovic (New York: Routledge, 2007), 81–95; and Martin King Whyte, "The Paradoxes of Rural-Urban Inequality in Contemporary China," in *One Country, Two Societies: Rural-Urban Inequality in Contemporary China*, ed. Martin King Whyte (Cambridge, MA: Harvard University Press, 2010), 7–13.

8 Jacob Eyferth convincingly explains this process of peasantization and rural deindustrialization in his *Eating Rice from Bamboo Roots: The Social History of a Community of Handicraft Papermakers in Rural Sichuan, 1920–2000* (Cambridge, MA: Harvard University Asia Center, 2009).

9 Eyferth, *Eating Rice from Bamboo Roots*, 223.

gains in education, electrification, health care, irrigation, and literacy. But even during the Cultural Revolution, Mao and his colleagues never wavered from the rural-urban divide's ideological justification (making China modern and strong through top-down state planning) and institutional underpinnings (the *hukou* system and grain rationing). As a result, cities and villages became more and more alienated from one another over the course of the Mao years.

The *hukou* and grain rationing regimes were crucial structural elements of rural-urban difference under Mao. Human interactions, however, were as important as government-imposed structures in creating the rural-urban divide. People themselves made the divide, and they constantly challenged and crossed it. If the *hukou* system indeed functioned as a "legal Great Wall," as Fei-Ling Wang writes,[10] it was a porous wall, not an impenetrable one. Alienation between village and city came about not through isolation, but through regular contact. During the socialist period, in spite of restricted mobility, people continued to travel between city and countryside in massive numbers.[11] Such movement – sometimes hidden and illicit, sometimes state-sanctioned – led to exchanges and interactions in which difference was negotiated on personal, familial, and professional levels. *Hukou* and grain rationing were only one factor in these moments of everyday contact. Language, physical appearance, work, family, food, and sex also came into play as people negotiated the rural-urban divide.

So did long-standing native place networks, which had been important resources for migrants during the late Qing and Republican periods.[12] Household registration and grain rationing failed to sever city dwellers' ties to their rural native places. During the Mao era, urban residents maintained ties with the countryside by hosting visiting relatives, and

[10] Fei-Ling Wang, "Renovating the Great Floodgate: The Reform of China's *Hukou* System," in Whyte, *One Country, Two Societies*, 335.

[11] On the substantial unsanctioned migration of the Mao period, see Diana Lary, "Hidden Migrations: Movements of Shandong People, 1949–1978," *Chinese Environment and Development* 7 (1996): 56–72.

[12] On native place identity during the Republican period, see S. A. Smith, *Revolution and the People in Russia and China: A Comparative History* (New York: Cambridge University Press, 2008), especially chapter 1; and Hanchao Lu, *Beyond the Neon Lights: Everyday Shanghai in the Early Twentieth Century* (Berkeley: University of California Press, 1999). On the late Qing see William T. Rowe, *Hankow: Commerce and Society in a Chinese City, 1796–1889* (Stanford: Stanford University Press, 1984), especially chapter 7. Byrna Goodman's *Native Place, City, and Nation: Regional Networks and Identities in Shanghai, 1853–1937* (Berkeley: University of California Press, 1995), covers the late Qing and Republican periods.

through visits home for the Chinese New Year. Ironically, the Communist bureaucracy also helped sustain rural-urban ties by including "native place" (*jiguan*) on paperwork in individuals' dossiers. During movements to reduce the city population (in the 1950s and early 1960s, covered in Chapters 2 and 4) or to purify urban space (in 1966 and 1968, discussed in Chapter 6), authorities used this information to determine where to deport people.

The administrative categories of "urban" and "rural" shaped life choices and opportunities, but they often clashed with lived reality. It is therefore useful to think of the categories as one of the "state fictions" described by James Scott, in that they "transformed the reality they presumed to observe, although never so thoroughly as to precisely fit the grid."[13] When the state's rigid rural-urban scheme was imposed on a complex human landscape, individuals and families had to sort out the mess. Labels pushed people into choices and situations that they might not have confronted otherwise. But surprisingly often, people took matters into their own hands and pushed back against the state-imposed binary between city and countryside. They did so through what Geoffrey Bowker and Susan Leigh Star call the "dynamic compromise" between "formal restrictions" and informal workarounds that is part of all classification systems.[14]

In other words, the state could never have maintained the rural-urban divide had it been consistently and inflexibly enforced at the local level. During the Mao period, negotiating the gap between city and countryside meant recognizing the power of state regulations while simultaneously finding ways around them. City and village, however, did not negotiate on equal terms. The city was the locus of economic and political power in Mao-era China. While peasants and rural cadres were not powerless to challenge directives from the metropole, they were at a distinct disadvantage. City-based officials were brutally coercive when they exiled people to the countryside, and they behaved like colonizers when they violently requisitioned grain from hungry peasants or dispatched work teams to occupy villages. Villagers resisted in small ways that tweaked the system but never really threatened it. Authorities, probably aware that "dynamic compromise" worked in their favor, often tolerated behavior that challenged *hukou* rules and grain rationing. For example, bureaucrats acted

[13] James C. Scott, *Seeing Like a State: How Certain Schemes to Improve the Human Condition Have Failed* (New Haven: Yale University Press, 1998), 24.

[14] Geoffrey C. Bowker and Susan Leigh Star, *Sorting Things Out: Classification and Its Consequences* (Cambridge, MA: MIT Press, 1999), 55, 53.

flexibly, even humanely, by turning a blind eye to grain smuggling or approving petitioners' requests to reunite their families in cities.

I would have never discovered the many examples of coercion, negotiation, and resistance described in this book if I had limited myself to reading newspapers and officially published sources, which tend to overstate the rigidity of the rural-urban divide and wash out human color. My source base of archival documents, unpublished manuscripts, personal diaries, and grassroots-level personnel records, supplemented by oral history interviews and memoirs, gets us as close as possible to how people in villages and city neighborhoods experienced the Mao years. Many of the documents I purchased at weekend flea markets or hand-copied in local archives, along with the interviews I conducted in villages, bring to light the experiences of people whose voices would not otherwise be heard.[15] Their stories show a society that was more diverse, complicated, and above all, more human than the simple institutional division into urban and rural spheres would suggest.

Using grassroots sources to focus on rural-urban interaction allows for fresh perspectives on such important events as the Great Leap famine, the Four Cleanups movement, the sent-down youth program, and the Cultural Revolution. The disastrous leap and its aftermath poisoned the relationship between city and countryside during the Mao era. This book shares Frank Dikötter's contention that the "pivotal event in the history of the People's Republic of China was the Great Leap Forward." Dikötter's argument that "the catastrophe unleashed at the time stands as a reminder of how profoundly misplaced is the idea of state planning as an antidote to chaos," however, is misleading.[16] His polemic against state planning makes it impossible to comprehend how China's society and economy developed after the leap in the 1960s and 1970s, because it is fundamentally at odds with how China's top economic planners understood and reacted to the famine. They saw the leap as a failure of state planning, and viewed better planning – including strict mobility control and food management – as the solution. Even though many central economic officials would fall during the Cultural Revolution, the *hukou* and grain rationing regulations they implemented in the aftermath of the famine remained in force during the 1960s and 1970s, despite the "chaos" of the period.

[15] I detail my strategies for digging up unique documents in Jeremy Brown, "Finding and Using Grassroots Historical Sources from the Mao Era," *Chinese History Dissertation Reviews* (December 15, 2010), http://dissertationreviews.org/archives/310.

[16] Frank Dikötter, *Mao's Great Famine: The History of China's Most Devastating Catastrophe, 1958–1962* (New York: Walker, 2010), xii.

A strengthened commitment to state planning was one consequence of the leap. Reemphasizing revolution was another. Mao Zedong blamed the failure of the leap on counterrevolutionaries in the countryside, claiming that China's "democratic revolution" (meaning the Communist Party's attempt to overthrow "feudal" forces and eliminate rural exploitation through land reform) was incomplete. For Mao, the answer was more class struggle – in his words, a "war of annihilation" against class enemies in the countryside.[17] This legacy of the leap is the key to understanding the Four Cleanups movement, which treated rural areas as "problems" to be solved by urbanites, and also the Cultural Revolution, which dumped city outcasts in the laps of rural people. By the 1960s and 1970s, revolution meant purifying urban spaces and dumping on rural ones. While urban industrial modernization continued to contribute to rural-urban inequality, calls for revolution – dictated by urban officials and often detrimental to rural interests – deepened alienation between city and countryside.

I refer to *Mao's China* in the title of this book because Mao's views, whims, and policy judgments were extremely important not only in pursuing a revolutionary modernization project that institutionalized rural-urban difference but also in launching key moments of rural-urban contact. Mao Zedong himself, however, only occasionally appears in this book. Mao and other central leaders' decisions help to explain why things happened when they did, but do not shed much light on how events unfolded at the grassroots level. The approaches of local leaders, including such top Tianjin officials as Wan Xiaotang (a public security chief in the early 1950s and top leader of the city from 1958 until his death in 1966) and Xie Xuegong (who led the city between 1967 and 1978), were often more relevant to the lives of the people who lived in and around Tianjin. At least as important as the Chairman in the Tianjin region were lieutenants who enjoyed proximity to Mao and who acted in his name, including ghostwriter and theorist Chen Boda and Mao's wife, Jiang Qing. Chen and Jiang's forays from their Beijing offices to the Tianjin countryside would have disastrous consequences for rural-urban relations.

I focus on Tianjin and its hinterland because the area is unique and significant, not because it is representative of China. No place is. Tianjin was the most important urban center and port in north China during the late Qing and Republican periods, but it remains understudied compared with Beijing and Shanghai, in part because of its relatively inaccessible

[17] ZGSX, 506.

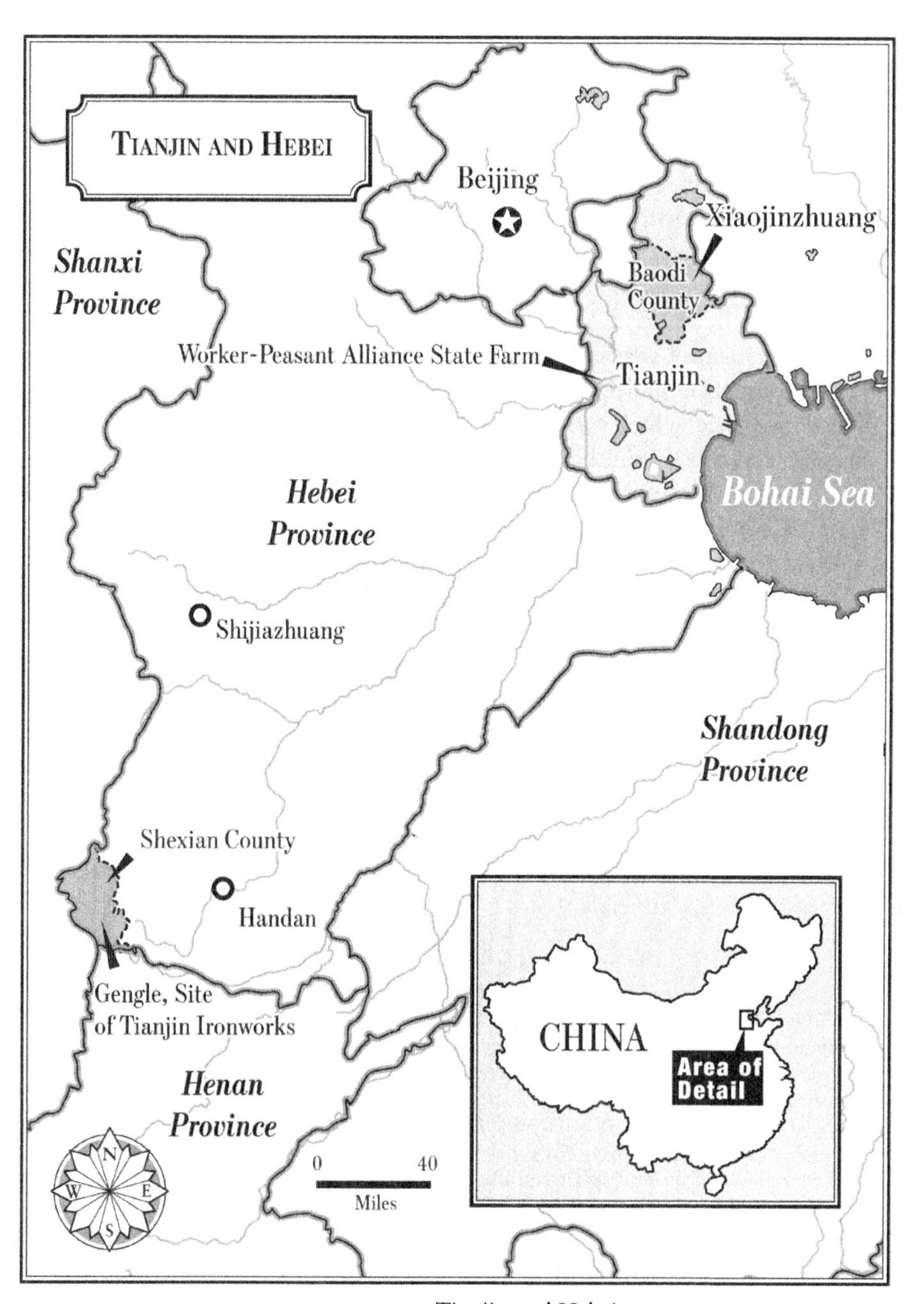

MAP 1. Tianjin and Hebei

archive. The city is best known for its status as what Ruth Rogaski calls a "hypercolony," a treaty port home to as many as eight foreign concessions in the early 1900s.[18] By the time the People's Liberation Army occupied Tianjin in January 1949, the concessions were no longer administratively significant. Tianjin was unique for other reasons during the Mao period. First, its proximity to Beijing meant that central leaders could easily visit to give speeches, test new policies, and try to establish a separate power base away from the capital. Second, its pre-1949 history of occupation by imperialist powers meant that many residents had "historical problems" that cadres and activists could focus on during political movements. Third, Tianjin constantly clashed over resources with Hebei province, which surrounded the city to the north, west, and south. Battles with mostly rural Hebei became especially pitched between 1958 and 1967, when Tianjin lost its status as a special municipality and became administratively subordinate to the province. Party center often sided with Tianjin when mediating disputes between the city and Hebei.

While Tianjin's particularities mean that I cannot extend my conclusions to all of China, its experiences do shed light on broader trends. Relationships between other large cities and their hinterlands unfolded on a timeline that corresponded to Tianjin's: migration during the 1950s accompanied by gradual restrictions on movement; protecting the food supplies of city dwellers at the expense of villagers during the Great Leap famine; deporting people to the countryside in the early 1960s and again during the Cultural Revolution; dispatching urban youth and work team members to villages; and cultivating model villages that served the interests of city-based officials.[19]

[18] Ruth Rogaski, *Hygienic Modernity: Meanings of Health and Disease in Treaty-Port China* (Berkeley: University of California Press, 2004). Other important works on late imperial and Republican Tianjin include Gail Hershatter, *The Workers of Tianjin, 1900–1949* (Stanford: Stanford University Press, 1986); Kwan Man Bun, *The Salt Merchants of Tianjin: State-Making and Civil Society in Late Imperial China* (Honolulu: University of Hawai'i Press, 2001); Liu Haiyan, *Kongjian yu shehui: jindai Tianjin chengshi de yanbian* [Space and society: The evolution of modern Tianjin] (Tianjin: Tianjin shehui kexueyuan chubanshe, 2003); and Brett Sheehan, *Trust in Troubled Times: Money, Banks, and State-Society Relations in Republican Tianjin* (Cambridge, MA: Harvard University Press, 2003).

[19] Lynn T. White III has written on migration to and from Shanghai in his *Careers in Shanghai: The Social Guidance of Personal Energies in a Developing Chinese City, 1949–1966* (Berkeley: University of California Press, 1978); and "The Road to Urumchi: Approved Institutions in Search of Attainable Goals during Pre-1968 Rustication from Shanghai," *China Quarterly* 79 (1979): 481–510. Chan, Madsen, and Unger discuss the experiences of city youth in a Guangdong village during the 1960s and 1970s; Anita

The following chapters are case studies of moments when people in and around Tianjin negotiated the rural-urban gap. They may not have known it at the time, but people who dealt with the rural-urban divide in their everyday lives were actually grappling with the interplay between revolution and modernization that was built into the Maoist development project. In the early 1950s, continuing and consolidating the revolution justified suppressing its potential enemies. Authorities initially set up the household registration system to allow the police to identify and keep track of "counterrevolutionaries." By the mid-1950s, Soviet-style modernization demanded more efficient ways to extract grain from the countryside, giving rise to new collective organizations and also to grain rationing rules that governed precisely how much food each person was entitled to in a month. When some peasants responded to collectivization and grain rationing by migrating to cities, household registration assumed the added function of restricting mobility. While grain rationing and the *hukou* regime served Mao's modernization goals, household registration was still a surveillance tool that remained the responsibility of public security officials and police officers: it served modernization by keeping people where the socialist planned economy needed them to be, but also protected Mao's revolution (for example, sometimes rural-urban migration was blamed on nefarious instigation by "class enemies"). Chapters 1 and 2 explain how this process unfolded during the 1950s and tell how people negotiated the gradually deepening but still permeable rural-urban gap.

By the late 1950s, household registration aimed to fix people in place, balancing China's "agricultural" and "non-agricultural" populations. An ideal balance would allow the state to invest the agricultural surplus in heavy urban industry, while still ensuring that everyone had enough to eat. But in 1958, this balance was ignored. So were migration restrictions. Why? A new revolutionary modernization movement called the Great Leap Forward promised the imminent arrival of utopia. With its large-scale communes, inflated bumper harvests and collective cafeterias, the leap is commonly understood as a rural event, but its push for rapid industrialization encouraged many farmers to leave villages in

Chan, Richard Madsen, and Jonathan Unger, *Chen Village: Revolution to Globalization*, 3rd ed. (Berkeley: University of California Press, 2009). On model villages, see Edward Friedman, Paul G. Pickowicz, and Mark Selden, *Chinese Village, Socialist State* (New Haven: Yale University Press, 1991); and Edward Friedman, Paul G. Pickowicz, and Mark Selden, *Revolution, Resistance, and Reform in Village China* (New Haven: Yale University Press, 2005).

search of better-paid urban or suburban jobs. This outflow of rural labor contributed to the spread of famine conditions in Tianjin's hinterland, examined in Chapter 3. Archival evidence reveals that top leaders including Mao and also local officials in Tianjin knew about the extent of the disaster in the countryside. Their response was to work energetically to shield city residents from food shortages while rural people starved. Tragically, urban leaders considered villagers more expendable than city dwellers. Rural lives were sacrificed at the altar of urban industrial development.

Leaders in Beijing responded to the disaster by ordering an unprecedented urban-to-rural population transfer called "downsizing" (*jingjian*), which is the subject of Chapter 4.[20] Workers who had arrived in Tianjin after 1958 were laid off, given severance funds, and told to return to their home villages. The downsizing movement triggered high-stakes interactions between urban officials and migrants, some of whom fiercely resisted the prospect of losing the benefits of city residency. Some villagers resented the downsized workers, who strained resources and created headaches for village officials. But the returnees were a more benign presence in north Chinese villages than two groups of urban visitors who spent time in villages in the mid-1960s: the first major wave of sent-down youth, and urban work teams conducting the Four Cleanups movement. Chapter 5 explores the intrusive behavior of these urbanites. Both groups went to villages as a result of problems that had emerged in the aftermath of the famine. Four Cleanups work teams attacked "class enemies" who had ostensibly usurped village leadership in an effort to restore capitalism. In Mao's view, the revolution in rural China had been left incomplete. The Four Cleanups movement was an attempt to finish what land reform had started.

Like work team members, the sent-down youth of 1964 were told that going to villages was revolutionary. But their migration was mostly about preserving urban stability. Thousands of jobless teenagers moved to villages to relieve post-leap employment pressures in Tianjin. Sent-down youth and Four Cleanups work team members clashed violently with villagers who were understandably suspicious of outsiders coming from a city that had turned its back on them during the famine. As a

[20] Most dictionaries define *jingjian* as "cut" or "reduce. I use "downsize" and "downsizing" because the euphemistic flavor of the English term, which began to be used in the 1980s to sugarcoat reports of corporate layoffs, applies quite well to the Chinese usage of the early 1960s.

result of these intense interactions between villagers and visitors from the city, rural-urban alienation worsened.

The famine's legacy was also a crucial element in the forced removal of political exiles from Tianjin during the first three years of the Cultural Revolution (1966–68). More than forty thousand Tianjin residents were forced into exile in their rural ancestral villages as punishment for stealing food, selling items on the black market, or having illicit sex during the early 1960s. During the Cultural Revolution, such transgressions represented "bourgeois" behavior that had to be penalized. Chapter 6 examines these "deportations" (*qiansong*). As an official policy governed by a sophisticated bureaucracy and supported by state funds, deportation shows a side of the Cultural Revolution quite different from the stock view of youthful red guards running wild. This was not chaos, it was state-sanctioned oppression that attempted to purify urban space. Officials justified deportation by pointing to the need to protect vital coastal industry during the heightened security environment of the Cultural Revolution. Only eight years after the heady days of the leap promised to eliminate the gap between cities and villages, the countryside had become a jail for urban outcasts who were poorly prepared for farm work and who strained village food supplies. Neither deportees nor the villagers who hosted them accepted this situation quietly.

By the 1970s, the household registration and grain rationing regimes (mostly justified by China's drive to modernize), combined with moments of rural-urban conflict like the leap, the Four Cleanups, and the deportations of the Cultural Revolution (all of which Mao launched in order to keep the revolution alive) to profoundly alienate cities from villages. The book's final two chapters examine unique spaces where people grappled with this alienation. In Chapter 7, I analyze two special sites: a state-run farm on the outskirts of Tianjin where workers tilled the fields but held non-agricultural *hukou*, and the Tianjin Ironworks, an enclave administered by Tianjin officials but located hundreds of miles away from Tianjin next to a remote mountain village in the far southwest corner of Hebei province.

The state farm and the ironworks show that space remained relational and contested in the Mao period. For peasants living next to the state farm or the ironworks, the proximity of administratively urban space offered opportunities for paid work (an avenue for upward mobility at the farm) or to steal valuable industrial materials (a regular trigger of conflict at the ironworks). But for people born and raised in Tianjin proper, an assignment to the farm or ironworks was seen as a demotion, or even as punishment.

Chapter 8 turns to the story of Xiaojinzhuang, a village north of Tianjin that was occupied by urban officials in June 1974. The officials transformed the village into a cultural theme park. Under the sponsorship of Jiang Qing and Tianjin authorities, Xiaojinzhuang became a rural model and tourist attraction famous nationwide for singing and poetry writing. While some villagers took advantage of their hometown's sudden prominence, many others had to endure living in a false utopia invented by urban politicians who disrespected rural residents. While publicly extolling the achievements and virtues of poor peasants, city-based officials treated villagers as inferiors and denied them political power.

The rural-urban alienation found in Xiaojinzhuang or at the Tianjin Ironworks by the late 1970s was certainly not what Mao had intended when he launched China down a road of revolutionary modernization. But whenever a policy decision led to problems that Mao and his colleagues might not have foreseen, they reacted with aggressive measures that themselves caused other unintended consequences. Let us now see how people coped with the fallout.

1

The City Leads the Village

Governing Tianjin in the Early 1950s

In late 1948 and 1949, residents of Tianjin awaited their impending "liberation" with uncertainty and trepidation. Many people's fears were allayed when the Communist takeover of Tianjin proceeded without massive disorder. The relatively disciplined soldiers and cadres who entered Tianjin in January 1949 were a welcome contrast to previous occupiers. This was no accident. In order to avoid embarrassment and conflict, Tianjin's new Communist leaders had taken pains to instruct rural cadres in urban manners and ways. The immediate takeover of Tianjin was an intense moment of rural-urban contact, both between Communist cadres and city residents, and also between cadres from diverse backgrounds. This chapter outlines the process by which officials and citizens defined and negotiated boundaries between city and countryside in 1950s Tianjin. Far from embracing its rural revolutionary past, in 1949 the party criticized rural characteristics and work methods and preferred people with urban expertise over what it called "purely village-born cadres." Throughout the 1950s party doctrine still mandated that cities would lead villages.

Within the party, cadres from urban backgrounds were privileged over battle-hardened officials from village backgrounds. In addition, well before the imposition of restrictions on migration, urban and rural became salient categories in the party's interactions with residents of Tianjin and its hinterland. Urban space became exclusive space, and not just anyone was eligible to live and work in Tianjin. The project of determining who was an acceptable urban resident evolved during the 1950s. Generally the most marginalized rural migrants – people fleeing famine who lacked close family ties or fixed employment in Tianjin – were the easiest to identify (by their clothing and accents) and deport during "return-to-village" movements in 1955 and 1957. But it was impossible for Tianjin authorities to fully regulate movement from city to countryside. Even as categories were fixed and lines drawn, the imperatives of survival, work, and family drove people to cross lines and defy categorization.

Takeover

The youthful People's Liberation Army soldiers who occupied Tianjin on January 15, 1949, were the first representatives of the Communist regime that city residents encountered, but they were not the ones running the show. A team of around seventy-five hundred cadres followed on the heels of the army, and like the young soldiers, they were under strict orders to make a good impression. Tianjin was the largest city that the Communists had occupied. How they carried out the takeover would be a key test of the party's shift from a rural to an urban policy. On the eve of the occupation, thousands of cadres assembled in Shengfang, a county town west of Tianjin already under Communist control. There, Tianjin's new mayor Huang Jing – scion of a prominent Nationalist family and Jiang Qing's former paramour – exhorted his underlings to leave their rural habits behind. "When you enter the city, you absolutely cannot find any old corner and urinate and defecate like you would in the village," Huang said in a speech in December 1948.[1] Other cadres from urban backgrounds gave lessons on how to operate flush toilets, with mixed results – after the takeover, some new cadres squatted precariously with their feet on the toilet seat.[2]

Mayor Huang Jing and his colleague Huang Kecheng, who was Tianjin's party secretary and chairman of military affairs in the months following the takeover, explained which rural attributes could be brought into the city and which were best left behind. They warned that imperialists and the bourgeoisie would try to seduce Tianjin's new rulers. The best way to fight against temptation was to "maintain the fine village tradition of hard work and plain living," Huang Kecheng told cadres in Shengfang. In the short term, this meant that "no one is allowed to change clothes or to seize property."[3]

1 Zhonggong Tianjin shiwei dangshi yanjiu shi, ed., *Chengshi de jieguan yu shehui gaizao (Tianjin juan)* [Urban takeover and social reform (Tianjin volume)] (Tianjin: Tianjin renmin chubanshe, 1998), 558.

2 TJJG, 2:351.

3 TJJG, 1:59.

In their interactions with city residents, rural cadres had trouble making themselves understood. Before entering Tianjin, Huang Jing told the cadres assembled in Shengfang to be polite in their dealings with city residents and to replace the friendly village salutations of "*lao xiang*" (fellow villager) or "*da niang*" (auntie) with the more formal "*nin hao*" (hello). To neglect such niceties would mean a loss of face, Huang said.[4] But even when cadres altered their vocabulary, their strong village accents caused misunderstandings. When two cadres went to a Tianjin neighborhood shortly after the takeover and asked residents for help in finding someone, the city people could not understand the men's rural patois. Aiming to please, the neighborhood residents assumed that the outsiders were like previous occupying forces and led them to the nearest brothel.[5]

Tense Encounters

In early 1949, public interactions between representatives of the new regime and Tianjin residents were mostly good-natured, albeit sometimes tinged with disapproval or incomprehension. Relations among Tianjin cadres from different backgrounds, however, were often more contentious. Officials from villages who had served the revolution in the countryside clashed with young urban cadres and other underground party members from Tianjin. Both of these groups had trouble getting along with the many bureaucrats who had worked for the Nationalists but who stayed on after the Communist occupation of the city. In interactions between rural cadres (*rucheng* or *jinshi renyuan*), underground party members (*dixia dangyuan*), and retained bureaucrats (*liuyong renyuan*), many rural officials, although numerically superior, were first embarrassed and then shunted aside as urban work progressed in Tianjin. This process calls into question Hong Yong Lee's contention that top leaders' "rural orientation" and "Mao's peasant mentality" characterized Chinese politics during the Mao era.[6]

In May 1949, there were 7,113 party members working in Tianjin. Of these, 5,389 had followed the army into the city, 1,564 were from the underground party, and 160 had joined the organization after takeover.[7]

[4] TJJG, 2:207–8.

[5] Ibid., 82.

[6] Hong Yung Lee, *From Revolutionary Cadres to Party Technocrats in Socialist China* (Berkeley: University of California Press, 1991), 1, 74, 388, 392.

[7] Zhonggong Tianjin shiwei dangshi yanjiu shi, *Chengshi de jieguan yu shehui gaizao (Tianjin juan)*, 581.

The largest group was mostly from villages, but also included some students who had left cities in order to attend the party-run North China University.[8] Poor coordination between rural takeover cadres and underground party members led to problems of mistrust and mistaken identity, which disappointed urban agents who felt that their sacrifices under Nationalist repression had not been properly recognized.[9] When takeover officials arrived at the Dongya Wheat Flour Company, they accosted underground party members who were guarding a warehouse, yelling, "you had better not be pretending!" and "what the hell are you up to?!" Similar scenes unfolded at banks and textile factories, where recently arrived cadres overheard rumors that "underground backbones" may have actually been "hidden traitors." These problems prompted the municipal party leadership to complain: "There is not enough trust in the underground party members. Being suspicious for no good reason has poured cold water on the moods of the enthusiastic underground comrades, and has damaged takeover work."[10] Although city-based underground party members were let down by their treatment in January 1949, a few months later they would be rewarded for their urban expertise.

So would the "retained personnel" kept on in work units, who also clashed with rural newcomers in Tianjin. Liu Fuji, General Manager and Chief Engineer of the Tianjin Water Works in the 1940s, was a Cornell graduate who had worked in New York City. He stayed on after ten Communist cadres took over his office. Liu's wife Grace wrote that the cadres were "green young country fellows without any experience in dealing with a large city's established organizations, and ignorant not only of the city but in a large measure, of the rest of the world. Situations arise that they cannot handle and they create unnecessary complications." One day, the top new Communist cadre at the water works questioned

[8] In his book on the takeover of Tianjin, Kenneth Lieberthal focuses on a divide between top party leader Liu Shaoqi's organization model of politics and Chairman Mao Zedong's mobilization model rather than emphasizing differences within the cadre ranks. But similar to the rift identified by Ezra Vogel in Guangzhou, tensions arose between the minority of urban insiders and the majority of rural outsiders in Tianjin's new government. Kenneth Lieberthal, *Revolution and Tradition in Tientsin, 1949–1952* (Stanford: Stanford University Press, 1980); Ezra F. Vogel, *Canton under Communism: Programs and Politics in a Provincial Capital, 1949–1968* (Cambridge, MA: Harvard University Press, 1969).

[9] On the student movement and underground party organization in Tianjin before 1949, see Joseph K. S. Yick, *Making Urban Revolution in China: The CCP-GMD Struggle for Beiping-Tianjin, 1945–1949* (Armonk, NY: M. E. Sharpe, 1995).

[10] TJJG, 1:124.

Liu's work. Liu exploded in rage, pounded a table, and yelled at the rural official for his temerity. Liu then went home and told his wife, "They can shoot me, hang me or cut off my head but no so and so farmer is going to call me a liar!" The next day, nobody was shot or decapitated. To the contrary, the Communist representative was deferential and apologetic. "'You know,' said the young man, 'we are just *tou bau tze* (country jacks). You must be patient and teach us so we can study and learn." Liu's wife wrote, "From that time he has been treated with the greatest respect by the comrades."[11]

Liu Fuji was named a model worker for three years in a row beginning in 1951, and continued to work at the water works until his death in 1955.[12] But it is unlikely that his clash with rural officials was resolved as neatly as his wife's rosy account suggests. Although Liu appeared to win the argument, his questioner's deference – executed with a dignity lacking in Liu's temper tantrum – was not entirely heartfelt. And rather than automatically giving Liu free reign over the water works, rural officials felt empowered to challenge a Cornell-trained engineer and to assert their authority.

Relations between takeover cadres and retained staff remained tense in urban work units. As Grace Liu's anecdote suggests, workplace battles were often recounted at home, and were then replayed in neighborhood squabbles long after 1949. In 1955, the Tianjin Civil Affairs Bureau (Minzheng ju) reported that at a shared dormitory for bank cadres and their families in Tianjin's former British concession, family members of rural cadres who had entered the city in 1949 formed a faction that clashed with relatives of retained urban employees. "The two groups are always opposed and look down on one another," the report noted. "Disunity among these family members leads to disunity among cadres themselves."[13] Beginning in spring 1949, a policy turn favoring urban expertise contributed to takeover cadres' feelings of resentment. This shift coincided with Vice-Chairman Liu Shaoqi's important visit to Tianjin. The visit and its aftermath meant that the new regime in Tianjin would have an urban orientation, not a rural one.

[11] Grace D. Liu, "Behind US-Made 'Bamboo Curtain': New Tientsin as Seen by an American," *China Digest* 6, no. 5 (June 14, 1949): 6–7. Grace Divine married Liu Fuji in New York in 1932. Liu Fuji moved to Tianjin shortly thereafter, and Grace joined him there in 1934.

[12] Eleanor McCallie Cooper and William Liu, *Grace: An American Woman in China, 1934–1974* (New York: Soho Press, 2002), 220.

[13] *Tianjin shizheng zhoubao* [Tianjin municipal government weekly] 127 (January 24, 1955): 9.

"Quality over Quantity"

According to Kenneth Lieberthal, Liu Shaoqi's speeches in Tianjin in April and May 1949 "shaped the contours of the Communists' penetration of Tientsin society during the years that followed."[14] Lieberthal is correct that Liu's emphasis on economic development, cooperative labor-capital relations, and centralized city government would have profound implications for Tianjin's residents, especially for newly arrived village cadres, who began to be shunted aside in favor of more technically adept officials. This trend actually began in March 1949, before Liu arrived.

A March report by the military commission governing Tianjin stated bluntly, "The quantity of cadres who entered the city far surpasses their quality." The solution was to "emphasize quality over quantity. Transfer in more politically reliable, richly experienced, old workers and staff who have worked in base areas; transfer fewer purely village-born cadres."[15] Only two months after the Communists occupied Tianjin, cadres' overwhelmingly rural backgrounds had become a liability and an embarrassment for the new regime. In May, Huang Kecheng repeated the quality over quantity phrase in a report to party center, stating that "peasant cadres" who had only worked in rural areas were "generally not suitable for city work." When cadres did not understand policy or lacked professional knowledge, Huang continued, they were "useless" (*qi bu liao zuoyong*) and "made fools out of themselves" (*naochu xiaohua*). This was particularly galling when "many cadres did not understand people's account books and English-language ledgers, causing retained staff to look down on us and say we have no talent," Huang wrote. In contrast, Huang praised underground party members as being better at urban work than village cadres, and called for more underground agents to be promoted.[16] In Tianjin, far from being wedded to a "rural orientation," party leaders found ruralness embarrassing. Liu Shaoqi's presence in Tianjin deepened the party's privileging of urban expertise.

Scholarly works and memoirs have highlighted Liu Shaoqi's remarks about the need for capitalists to continue exploiting workers in the short term for the sake of fighting unemployment and promoting production.[17]

14 Lieberthal, *Revolution and Tradition*, 50.

15 TJJG, 1:109.

16 Ibid., 101–2.

17 Lieberthal, *Revolution and Tradition*; James Zheng Gao, *The Communist Takeover of Hangzhou: The Transformation of City and Cadre, 1949–1954* (Honolulu: University of Hawai'i Press, 2004), 76–77; Bo Yibo, *Ruogan zhongda juece*, 1:49–50.

This was indeed a central element of Liu's visit to Tianjin, but was blown out of proportion during Cultural Revolution-era attacks on Liu, coloring later accounts and obscuring Liu's important comments on rural-urban relations. After a week of tours and meetings in mid-April, Liu critiqued village work style, discussed peasant burdens, and outlined his vision of rural-urban difference in series of speeches to businesspeople, workers, and cadres.

In a talk with the Tianjin party committee on April 18, Liu told leaders that they should centralize city government by having the municipal bureaucracy assume tasks that local districts had been handling. Neighborhood organizations were in charge of too many things, Liu said, which wasted time and resources and was an example of "village work style." "The city is concentrated, so work should also be concentrated," Liu said.[18] Liu was chiding Tianjin's leaders for failing to recognize fundamental differences between urban and rural administration.

In his talks with capitalists and workers, Liu emphasized another type of difference, this time between city people and peasants. Speaking with capitalists on May 2, Liu referred to the tough plight of peasants in order to convince the businessmen to contribute their fair share to the revolution. Liu admitted the validity of peasant complaints that grain taxes, military service, labor conscription, and various fees imposed a heavy burden. He noted that capitalists shouldered a lighter burden than peasants, and asked them to sacrifice a bit more.[19] Liu had used a similar strategy on April 28, when he told workers that if their wages were raised too high, prices would increase for everyone, hurting peasants the most. "When peasants come to the city to buy things like towels, socks, and shoes, items are very expensive and they will be unhappy," Liu said. "The peasants will raise the 'reasonable burden' problem, so increasing wages is also connected with the peasants."[20]

It was convenient for Liu Shaoqi to invoke peasant hardships when he was asking urban workers to forego immediate economic benefits. But only a few days later, Liu changed his emphasis. He said that while workers should recognize peasants' heavy burden, actually peasants were the main beneficiaries of the revolution because they had received property during land reform, while "basically, workers did not get anything."

[18] Tianjin shi dang'anguan, ed., *Jiefang chuqi Tianjin chengshi jingji hongguan guanli* [Tianjin city macroeconomic management in the initial stage after liberation] (Tianjin: Tianjin shi dang'an chubanshe, 1995), 51–52.

[19] Ibid., 90.

[20] Ibid., 77.

Therefore, Liu argued, "peasants cannot keep up with workers, and asking to be the same is wrong and unreasonable."[21] Not only were workers and peasants different, Liu was saying, but the former deserved to be rewarded for their contributions to urban modernization. It made sense, then, that cities and workers would lead the countryside until some indefinite point in the future. Liu said:

> Not only does today's Tianjin lead villages, it has always led villages. In the past it was this way, and in the socialism of the future it will also be this way. It will be like this until we change villages to make them look like cities, eliminate the gap between city and countryside, and electrify and mechanize everything. At that point, cities and villages will be about the same.[22]

Liu's message was multifaceted but clear. Village methods were ill-suited to the city, peasants had made some sacrifices but had been compensated in land reform and should not be too demanding, and for the time being, cities would lead the way forward to socialism.

Tianjin leaders took Liu's critique to heart. In response to Liu's speeches, the city party committee issued an apologetic report blaming rural cadres and peasant shortcomings for most of the problems that had arisen since January. "Because of our many years of working in villages, we are not familiar with cities," the June 1949 document explained. "We unconsciously brought a village work style to the city." Cadres of peasant background were responsible for a litany of errors and foibles, from being afraid to meet with capitalists and workers to announcing the start of meetings by banging loudly on gongs. Even worse, the report continued, many rural cadres thought that the party's new policy of cities leading villages was "unreasonable." In response, some asked to be transferred back to villages, and a few even ran off on their own.[23] But most other officials in Tianjin eventually came to accept Liu Shaoqi's notion that cities should lead villages. They adjusted to city life and adopted urban identities. The city, however, was not without dangers.

The Liu Qingshan-Zhang Zishan Corruption Case

In the party's reckoning, cities were advanced and modern, but, as home to imperialists and capitalists, were also potentially corrupting. Mao's

[21] Ibid., 114.
[22] Ibid., 100.
[23] Zhonggong Tianjin shiwei dangshi yanjiu shi, *Chengshi de jieguan yu shehui gaizao (Tianjin juan)*, 121–22.

March 1949 warning that some leading cadres might succumb to the "sugar-coated bullets of the bourgeoisie" is well known.[24] On the eve of the takeover of Beijing, Mao told Premier Zhou Enlai, "We won't be another Li Zicheng," referring to the peasant rebel who overthrew the Ming Dynasty in 1644 but whose undisciplined forces lost control of the capital in only a month.[25]

According to Bo Yibo, top party secretary of the North China Bureau in the early 1950s, the execution of Tianjin prefectural leaders Liu Qingshan and Zhang Zishan in February 1952 was a second message from Mao that the party could not allow urban temptations to turn it into Li Zicheng.[26] Liu and Zhang were the highest ranking Communist officials to be executed since 1949, and their case was presented as an example of how the city could corrupt previously upright revolutionaries.

To a certain extent, all top party leaders enjoyed perks and privileges after the takeover. In Tianjin, leaders' residences and offices were (and still are) in lavish colonial compounds and mansions confiscated from the previous regime and from foreign property holders in 1949. City leaders traveled in chauffeured cars, and a hierarchical ranking system determined the quality and amount of food they ate. What set Liu and Zhang apart was their ostentation, their entrepreneurial zeal for profit-making, and their inability to get along with each other and keep secrets. In addition, the two had bad timing: their case coincided with the beginning of the Three Antis (*sanfan*) anticorruption drive in 1951.[27]

Liu Qingshan was from a village in Boye county in central Hebei, and he started working as a hired laborer there at a young age. In 1931, when he was fourteen, another laborer introduced him into the Communist Party, and Liu then joined the Worker-Peasant Red Army. Liu barely escaped death after a failed uprising against Nationalist authorities in Gaoyang and Li counties. In response to the uprising, Nationalist soldiers had decapitated nineteen red army fighters and were about to cut off Liu Qingshan's head when their leader noticed how young the boy was and let him go. After this, Liu returned to his village and later made his way to Yan'an, where he rejoined the Communists.

Unlike Liu Qingshan, who was uneducated, Zhang Zishan left his Hebei village and excelled at the Shenxian county school. After 1931,

[24] Lieberthal, *Revolution and Tradition*, 154.
[25] Gao, *The Communist Takeover of Hangzhou*, 38.
[26] Bo Yibo, *Ruogan zhongda juece*, 1:152.
[27] On the Three Antis, see Lieberthal, *Revolution and Tradition*, 142–79. Lieberthal does not mention the Liu Qingshan-Zhang Zishan case.

Zhang became a leading agitator against Japanese aggression. He joined the Communist Party in 1933. The next year, a turncoat revealed Zhang's name to Nationalist authorities and he was imprisoned in Tianjin, but he refused to bend under torture and eventually escaped. By the time they were appointed to top prefectural positions in 1949, Zhang and Liu had proven their revolutionary mettle.[28]

Officially, Liu Qingshan and Zhang Zishan were not supposed to have much to do with urban Tianjin. Respectively party secretary and commissioner of Tianjin prefecture, which was established in the small town of Yangliuqing in August 1949, the two men were responsible for eleven rural counties and three townships in the Tianjin region. Although their offices were in Yangliuqing's famous Shi Family Courtyard, the two men spent much of their time in Tianjin, only ten miles to the east. During the early 1950s, government and party work units were urged to carry out "office production" (*jiguan shengchan*) as a way to supplement tight official budgets. After 1949, Liu and Zhang threw themselves into profit-making and investing, setting up a prefectural "Office Production Management Department" in Tianjin with interests in factories and construction companies. In order to supervise these business projects and also to "recuperate" from an illness, Liu Qingshan took up residence in a mansion on exclusive Machang Road in Tianjin's former British concession.[29]

The bulk of Liu and Zhang's crimes involved embezzling and misappropriating state funds and bank loans, most of which were then invested in office production projects. Liu Qingshan reportedly told a county party secretary, "now that it is peacetime, we do not have to be so stingy. If office production is done well, all expenses can be taken care of."[30] But Liu and Zhang did office production too well, enlisting the help of Tianjin businesspeople who had shady pasts, sending agents on purchasing trips to the northeast and to Hankou, and giving gifts of watches, pens, and cash to keep colleagues happy and quiet. By mid-1951, though, the two men's relations had worsened. Zhang complained to Hebei provincial authorities about Liu's wasteful behavior and undemocratic

[28] Zhou Licheng and Li Keyi, "Liu Qingshan, Zhang Zishan tanwu an jishi" [Record of the Liu Qingshan, Zhang Zishan corruption case], pt. 1, *Tianjin shi zhi* 2 (April 2001): 37.

[29] Zhou and Li, "Liu Qingshan, Zhang Zishan tanwu an jishi," pt. 3, *Tianjin shi zhi* 4 (August 2001): 38–40.

[30] Zhou and Li, "Liu Qingshan, Zhang Zishan tanwu an jishi," pt. 3, 38.

leadership. Liu was transferred to Shijiazhuang, where he became a vice party secretary, while Zhang was promoted to top party secretary of Tianjin prefecture. On his way out of Tianjin, Liu Qingshan told a confidant, "Shijiazhuang is an okay place, but it is a real loss of face for Zhang Zishan to get rid of me like this. There is a future in Tianjin work, I kind of hate to leave."

It looked like Zhang's maneuvering had been successful, but he was unable to keep his mouth shut during a drinking session, when one of his subordinates learned of Liu and Zhang's business dealings with Tianjin capitalists. Correctly sensing an opportunity for a promotion, the subordinate reported his suspicions of corruption to Hebei provincial authorities, who, after a brief initial investigation, recommended to Bo Yibo that the two men be arrested. Mao Zedong quickly approved of this decision, writing that the case was a warning that the party should deal harshly with cadres "corrupted by the bourgeoisie."[31] Zhang and Liu were both imprisoned in the Hebei provincial capital of Baoding. On February 10, 1952, their death penalty verdict was read there at a huge public rally, and was also broadcast live in Tianjin.[32] Immediately after the rally, the two were driven to an athletic field on the outskirts of Baoding and shot through the heart. Apparently Mao had ordered that because of the two men's previous contributions to the revolution, they should be shot in the heart, not the head.[33]

Even after Liu and Zhang were arrested in late 1951, officials in and around Tianjin disagreed on how to characterize the men's misconduct. A special investigation team was formed in Tianjin, because most of Liu and Zhang's problems had arisen there. At an all-night meeting, team members from Tianjin and Hebei province debated how to deal with Liu and Zhang. One faction argued that the two men's expropriation of funds for office production arose from "the bad habit from guerrilla warfare of acting on one's own." This was a variation of the critiques lodged against rural cadres who had been unable to adapt to city work in 1949. While this group acknowledged the seriousness of Liu and Zhang's mistakes, it emphasized their revolutionary valor and lobbied for lenient

[31] MWG, vol. 2 (1987), 528.

[32] Zhou and Li, "Liu Qingshan, Zhang Zishan tanwu an jishi," pt. 2, *Tianjin shi zhi* 3 (June 2001): 37–38; Zhou and Li, "Liu Qingshan, Zhang Zishan tanwu an jishi," pt. 5, *Tianjin shi zhi* 6 (December 2001): 41.

[33] Sun Hongquan, "Liu Qingshan yi an buyi" [Addendum on the case of Liu Qingshan], *Wenshi chunqiu* 3 (2000): 7.

treatment. The second faction played up the urban nature of Liu and Zhang's misdeeds, focusing on their ties with shady Tianjin profiteers and their appropriation of grain intended for rural flooding victims and public works laborers. For this group, it mattered most that Liu and Zhang had made illicit business deals with urban capitalists and siphoned resources from suffering peasants. By morning, the viewpoint stressing the urban character of their crimes had won the day, and the investigation group's final report, in line with the escalating Three Antis anticorruption campaign, recommended severe punishment.[34]

Even after Mao had signed off on Liu and Zhang's execution in early 1952, high officials pleaded for clemency. Tianjin mayor Huang Jing, who had worked alongside the men in the Central Hebei party committee during the war against Japan, asked Bo Yibo to approach Mao and tell him that the men should not be shot, but should instead be given a chance to reform themselves. Bo was reluctant to argue against a decision that already seemed final, but Huang Jing persisted and Bo finally went to Mao. Mao responded that precisely because Liu and Zhang were so high ranking, they had to be killed. Only by killing them could the party save thousands of other cadres from making similar mistakes, and comrade Huang Jing ought to understand this logic, Mao said.[35]

Official portrayals of Liu and Zhang made it clear that the decadent urban environment – and not the two men's rural upbringing – was ultimately responsible for leading them astray. *People's Daily*, acting directly on Mao's orders, issued the first public reports on the case on December 30, 1951.[36] A front-page story concluded that "after leadership moved from villages to cities, [Liu and Zhang] could not withstand the sneak attack of bourgeois ideology." Laborers on public works projects from which Liu and Zhang had profited complained, "they got rich, sat in nice cars, and watched plays while we suffered hardship."[37] Internal propaganda outlines targeting Hebei peasants adopted a similar

[34] Hao Shengde, "Tianjin neimao xitong 'sanfan yundong' pianduan jishi" [Partial report of the Three Antis movement in the Tianjin domestic trade system], *Tianjin wenshi ziliao xuanji* 62 (June 1994): 45–46.

[35] Bo Yibo, *Ruogan zhongda juece*, 1:152. Half a year later, Huang was transferred out of Tianjin and assigned to a ministerial post in Beijing; Donald W. Klein and Anne B. Clark, *Biographic Dictionary of Chinese Communism, 1921–1965* (Cambridge, MA: Harvard University Press, 1971), 1:392.

[36] Bo Yibo, *Ruogan zhongda juece*, 1:150.

[37] RMRB, December 30, 1951, 1.

nurture-over-nature line, dwelling on Liu's opium smoking and whoring, castigating Zhang's profligacy, and concluding:

> After they entered the city, their capacity for clear thinking was torn asunder by the world of sensuality. They became arrogant and thought that they had made contributions to the revolution and could enjoy comforts. Seeking pleasure, they became good friends with the bourgeoisie and learned their evil tricks of boasting and toadying.[38]

After hearing about Liu and Zhang's metamorphosis, peasants were quoted calling for the two to be hauled out and shot in public, and peasant representatives, including some from Baodi county, were bused in to make aggrieved denunciations at rallies.[39]

In early 1949, rural backgrounds had been liabilities for many cadres charged with administering Tianjin. When Liu Shaoqi visited the city in April 1949, rural traits and work methods made sense as targets for a party emphasizing expertise and stability in the city. But in 1951 and 1952, the urban environment itself became a liability and was excoriated in the context of the Liu-Zhang case and the Three Antis campaign. Villages and cities and the people who inhabited them had both positive and negative attributes in the official lexicon. These sometimes contradictory messages coexisted, with certain characteristics of urbanity or ruralness receiving more emphasis depending on the political moment. Villagers were hard-working and honest but uneducated and prone to rashness. Cities were advanced and modern, but as home to the bourgeoisie, were polluting dens of iniquity. Cities and villages also required different approaches to governance. Rural work was ad hoc, decentralized, and open to local rules and solutions. Urban management was centralized, rule-based, and required complex but uniform structures of decision-making and control. During the turn toward cities in 1949, rural work styles seemed inappropriate, while the anti-corruption campaign of 1952 demanded an attack on city life. Yet even though it was evident that cities still needed to be transformed and cleaned up in 1952, the

[38] Chun Hua, "Yonghu Zhonggong Hebei shengwei guanyu kaichu da tanwu fan Liu Qingshan, Zhang Zishan dangji de jueyi" [Support the Hebei party committee's decision to expel big embezzlers Liu Qingshan and Zhang Zishan from the party], *Nongcun xuanchuanyuan* (Baoding) 3 (February 5, 1952): 7–8.

[39] Luo Xianming, "Kaiguo fanfu diyi an quanjing xiezhen – chujue Liu Qingshan, Zhang Zishan gaoceng juece zhuiji" [Full description of the first anti-corruption case since the founding of the state – a record of top-level policy decisions on executing Liu Qingshan and Zhang Zizhan], *Yanhuang chunqiu* 4 (1994): 17; RMRB, February 13, 1952, 2.

notion that cities and urban industry should lead villages and agriculture had been drilled home in 1949 and remained dominant throughout the 1950s. This became increasingly clear after 1953, when a new grain rationing policy confirmed that the socialist planned economy offered concrete benefits to city dwellers while denying them to villagers.

2

Eating, Moving, and Working

One day in 1949, a police officer walked the streets of Tianjin's former British concession. His task was to inspect the household registration (*hukou* or *huji*) of residents in the exclusive neighborhood, which had intimidating "tall walls and deep courtyards." The officer often encountered resistance when he tried to check for unauthorized guests. Some "upper-crust elements" (*shangceng fenzi*) tried to drive him away by asking difficult questions, like why the new national flag had five stars. Others made him wait outside for upwards of fifteen minutes, or did not allow him past the entry hall. In one home, the officer saw more than ten people playing cards. Most of them were not registered residents or authorized guests. They claimed that they would not be sleeping over, but it turned out that some had already stayed for three nights. According to an annual report on *hukou* management by the Tianjin Public Security Bureau (PSB), many officers "hung back in fear" when faced with such situations, leading to a "big loophole" in public security work.[1]

Household registration in the years immediately following the Communist takeover of Tianjin was meant to ensure public security, not to restrict movement between city and countryside. Rural-urban difference only came into play if a *hukou* inspector happened to be a newly arrived villager in the city, easily intimidated by well-educated urbanites who laughed at "incompetent" cops (*zhengce shuiping di*).[2] But over the course

[1] "1949 nian hukou gongzuo baogao" [Report on *hukou* work in 1949], *Tianjin gongan* 1, no. 4 (1950): 3.

[2] "1949 nian hukou gongzuo baogao," 3, does not specify whether the officer was from a village, but because the description of the police officers' incompetence sounds much like the "quality over quantity" rhetoric described in Chapter 1, I suspect that he was.

of the 1950s, household registration took on additional functions. What began as a tool to protect the revolution by identifying and managing its enemies ended up assigning an urban or rural identity to everyone in Chinese society. When central planners expanded the role of the *hukou* system, they did not intend to create a divide between villagers and urbanites. Above all, they were concerned about food. To fuel industrial modernization, grain had to be exported and traded for advanced machinery, but enough had to be left over to somehow feed everyone in China. Centralized grain management forced the state to clarify the relationship between food producers (rural people, with "agricultural" *hukou*), and consumers (city people, who held "non-agricultural" *hukou*). This chapter charts how officials in and around Tianjin attempted to increase control over food and residence between 1949 and 1958, and describes how villagers and urbanites responded.

Producers versus Consumers

In the first four years of Communist rule in Tianjin, household registration had little to do with limiting rural-to-urban migration. In October 1949, Public Security vice director Wan Xiaotang, who would assume an increasingly important role in Tianjin later in the 1950s, ordered his force to link household registration with the struggle against enemy operatives.[3] *Hukou* police busied themselves with door-to-door checks, paying special attention to people suspected of being counterrevolutionaries.[4] Rather than excluding people from rural backgrounds, Communist leaders' plan for Tianjin during the early 1950s stressed social order. It also emphasized "producers" over "consumers."

Tianjin officials identified refugees who had fled rural hardship as a group that threatened social order and consumed more than it produced. Refugees (*nanmin*), disaster victims (*zaimin*), vagrants (*youmin*), and peasants (*nongmin*) had sought relief in Tianjin for hundreds of years, and despite efforts to stop them, they continued to appear in the city during the 1950s. As soon as the Communists took over Tianjin they were confronted with crowds of refugees in dire straits. The Nationalist

[3] "Jin yi bu zuo hao huzheng gongzuo – Wan fujuzhang zai hukou gongzuo huiyi shang de jianghua" [Improve residential administration work – Vice director Wan (Xiaotang)'s speech at the *hukou* work meeting], *Tianjin gongan* 1, no. 4 (1950): 4–5.

[4] According to Fei-Ling Wang, even after the *hukou* system assumed new functions, it continued to monitor and control specially targeted individuals. Wang, *Organizing through Division and Exclusion*, 46.

army had destroyed tens of thousands of homes on the outskirts of the city in order to construct a defense perimeter, leaving more than one hundred thousand residents homeless. After January 1949, the city's new rulers provided relief grain to the homeless and helped to rebuild the dwellings.[5] By March, tens of thousands of rural refugees, Nationalist soldiers, and landlords and students from northeast China had been sent back to their home villages. The government gave the travelers funds for transportation and food for the road.[6] But a spring drought followed by heavy summer rains in north China led to a new influx of rural people fleeing disaster. In August 1949, the Hailuan river overflowed its banks. In Baodi county just north of Tianjin, 808 villages were flooded, 56,000 homes were destroyed, and 97 percent of the fields were inundated.[7]

Beggars appeared on the streets of Tianjin, prompting complaints from businessmen, who wrote letters to *Tianjin Daily* and appealed to the new government to restore social order.[8] City hall continued the imperial and Nationalist governments' practice of opening porridge stations, which gave refugees two daily meals.[9] City officials also got in touch with the leaders of nearby counties, who dissuaded rural residents from coming to the city and encouraged them to move permanently to the more sparsely populated Northeast.[10] Officials set quotas: two thousand Baodi residents and five thousand from low-lying Ninghe county were slated to migrate to the Northeast. Flood victims were understandably reluctant to leave the Tianjin region for faraway, unfamiliar places. One woman from the outskirts of Tianjin went to a porridge station and yelled, "these cadres had better not deport us to the Northeast!"[11] In September 1949, Tianjin prefectural commissioner Zhang Zishan ordered local counties to smash the "conservative provincialism" that was keeping the refugees from moving away from the Tianjin area. "Explain that all peasants in China are one family," Zhang urged.[12]

[5] TJJG, 1:10; Lieberthal, *Revolution and Tradition*, 32.

[6] RMRB, March 2, 1949, 1; Lieberthal, *Revolution and Tradition*, 32.

[7] Tianjin shi dang'anguan, ed., *Tianjin diqu zhongda ziran zaihai shilu* [Record of major natural disasters in the Tianjin region] (Tianjin: Tianjin renmin chubanshe, 2005), 498.

[8] TMA, X70–4C, 7.

[9] In January 1950 there were four such stations in Tianjin. One was designated for refugees from counties in Tianjin prefecture, another was open to people from the Cangxian area; the other two served urban street beggars and people from other areas. Tianjin shi renmin zhengfu yanjiu shi, ed., *Minzheng shehui shizheng ziliao* [Municipal government materials on civil affairs and society] ([Tianjin]: 1950), 47.

[10] TMA, X63–28C, 39.

[11] Tianjin shi renmin zhengfu yanjiu shi, *Minzheng shehui shizheng ziliao*, 47.

[12] TMA, X63–20C.

Not only did the city government urge short-term refugees in Tianjin to return to their villages or to migrate, authorities also tried to remove "unproductive" city residents. In a September 1949 speech, Mayor Huang Jing proclaimed, "in order to transform the consumer city into a productive one, we must disperse the population."[13] By April 1950, almost fifteen hundred Tianjin residents had moved to the Chabei area (along the border of today's Hebei province and the Inner Mongolia autonomous region). A third of them were peddlers, more than a quarter were unemployed factory workers, and some were rickshaw pullers.[14] Such small numbers of people were a drop in the bucket of Tianjin's unemployment problem, and many city residents resisted efforts to make them leave. Rumors spread through city neighborhoods about poor quality land, man-eating wolves, and fierce Mongols in Chabei.

Yet when a group of more than ten peasants from Shandong province heard about the migration program, they jumped on a train to Tianjin and tried to sign up to go to Chabei. According to the Tianjin Civil Affairs Bureau, this was not permitted. Migrants were not supposed to travel to Tianjin for the purpose of getting a free ride to a new home.[15] Tianjin's programs to deport refugees and disperse "unproductive" people were costly upfront, with the government covering deportees' transportation costs, several months of food, and accommodations in the receiving village. The hope was that getting rid of burdensome residents who did not fit the needs of urban industrial development would eventually make up for such initial outlays. But throughout the early 1950s, enterprising people took advantage of migration and deportation programs to get free tickets and stipends. If the government was going to label them unfit for urban residence, these entrepreneurs would work the system as much as they could.

A group of seven peasants from Huanghua county, directly south of Tianjin, traveled to the city in 1953 in search of work. When they failed to find jobs, they approached the Civil Affairs Bureau and asked to be deported back to Huanghua. Hoping to get transportation and food stipends, they pretended that they had no money, but a search of their

[13] Zhonggong Tianjin shiwei dangshi yanjiu shi, *Chengshi de jieguan yu shehui gaizao (Tianjin juan)*, 135. Huang's speech echoed a *Tianjin Daily* commentary, republished in *People's Daily* on March 17, 1949.

[14] Guo Fengqi, ed., *Tianjin tong zhi: minzheng zhi* [Tianjin gazetteer: Civil affairs gazetteer] (Tianjin: Tianjin shehui kexueyuan, 2001), 176.

[15] Tianjin minzheng ju, "Dui yimin gongzuo jiancha baogao" [Investigation report on migration work], *Tianjin shizheng yiye* 42 (May 13, 1950): 7.

pockets revealed enough cash for the trip, so they were sent away empty-handed. Other migrants repeatedly requested to be deported, received free train tickets, and scalped them for a profit at the main Tianjin station.[16] Such people, some of whom actually earned a living by traveling back and forth between large cities in north China at government expense, posed a headache to urban authorities. In 1953, Tianjin's Civil Affairs Bureau complained to central authorities that Beijing, Shenyang, and Tangshan were dumping vagrants in Tianjin instead of sending them home to villages. Over the course of three weeks in November 1953, Shenyang officials deported 305 people to Tianjin, only 9 of whom were actually from Tianjin. The rest were people from villages and other cities who were seeking work. At the end of 1953, Tianjin civil affairs officials asked the municipal government to remove deportation work from their portfolio because it was too much trouble. The request was denied.[17]

In addition to creative freeloaders, the economic gap between city and countryside stymied city officials charged with separating "producers" from "consumers." By the early twentieth century, Tianjin had become north China's financial and trade center and was home to eight foreign concessions, but after the founding of the People's Republic in 1949, the city faced uncertainty and found its role diminished. The First Five-Year Plan funneled resources to interior cities, but dictated that coastal Tianjin's existing industrial infrastructure was to be "fully exploited but not further developed."[18] Even so, economic recovery following the Communist takeover made the city a magnet for rural migrants seeking jobs.

In early 1954, bad weather and dissatisfaction with changes in the rural economy pushed many more migrants to Tianjin. Massive summer flooding in Hebei province was exacerbated by a 3.5 billion kilogram increase in state grain purchases compared with the previous year.[19] The imposition of a state monopoly on the buying and selling of grain (*tonggou tongxiao*) in late 1953 fundamentally changed the relationship between city and countryside. The new grain policy ordered peasants to sell "excess" grain to the state at a fixed low price, while providing

[16] TMA, X65-309Y, 9, 12.

[17] Ibid., 26.

[18] Dangdai Zhongguo congshu bianjibu, ed., *Dangdai Zhongguo de Tianjin* [Contemporary China's Tianjin] (Beijing: Zhongguo shehui kexue chubanshe, 1999), 1:100–101.

[19] Wu Li and Zheng Yougui, eds., *Jiejue "san nong" wenti zhi lu – Zhongguo gongchandang "san nong" sixiang zhengce shi* [The path of solving the problem of agriculture, villages, and farmers – a history of the Chinese Communist Party's ideology and policy on agriculture, villages, and farmers] (Beijing: Zhongguo jingji chubanshe, 2004), 407.

city residents with guaranteed rations. Some villagers resisted the grain monopoly by fleeing to cities. This led to new restrictions against migration, eventually including the use of the *hukou* system to limit mobility.

Getting the Grain

During the first half of 1953, economic planners in Beijing became increasingly concerned about grain supplies. National grain output in 1952 was up 10.6 percent from the previous year, and up 44.8 percent from 1949, but food supplies to cities were still tight because urban populations had grown so rapidly. Mao Zedong asked finance officials to address the conflict between grain supply and demand, and during the summer of 1953, top economic leaders Bo Yibo and Chen Yun considered their options.[20] Chen quickly ruled out cutting grain exports, because he thought that China needed foreign currency to buy industrial machinery and equipment.[21] Chen then considered approaches that would allow China to continue exporting grain. He reckoned that the private grain market had to be eliminated, because the status quo was leading to "chaos." He deemed rationing in cities but not requisitioning in villages unworkable because peasants might refuse to sell grain if they thought the urban sale price was set too low. Similarly, requisitioning in villages while keeping a free market in cities would not work because peasants would go to cities to repurchase grain that they had already sold to the state. Chen also ruled out three other options: leaving grain management up to localities, "digging a well when on the verge of thirst" (requisitioning from highly productive areas only when supplies got tight), and using advance-purchase contracts (which peasants tended to breach in lean years).[22]

Chen Yun said that economic planners were left with only one choice: replace the private grain market with centralized management that requisitioned grain from villages and supplied it to city residents through rationing (this would become known as "unified purchasing and marketing," or *tonggou tongxiao*). At a Politburo meeting on October 2, 1953, Chen warned what might transpire without a centralized system: prices would fluctuate, forcing wages up and damaging the First

[20] Bo Yibo, *Ruogan zhongda juece*, 1:181, 183.

[21] Jin Chongji and Chen Qun, eds., *Chen Yun zhuan* [Biography of Chen Yun] (Beijing: Zhongyang wenxian chubanshe, 2005), 1:845.

[22] Bo Yibo, *Ruogan zhongda juece*, 1:183–84.

Five-Year Plan. Chen admitted that his proposal to centralize requisitioning and rationing was not perfect, but insisted that there was no alternative. "Are there shortcomings?" he asked. "Yes. It might dampen production enthusiasm, hound people to death . . . and cause insurrections in certain areas. But it would be worse if we do not implement it. That would mean going down the old road of old China importing grain," which would cause socialist construction to fail, and might even lead to war against the imperialists.[23] Chen Yun was arguing that the success of China's revolutionary modernization project depended on implementing a state grain monopoly.

Mao Zedong agreed. At the end of the Politburo meeting, Mao approved Chen Yun's report, saying that putting a unified grain policy in place would be a "war" that required urgent mobilization. Sensing that requisitioning and rationing might make peasants, city people, and foreign opinion all "unhappy," Mao called for a big propaganda show, but ordered that "not one word" about the grain monopoly appear in newspapers.[24] Promoting state control over food required face-to-face contact between propagandists and people who would be affected by the new policy, while newspaper articles might raise anxieties, leading to rumors and hoarding.

Even without newspaper publicity, people in and around Tianjin rushed to store up grain when they heard that the city would begin rationing flour on November 1, 1953. One Tianjin grain shop that normally sold ten bags of flour per day sold fifty bags on October 29. When informed that some residents would receive more grain than others based on presumed differences in levels of physical exertion required in various occupations, people complained about arbitrary unfairness: workers in large factories with more than one hundred employees would receive nine kilograms of flour per month, while those in smaller factories would get six kilograms. "Since we are all members of the working class," some party members said, "might two different ration levels affect the unity of the working class?" Others remarked, "After liberation the standard of living went up. Why is it going down now?"[25]

Requisitioning in villages was at least as nerve-wracking for villagers as rationing was for city residents. Peasants hoarded grain in counties surrounding Tianjin, including Baxian, Baodi, Jinghai, and Wuqing. One

[23] Ibid., 1:185–86.

[24] Ibid., 1:186.

[25] NBCK 257 (November 3, 1953): 27–28.

man in Wuqing, anxious that the state would take his crops, distributed a cartful of corn and peanuts to three different relatives before changing his mind and taking the cart back home. Other peasants in Wuqing rushed to grind their wheat into flour, which was easier to store.[26]

It turned out that villagers had more reason to worry than urbanites did. After initial problems preventing grain from flowing out of Tianjin to hungry villages (train passengers carried 125,000 kilograms of grain out of the Tianjin station each month in early 1954),[27] the state grain monopoly guaranteed sufficient rations to city residents while leaving peasants in an increasingly perilous position. Kenneth Walker has calculated rural Hebei's grain consumption as a percentage of Tianjin's consumption during the first years of the state grain monopoly. Villagers consumed considerably less than people in Tianjin:

- 1953: 73.3%
- 1954: 67.5%
- 1955: 90%
- 1956: 83%
- 1957: 90.5%
- Average Hebei grain consumption as a percentage of Tianjin grain consumption, 1953–1957: 80.2%[28]

In comparison with the countryside, Tianjin offered job opportunities, protection from natural disaster, and plentiful and secure food supplies. It is therefore not surprising that villagers continued to move to the city after the state grain monopoly began in late 1953.

Rural-to-urban migration in the mid-1950s threatened the new state monopoly on grain and pushed central planners to make what historian Wang Haiguang has called the "passive choice" to restrict mobility by linking household registration to grain rationing.[29] The decision was

[26] NBCK 297 (December 19, 1953): 355.

[27] Guo Fengqi, ed., *Tianjin tong zhi: shangye zhi, liangshi juan* [Tianjin gazetteer: Commerce gazetteer, grain volume] (Tianjin: Tianjin shehui kexueyuan, 1994), 111.

[28] Kenneth R. Walker, *Food Grain Procurement and Consumption in China* (New York: Cambridge University Press, 1984), 123. Robert Ash shows that villagers consumed considerably less food than city people nationwide throughout the Mao period. The gap in consumption of vegetable oil, sugar, and pork was even more striking than inequality in grain consumption. See Robert Ash, "Squeezing the Peasants: Grain Extraction, Food Consumption and Rural Living Standards in Mao's China," *China Quarterly* 188 (2006): 991.

[29] Wang Haiguang, "Dangdai Zhongguo huji zhidu xingcheng yu yange de hongguan fenxi" [A macroscopic analysis of the formation and evolution of contemporary China's household registration system], *Zhonggong dangshi yanjiu* 4 (2003): 23.

TABLE 2.1. *Population Moving in and out of Tianjin's Urban Districts, 1951–1957*

	Moved In	Moved Out	Net Change
1951	235,958	175,424	60,534
1952	193,458	167,638	25,820
1953	195,692	138,445	57,247
1954	162,390	108,059	54,331
1955	126,286	215,426	−89,140
1956	221,038	161,046	59,992
1957	168,968	83,823	85,145

Source: Tianjin shi dang'anguan, ed., *Jindai yilai Tianjin chengshihua jincheng shilu* [Record of the process of urbanization in modern Tianjin] (Tianjin: Tianjin renmin chubanshe, 2005), 715.

"passive" in that it reacted to the unintended consequences of the grain monopoly. Its starting point was "let's address a grain crisis that might threaten the revolution," rather than "let's limit freedom of movement between city and countryside." Throughout the mid-1950s, officials in Tianjin had new rules and tools at their disposal to restrict migration to the city. As Table 2.1 shows, Tianjin authorities did manage to reverse the flow in 1955, but overall they found themselves fighting a losing battle.

A "Bad Influence"

According to an internal labor bureau report from April 1955, around seven thousand of the more than one hundred thousand villagers who moved to Tianjin in the previous year had found jobs. The prospect of steady work in Tianjin, the report noted, "encouraged even more farmers to flow blindly into the city." Other migrants had not found formal employment, but stayed in the city nonetheless, and some even resorted to selling their belongings, collecting junk, begging, thieving, or turning to prostitution.[30] Some of the migrants explicitly linked their difficulties to the state grain monopoly. One woman said that the government had "talked a good line about buying our grain, saying that it would guarantee that we would have enough to eat," but then it sold millet to peasants at a higher rate than it had paid them for grain the previous year. "How is that reasonable?!" she asked. In January 1955, another "disaster victim" who had come to Tianjin said, "once the grain is sold, you cannot buy it back," which he claimed had led to a situation even worse than the years

[30] TMA, X53-1002C, 4.

of famine before 1949: "people are eating weeds, wheat husks, and corn stalks in villages now."[31]

City officials attempting to manage the urban food supply did not welcome villagers who had fled the effects of grain requisitioning. On May 3, 1955, the Tianjin municipal government sent a notice to all urban districts on "mobilizing vagrant begging disaster victims to return to their villages and produce" (*dongyuan liulang qigai de zaimin huixiang shengchan*):

> Since February, vagrant disaster victims begging on the street have gradually increased. These people often ask for food at people's homes or on the streets. Some use the excuse of selling ash paper (*huizhi*) or firewood to enter residences and when no one is home they steal things. Some push their bawling children down the street on small carts, causing many people to gather and stare, which has a bad influence.[32]

Poor peasants on Tianjin streets were a "bad influence" because they attracted attention and raised questions among city residents, some of whom wondered: What was wrong in the countryside? Why were peasants so much worse off than urbanites? Destitute migrants made city residents aware of rural grain requisitioning and inequities in food consumption.

One report sent to top leaders in Beijing detailed the "chaotic thoughts" of Tianjin residents who heard peasants complaining about unified grain purchasing. A man named Dong said, "There is so much flour in Tianjin that we cannot eat it all, but in villages the peasants do not have any flour at all. The government should pay more attention to the whole picture." Other city residents commented on the specifics of unequal rationing levels. A woman named Li told a police officer that while her family received a monthly ration of 700 grams of cooking oil, "peasants only get 150 grams per person per month. Isn't that too little? Take some of our oil and give it to them to eat."[33] Policy makers did not adopt Li's suggestion. Instead, they removed poor migrants from the city.

Two weeks after first circulating the notice to "mobilize vagrant begging disaster victims" to return to their villages, Tianjin authorities publicized the same policy more widely, but this time the reference to "vagrant beggars" was removed from the title, implicitly broadening the scope of

31 NBCK 5 (January 7, 1955): 124.
32 TMA, X53-1002C, 2.
33 NBCK 5 (January 7, 1955): 124.

people targeted for removal.[34] Neighborhood offices were to work with local police stations to investigate poor migrants in Tianjin. Beggars and those with "improper income" were to be mobilized to return home and, if necessary, provided with travel funds. If an individual declined to return home voluntarily, he or she could be detained and the mobilization effort could continue in a detention center.[35]

Later in May 1955, police officers and civil affairs cadres in the Wandezhuang neighborhood surveyed 1,699 "disaster victims" (864 women and 385 men mostly from nearby rural counties).[36] Almost anyone with a rural background who scraped together a marginal living in the city was counted in the survey, including people who came seasonally or even those who had lived in the city for more than ten years. More than three-quarters of the migrants stayed with family or friends. Ms. Liu, a fifty-one-year-old woman from Wuqing county, moved in with her daughter and son-in-law Zhang Shiqing, who worked as an inspector at the Tianjin Streetcar Company. Liu's daughter said that thanks to Zhang's monthly salary of fifty yuan, it was not a problem to feed one more mouth in the city. It would have been more of a burden to send money back to Wuqing, she said. Although Liu was identified in the survey, city cadres did not ask her to return to her village. Urban residents were implored to discourage their family members from coming to Tianjin, but the Civil Affairs Bureau instructed cadres not to "directly mobilize" refugees living with city relatives to return to villages.[37] Officials probably feared the potentially destabilizing effect of forcibly splitting up families. As we will see in future chapters, government recognition of family ties assisted villagers who hoped to become long-term city residents.

The report about "disaster victims" in Wandezhuang noted that many of them were making and saving money. Officials counted 118 peddlers who lived in small inns or stayed with fellow villagers. Twenty-three-year-old Feng Laofu carted peanuts to Tianjin from his village in March

[34] "Shi renmin weiyuanhui tongzhi ge qu dongyuan liuru chengshi de zaimin huanxiang shengchan" [The municipal people's committee informs each district to mobilize disaster victims who have flowed into the city to return to villages and produce], *Tianjin shizheng zhoubao* 144 (May 23, 1955): 5.

[35] TMA, X53–1002C, 2.

[36] The following paragraphs on the civil affairs survey are from TMA, X53–1003C, 23–28. The survey was conducted as a first step in identifying and removing undesirables who were affecting social order in Tianjin.

[37] In December 1955, a city order continued the practice of not removing wives, children, and parents who had come to stay with relatives in Tianjin. Nannies from villages were also allowed to stay. *Tianjin shizheng zhoubao* 172 (December 5, 1955): 2.

1955 and roasted them at a street stand, earning around 1.5 yuan a day. An additional 194 of those surveyed had found temporary or long-term work, some through the Wandezhuang labor market, others through small factory proprietors or family connections. Another group of people who said they regularly came to the city during the slack agricultural season were counted as disaster victims, including fifty-five who collected and resold junk. Xing Qiulu, a forty-seven-year-old man from Cangxian, lived in a small communal dwelling and saved around 0.3 yuan every day from junk recycling, enough to send five yuan home to his family shortly before city officials interviewed him.

Only eleven of the outsiders counted in Wandezhuang admitted to begging. All of them lived in inns, and four were labeled "professional beggars" (*zhiye qigai*). Liu Zhanyuan, a thirty-six-year-old from neighboring Jinghai county, had lived in a Tianjin inn since 1945. He went out early each morning to an area of workers' dormitories, where he would "tell the masses that he had been hit by disaster and could not survive. If the masses do not give him money he pretends that he is dying." Liu earned up to three yuan by the end of each workday, when he took a bus back to his inn. He told his interviewers that he wanted to become a peddler but did not have the capital to get started.

At the end of their report, officials analyzed why people had come to the city. They concluded that because Tianjin's "urban people" and the "masses" from nearby counties had strong family ties, villagers came not only to find food, but also to visit family. Others came seasonally to peddle or do odd jobs.[38] The problem, the report claimed, was that after coming to Tianjin, rural people found work and became dissatisfied with agricultural production. Their presence "adds to the labor force and definitely affects the employment of unemployed workers, market management, the grain and oil supply, and social order." In effect, the Wandezhuang report's author was blaming migrants for disrupting key elements of the socialist planned economy, including labor allocation and grain rationing. In the eyes of city officials, migrants were messing up the plan.

Linking *Hukou* to Food and Mobility

As spring 1955 turned to summer, Tianjin officials made adjustments to both food and migration policy. They were following directions from

[38] Liu Haiyan has shown that this was a longstanding practice during the Qing and Republican periods. Liu Haiyan, *Kongjian yu shehui*, 264.

central authorities who had become convinced that in order to function effectively, the grain monopoly needed to be accompanied by tighter restrictions on mobility. Before implementing changes, officials studied problems and loopholes in grain policy. While civil affairs cadres surveyed migrants in Wandezhuang, grain bureaucrats collaborated with Tianjin police to investigate "suspicious travelers" (*keyi de lüke*) transporting food. Between May 21 and 28, cadres discovered 309 people, mostly peasants from near Tianjin, carrying almost four thousand kilograms of grain. When questioned, the peasants explained that they had bought cornmeal from city residents. They said they could not buy grain in their own villages. Once back home, they intended to mix the cornmeal with wheat chaff or stalks, in order to survive the spring food shortages. City officials confiscated goods from sixteen travelers who were suspected of reselling at a profit; the grain bureau compensated the others by buying back cornmeal "at a reduced price."[39]

A few weeks later, in mid-June 1955, Tianjin grain officials set up thirty-nine checkpoints on roads and waterways leaving the city. Not much happened until dark fell. After midnight, cadres discovered "quite a few people" transporting grain in groups. Some pulled wagons, using layers of clothes or dried grass to conceal packages of crackers and vermicelli. In a single day, eighteen people, many of them "old men" (*laotou*), transported grain from one spot in the south suburbs. Not surprisingly, smugglers reacted unhappily when officials confiscated their cargo at checkpoints. A report sent to central leaders in Beijing about the "severe" outflow of grain from Tianjin noted that, "in a few places, peasants beat inspectors with shoulder poles."[40]

Convinced of the need to get tough, city officials introduced new policies on grain management and migration control in July 1955. Investigators went house to house and established new ration standards based on what Tianjin families had actually consumed in the previous month. Grain authorities claimed that new rules passed on July 9, 1955 reasserted control over food supplies by "attacking illegal buying and reducing the outflow of grain."[41] Then on July 20, 1955, Tianjin's PSB sent a "Measure to Use *Hukou* to Restrict the Blind Flow of Population into Tianjin"

[39] NBCK 130 (June 7, 1955): 71.

[40] NBCK 148 (June 28, 1955): 461.

[41] The new rationing rules passed on July 9, 1955, known as "set the ration by household" (*yi hu dingliang*), were replaced by a new policy, called "set the ration by person" (*yi ren dingliang*) in November 1955. Guo Fengqi, *Tianjin tong zhi: shangye zhi, liangshi juan*, 111.

to the city's police stations.[42] The policy formally linked household registration to mobility control. The PSB instructed police stations to ask people entering the city about their "'occupation,' 'reason for entering,' 'native place,' 'previous address,' 'occupation at native place or previous address,' 'economic circumstances,' and 'on whom are you relying' in the city." Migrants who belonged to five restricted categories – specifically, people "blindly coming to Tianjin looking for work," people coming to the city to rely on friends or family, peasants privately hired by city enterprises without permission from the Labor Bureau, and "other consumers who have improper employment or lost their means of living in their original homes" – were to be denied Tianjin *hukou*.[43] Without city *hukou*, people affected by the new policy would be ineligible for urban food rations.

Tianjin was following national policy as it tightened restrictions on mobility in 1955. The city's policy of using *hukou* to control population movement was issued less than a month after the State Council circulated its "Directive Concerning the Establishment of a Permanent System of Household Registration." Later in the year, the State Council issued policies governing grain rationing in cities (on August 25, 1955), and demarcating between urban and rural areas (on November 11, 1955).[44] Together, these rules attempted to define urban and rural spatial categories, restrict people from moving between the two spaces, and ensure that rural areas provided grain to cities and towns.

It is no coincidence that new rules tightening state control over grain and mobility coincided with Mao's all-out push to collectivize agriculture in the second half of 1955. Mao saw rapid cooperativization as a revolutionary movement that would ensure China's transition to socialism. But according to Bo Yibo, some of Mao's colleagues in the central leadership ended up supporting collectivization for a different reason. They thought it would help increase China's grain supply, in turn fueling urban industrialization. Bo writes, "After land reform, everyone recognized that a small-scale peasant economy would not satisfy China's ever-increasing grain needs."[45] In other words, economic planners hoped that organizing farmers into bigger collectives would increase the food supply. Mao's call to collectivize the countryside in 1955 meshed revolutionary impulses

[42] TMA, X53-1002C, 38, 46–49; Guo Fengqi, *Tianjin tong zhi: gongan zhi*, 37.
[43] TMA, X53-1002C, 47.
[44] Cheng, "Dialectics of Control," 95–102, 396–400.
[45] Bo Yibo, *Ruogan zhongda juece*, 1:256.

with modernization efforts. In order for this revolutionary modernization project to succeed, people had to move on the state's terms, not as they pleased. In Tianjin, officials worked to get rural migrants back to the countryside.

Shock Mobilization

Part of Tianjin's effort to restrict migration in the mid-1950s involved setting up ad hoc committees to periodically push migrants back to their home villages. In July 1955 the municipal government established a "Population Office" staffed by cadres transferred from the public security, civil affairs, labor, and commerce bureaus, the women's league and youth league, and the party-run union. Each city district also responded. Neighborhood offices formed work teams to persuade migrants to depart Tianjin. Between July 1955 and March 1956, 128,200 people left the city and returned to villages. The Tianjin government declared that the project had successfully "increased the power of agricultural production, and also decreased the nonproductive population and appropriately laid the base for a socialist city."[46] In other words, urban employment pressures had been eased by this transfer of labor power to the countryside at the height of the collectivization campaign.

After mid-1956, city population offices disbanded and cadres returned to their original work units. Forcing migrants to leave the city was a difficult and unwelcome task for city cadres, who only sprung into action when prodded by directives from above. At this point, deporting migrants was episodic and not part of the daily portfolio of urban officials. Rural people still came to Tianjin. Another wave of damaging floods and hailstorms assailed the countryside surrounding Tianjin in summer 1956. To the north, Anci, Baodi, and Wuqing counties were hit hard; in Cangxian to the south, flooding was even worse than in 1954.[47] Refugees built six hundred new shacks in Tianjin during the second half of 1956, and by spring 1957 city officials estimated that the number of peasants in the city had doubled since December 1956.[48] In 1956 and 1957, more than 205,000 rural people had moved into Tianjin.[49]

[46] TMA, X53-1002C, 82-83.

[47] Wang Wei and Zhao Jihua, eds., *Wuqing xian zhi* [Wuqing county gazetteer] (Tianjin: Tianjin shehui kexueyuan, 1991), 41; TMA, X53-751Y, 112.

[48] TMA, X53-684Y, 50, 12.

[49] "Shi renmin weiyuanhui guanyu dongyuan liuru chengshi nongmin huixiang canjia shengchan de fang'an" [Municipal people's committee's program for mobilizing farmers

Flooding was not the only factor pushing migrants out of the countryside. Collectivization and grain procurement may have also played a role. The summer 1957 harvest in Tianjin prefecture failed to meet state planners' quota. According to an internal New China News Agency report, the main reason for the disappointing numbers was that rural cadres had "opposed grain work" by falsely reporting yields in order to hand over less grain to the state (thereby keeping more for themselves).[50] Similar problems plagued the Tianjin suburbs, where a Tianjin Grain Bureau employee reported that the amount of wheat collected by the state would only meet 60 percent of the quota. More than 10 percent of farmers actively resisted requisitioning, and some sold grain at higher prices on the black market instead of giving it to the state.[51] Given this situation, it is no surprise that some villagers decided that trying to gain a foothold in the city was preferable to fighting for a share of the harvest in the countryside.

In April 1957, vice mayor Wan Xiaotang established another temporary organization to remove the new arrivals from Tianjin. As in 1955, city officials attempted to ease the task by focusing on the most vulnerable populations: people staying with distant relatives or friends were targeted, while people living with close relatives were not. Those who had found temporary work could finish out their contracts. But people living out in the open, either in homemade sheds or on the floors of waiting rooms in the city's train stations, were sitting ducks. This is what city officials discovered when they carried out "shock mobilization" (*tuji dongyuan*) roundups at Tianjin's train stations and street corners. In 1957, there was no "great wall" separating Tianjin from its hinterland. It was impossible to completely stop people who wanted to enter the city. How could authorities be entirely certain who was a "peasant" or "disaster victim" and who was in the city legitimately? Some migrants to Tianjin exploited this confusion.

Between May 16 and May 26, 1957, the number of people living at Tianjin's three train stations increased precipitously. At the main east station there were around two thousand rural people sleeping on the floor, and there were six hundred more at the north and west stations. Around 80 percent of the disaster victims were from Wuqing county;

who flowed into the city to return to villages to participate in production], *Tianjin shizheng zhoubao* 281 (January 6, 1958): 2.

[50] NBCK 2278 (August 8, 1957): 23.

[51] Ibid., 24–25.

most of them were women, elderly people, and children. Aside from a few young people who cut grass or worked odd jobs, the refugees went out early each morning to beg. Officials from Tianjin and others from Hebei province traveled to Anci, Baodi, and Wuqing to demand that local governments transfer relief grain to needy areas and establish "dissuasion stations" (*quanzu zhan*) to stop potential migrants before they left their home counties. Tianjin officials also formed a work team of cadres and railway police to handle refugees at the train stations.[52]

During the last five days of May 1957, around thirty city officials placed 2,722 residents of Tianjin's railway stations on trains back to their home counties. But the total number of people lying on the floors held steady. The problem was that as soon as a train left Tianjin, another arrived with more refugees. In early June, the number of city cadres assigned to railway deportation work jumped to sixty, and their strategy shifted. Instead of emptying out the waiting rooms, city cadres focused on arriving trains. They rounded up passengers as soon as they disembarked, offered food to "temporarily allay their hunger," and put them on the next train out. This method was more effective, and the number of people living at Tianjin's east station shrunk from 1,521 on May 31 to 691 on June 4. Prospective migrants got the message that they would not be welcomed at city train stations. Unfortunately, a work report admitted, "we discovered that during dissuasion work on the platforms, the scope of those rounded up was too broad and some masses who were not disaster victims were held and delayed for a while. Pay attention to correcting this erroneous tendency from now on."[53]

How were officials to discern who was an unacceptable migrant and who was simply a legitimate traveler taking a train to Tianjin? They profiled deportation targets based on their appearance. Rural people attempting to get to Tianjin by train in June 1957 were aware of this and took advantage of it. Officials at the train station reported that some migrants had begun "playing tricks" to avoid getting rounded up. Some wore new clothes and claimed that they had come to Tianjin to see relatives. Further questioning revealed that the gussied up visitors had no family or friends in the city. Savvy rural people tried to pass as legitimate travelers. They realized that they could not look like refugees if they wanted to avoid the cadres on the platform. We do not know how many newly tailored rural people were able to convince the city work team to let them proceed. But

[52] TMA, X53-684Y, 26.

[53] Ibid., 31.

the migrants knew that they were being profiled based on appearance. In the 1950s, urban and rural identities were cultural categories as well as state-imposed labels.[54]

In spite of awkward cases of mistaken identity, authorities were so pleased with the results at the train station that later in June they attempted the same strategy in the city at large. Quick round-ups of suspected disaster victims on Tianjin streets were not free of problems. According to the summary bulletin of the weeklong "shock mobilization and detention of disaster victims sleeping on the streets and begging," 337 people returned to villages and 106 were sent to detention centers. The problem was that some cadres "did not check people's status carefully enough" and could not distinguish between different types of people. Some pedicab drivers, temporary workers, and legitimate residents of guest houses were rounded up and sent out of the city, "causing great unhappiness."[55] In their zeal to rid the city of disaster victims, city cadres cast their nets too wide. Anyone who looked rural,[56] was engaged in outdoor physical labor, or with a non-fixed residence could have been suspect, even if he or she was contributing to Tianjin's socialist modernization in an officially sanctioned manner.

Had the detainees been working inside factories, they would not have been mistaken for return-to-village targets. Industrial work remained a legitimate reason to migrate from villages to Tianjin during the 1950s.

54 These cultural categories were shaped by the changes of the early twentieth century. According to anthropologist Myron Cohen, that is when urban intellectual elites "invented" the Chinese peasantry as a cultural category. A vast, undifferentiated mass of backward rural residents was seen as one of the primary obstacles on China's path to modernization. Myron Cohen, "Cultural and Political Inventions in Modern China: The Case of the Chinese 'Peasant,'" *Daedalus* 122, no. 2 (1993): 151–70. For other works about the formation of rural and urban identities in the Republican period, see Yi-tsi Mei Feuerwerker, *Ideology, Power, Text: Self-Representation and the Peasant "Other" in Modern Chinese Literature* (Stanford: Stanford University Press, 1998), Xiaorong Han, *Chinese Discourses on the Peasant, 1900–1949* (Albany: State University of New York Press, 2005), and Susan Mann, "Urbanization and Historical Change in China," *Modern China* 10, no. 1 (1984): 94.

55 TMA, X53–684Y, 56. Another category of "return to village targets" in 1957 and 1958 consisted of longtime city residents who had migrated to Qinghai province in 1955 and 1956. More than half of the over ten thousand migrants had "flowed back" to Tianjin without permission by 1957.

56 I discuss the socially constructed physical markers of rural identity, including dark skin, homespun clothing, and "bearing" (*fengdu*), in Jeremy Brown, "Spatial Profiling: Seeing Rural and Urban in Mao's China," in James Cook, Joshua Goldstein, Matthew David Johnson, and Sigrid Schmalzer, eds., *Visualizing Modern China* (Lanham, MD: Rowman & Littlefield, forthcoming).

Yet just as disaster victims and other farmers resisted or subverted official efforts to categorize and deport them by moving in with relatives, cheating free tickets, donning disguises, or simply refusing to leave, many migrants in factories based their decisions on work and family, often ignoring (or simply unaware of) the Communist regime's restrictions.

At the end of 1957, urban cadres in charge of "return to village" mobilization summarized the year's work and outlined plans for the future. Hexi district officials acknowledged the challenges in removing villagers from the city: "Several times over the past years we have mobilized peasants to return to villages to produce, but the inflow phenomenon still continues to increase. Aside from flooding in some areas, and some peasants not being satisfied with agricultural production and envying city life, the reason for the inflow has to do with problems in our work." Such problems included hiring peasants without approval from the city Labor Bureau (16,666 people between 1956 and September 1957 citywide, including 308 in Hexi) and city people helping their relatives get formal urban employment.[57] It is telling that city officials identified urbanites' finding jobs for migrants as one of the main obstacles in their efforts to manage Tianjin's population.

Work and Family

During the 1950s, many rural migrants used family connections to get factory work, or responded to recruitment by city work units that actively sought out migrants. Between 1951 and 1957 more than 780,000 people entered Tianjin in search of work or to move in with family members, and urban enterprises recruited an additional 409,000 workers from villages.[58] They crossed the rural-urban divide just as state-imposed laws and categories reified the gap. Those who found jobs during this period made the gradual transition from farmer to factory worker. City authorities tried to regulate this movement, but some migrants and urban recruiters circumvented *hukou*, labor, and grain rationing rules and continued to make work arrangements based on family or native place connections.

[57] Tianjin shi Hexi qu renmin weiyuanhui, "Hexi qu guanyu dongyuan liuru chengshi nongmin huanxiang shengchan de gongzuo jihua (caogao)" [Hexi district draft work plan on mobilizing peasants who flowed into the city to return to villages to produce], December 24, 1957, AC.

[58] Li Jingneng, ed., *Zhongguo renkou, Tianjin fence* [China's population, Tianjin volume] (Beijing: Zhongguo caizheng jingji chubanshe, 1987), 157.

Immediately after the takeover of Tianjin in 1949, the new government's labor bureau attempted to register tens of thousands of unemployed workers (*shiye gongren*) who had lost jobs during the turbulence of the late 1940s. After signing up, unemployed workers received welfare stipends and waited for the labor bureau to assign them to new jobs. The question of who was eligible for registration was contentious. Not only were peasants ineligible, former factory workers who had returned to their native villages after losing city jobs were not allowed to register.[59] By going home and farming after factory closures, migrants had unwittingly disqualified themselves from officially sanctioned urban futures. The only peasants eligible to register for city job assignments were farmers in the immediate suburbs whose land had been appropriated for urban construction.[60]

Migrants accustomed to traveling between villages and Tianjin as rural harvests and urban job opportunities fluctuated were surprised when doors were shut. In December 1952, the Hebei journal *Village propagandist* published a letter to the editor about a disappointed villager named Kong Zhiqiang, who had worked in a Tianjin factory until 1951, fell ill and returned to his village to recuperate, but was not allowed to register for a job assignment when he returned to the city in 1952. The editor responded that the vestiges of imperialist, reactionary rule in cities (potent issues in Tianjin, where foreign architecture still dominated the former concessions and where the Japanese and Nationalists had ruled for twenty consecutive years before 1949) meant that urban unemployment was still a problem:

> The party and government decided on the following policy: solve city problems in the city, solve village problems in the village. Blindly running to cities without planning causes more difficulty in solving the unemployment problem. Actually, this is also taking care of peasants, because when you do not find a job in the city and go back and forth in a futile effort, it is a big waste, and not as good as just finding a way to get by in the village in the first place.

But after the situation in cities improved, the editor added, jobs would be plentiful for everyone. "It is not like some people think, that there is no future for peasants going to the city," he wrote. "Please tell returned

[59] TMA, X68–84Y, 2.

[60] "Tianjin shi laodong jiuye weiyuanhui guanyu shiye ji qiuzhi renyuan tongyi dengji banfa gongzuo xize" [Tianjin municipal labor employment committee's detailed work regulations on unified registration of unemployed and job-seeking personnel] *Tianjin shizheng zhoubao* 7 (October 27, 1952): 6.

workers in villages to not get anxious. In the future they will be invited to work in factories and mines."[61]

Many villagers were unwilling to wait. They came to Tianjin anyway and ignored official job assignment regulations. Several months after Kong Zhiqiang's story appeared in print, more than two thousand peasants and demobilized soldiers attempted to register for jobs in Tianjin but were denied. In one district of the city, half of the denied migrants remained in Tianjin and fended for themselves.[62] Throughout the 1950s, even following the implementation of rural grain procurement and urban rationing in 1953 and regulations linking *hukou* to mobility in 1955, some rural people landed jobs in Tianjin before they left their villages. In December 1954, cadres at a state-operated knitting and dye factory decided on their own to hire thirty-one people from a single village in the Xushui area of Hebei. A good portion of the village's leadership departed for Tianjin, including fourteen militia members, five vice–village leaders, and five production team leaders. It is likely that dye factory management had family ties to Xushui, because it was not necessary to look so far afield for new workers. When flood refugees entered Tianjin in 1955, it was easy for factories to find migrant workers. Tianjin's Daming Steel Mill, which had already been nationalized, bypassed the city labor bureau's introduction of temporary workers and went straight to small guesthouses to hire "disaster victims" at a cheaper rate. Some flood refugees were even hired on as long-term workers, including eight people who used family connections to get jobs at cotton processing factories.[63]

Family ties remained the best way to get a job and establish residency in 1950s Tianjin. Wei Rongchun was a typical case. Around midday one afternoon in 1951, the seventeen-year-old boarded a small boat in Baodi county.[64] After a full twenty-eight hours of floating and paddling down the canals and rivers north of Tianjin, he disembarked. For the first time in his life Wei laid eyes upon what was then the largest city in north China. Dazzled and overwhelmed by Tianjin's electric lights, tall buildings, and wide roads, Wei felt thankful that he was not alone. He had made the

[61] "Nongcun li de shengyu laodongli bu neng mangmu de xiang chengshi li pao" [Excess labor in villages cannot blindly run toward cities], *Nongcun xuanchuanyuan* (Baoding) 23 (December 20, 1952): 25. This journal, aimed at rural propaganda workers, featured question-and-answer articles and letters to the editor instructing village officials how to respond appropriately to thorny questions like the one posed by Kong Zhiqiang.

[62] TMA, X67–31Y, 1.

[63] TMA, X53–1002C, 27.

[64] Interviewee 1.

trip with a cousin who worked at a hat workshop, and he stayed at his uncle's house in the city. Wei had originally hoped to work alongside his cousin making hats, but there were no jobs available. After a few days in the city, Wei was ready to give up and make the long journey back to his village. But his uncle happened to work at a belt factory, and he found Wei a position as an apprentice.

For his first six months on the job, Wei did not leave the confines of the belt workshop. He worked and slept in the same space, often rising as early as four in the morning and working until almost midnight. As an apprentice, he earned one hundred kilograms of millet per month, half of what regular workers did, and payday only came once a year. By the mid-1950s, when urban officials began efforts to remove unwanted farmers, disaster victims, and vagrants from the city, Wei was not a target. He had become an acceptable urban resident, a worker in a newly nationalized, consolidated, and expanded knitting and dye factory. In 1956 he joined the Communist Party, and his salary was enough to support his parents, his younger brother's schooling, and his wife back in Baodi.

Most of Wei's colleagues were originally from villages, including a couple from Raoyang county in Hebei who met at the factory in 1952 and married two years later. The wife had moved in with her uncle's family in Tianjin to help with household chores before finding a job at the belt factory. The couple worked in Tianjin until retirement.[65] But while some newly formed families built lives in the city, other migrants returned to villages because of domestic issues, or simply because they could not handle working in Tianjin.

Liang Yangfu grew up in the same Baodi village as Wei Rongchun, who was four years Liang's senior. In 1955, the year when new policies directly linked *hukou* to mobility control, Liang's father drove him into Tianjin on a horsecart. It was a slow, bumpy, overnight trip. Liang began what was supposed to be a three-year apprenticeship to a family friend who was an itinerant barber. The teenager hated the work, and after a year of going from house to house cutting hair, he quit and returned to his village to work the fields. He would have preferred a city factory job over agricultural work ("who wants to suffer the exhaustion [of farming]?" he asked), but he had no idea how to find one. It seemed impossible to the seventeen-year-old. As an unpaid apprentice he was completely dependent on his master barber. He was afraid to approach strangers in Tianjin. "I

65 Interviewee 2, interviewee 3.

felt restrained and did not know what to do," Liang remembered, "I even looked down on myself."[66] Liang gave up on Tianjin and went home on his own, without any prompting from the various official agencies charged with limiting rural migration.

Another Baodi resident's migration decisions during the 1950s also had little to do with state regulations and categories. Right around the time of the Communist takeover of Tianjin, a village woman named Zhang went to visit her husband, who was working in the city. Her husband used his connections to get her a job at a hat workshop. Zhang liked the work, even though she had to stay in a dormitory apart from her husband. One day her husband dropped by for a visit, an event that cut short Zhang's future in Tianjin. "Some male colleagues of mine were passing by and came in and sat down," she remembered. "As soon as [my husband] saw this he got mad and thought that I had something going on with someone else. I was so upset that I didn't eat for two days, and he didn't let me work anymore, so I came back [to the village]." She lived in Baodi for the rest of her life, only returning to Tianjin temporarily when food was short in the village during the Great Leap famine.[67]

In January 1958 the National People's Congress adopted stricter household registration regulations which tied families to their rural or urban residence, but the rules were ignored when the leap began several months later. In addition to its well-publicized goals of rural communization and miraculous bumper harvests, the leap also called for rapid urban industrialization. The path to utopia ran through both city and countryside. The leap's emphasis on urban industry meant that Tianjin's population would continue to grow, as it had throughout the 1950s. The volume of migrants coming to Tianjin ebbed and flowed during the 1950s, and the leap ushered in another major influx. Even during relatively restrictive periods like the return-to-village movement of 1955 and the shock mobilizations of 1957, many people in Tianjin successfully negotiated state-imposed obstacles between city and village by resisting deportation and challenging categorization. During the leap, even more people crossed the rural-urban divide. As we shall see in the following pages, the tragic injustice of the leap was that urban-based authorities allowed villagers to starve while guaranteeing the survival of city residents. The rural famine was an unintended consequence of the leap, but

[66] Interviewee 4.
[67] Interviewee 5.

the steps taken to prioritize urban industry by taking grain from peasants during the 1950s suggest that we should not be surprised by how unevenly the disaster unfolded. The famine, contributed to in part by untrammeled rural-to-urban migration, convinced state planners that more control was the answer.

3

Tianjin's Great Leap

Urban Survival, Rural Starvation

In 1959, in response to food shortages in Wuqing county just northwest of Tianjin, a member of an opera troupe in the village of Zaolin composed a "clappertalk" (*kuaiban*) routine called "Suffering from Famine" (*Nao liang huang*). The piece was performed openly in the village. The composer charged that there were all kinds of obstacles to getting sufficient food, and that no matter how good the crops were, there was never enough to eat. In contrast, he continued, people in Beijing and Tianjin always had plenty to eat. After hearing the performance, villagers proposed organizing a caravan to Tianjin. Some peasants expressed doubt that food was more abundant in the city, and did not want to go, but the clappertalk composer, insinuating that certain families might be hoarding grain secretly, said, "whoever does not go to Tianjin must have food in their house." Persuaded by this argument, more than 180 villagers clambered on eight large carts and embarked for Tianjin. When the villagers arrived in the city, they begged for food on the streets.[1] They were indeed correct in their impression that food was more plentiful in Tianjin.

The desperately hungry peasants from Wuqing knew that cities were better off than villages during the famine. They may not have paused to wonder why the demands of rapid modernization gave cities priority in

[1] Zhonggong Hebei shengwei *Hebei siqing tongxun* bianji bu, ed., *Hebei nongcun jieji douzheng dianxing cailiao* [Representative materials on class struggle in Hebei villages], vol. 1 (February 1966), 169–70. This collection of "negative examples" (*fanmian jiaocai*) produced during the Four Cleanups movement featured many stories of illicit migration, grain smuggling, and hoarding that occurred during the leap.

the socialist planned economy, but they knew that food would be easier to find in Tianjin. As centers of heavy industry, cities played a leading role in the Great Leap Forward's push toward utopia, and the people who lived in them were protected.

Focusing on the city does not mean discounting the rural nature of the famine. But in order to understand how the famine struck China so unevenly, we cannot ignore cities. In this chapter I draw on archival materials to describe how Tianjin and its hinterland weathered the famine. The leap's call for rapid urban industrialization drew many peasants away from communes and into Tianjin factory jobs. This rural-to-urban population transfer contributed to an imbalance in the supply system, exacerbating food shortages caused by inflated harvest reports and excessive state grain requisition. Simply put, because of the leap, there were fewer agricultural workers in the countryside and more people eating state grain in cities. Ironically, a movement that promised rural utopia resulted in one of the largest waves of out-migration from villages since the founding of the People's Republic. The uneven toll of the disaster that followed confirmed that the lines that had been drawn between urban and rural during the 1950s favored cities and the people who lived in them.

As early as 1958, Mao Zedong and other top leaders in Beijing were aware of famine conditions caused by leap policies.[2] Tianjin leaders also knew. The view from Tianjin's offices and neighborhoods confirms that it is not plausible to claim that urban officials were unaware of famine in the countryside. Average Tianjin residents knew about rural starvation because they saw beggars on the streets or hosted hungry relatives in their homes. City leaders, including top party secretary Wan Xiaotang, had an even clearer picture of the problem. They received daily reports about deaths and illnesses caused by the famine, and they traveled to villages to assess the situation firsthand. They knew how bad it was, but they were more vigorous in fighting for food for urban residents than in addressing the rural famine.

Urban residents did feel the pinch. Food rations were cut and hundreds of thousands of Tianjin people were malnourished. Tensions ran high as urbanites fought over food at grain shops, and urban crime – from illicit market activity to petty theft to brazen armed robbery – escalated as people struggled to stay afloat. City residents tightened their belts

[2] Thomas P. Bernstein, "Mao Zedong and the Famine of 1959–1960: A Study in Wilfulness," *China Quarterly* 186 (2006): 421–45.

but survived, while people in villages were allowed to starve in massive numbers.

"We Want Peasants"

One of the ironies of the Great Leap Forward was that a movement aimed at radically increasing rural production ended up draining the countryside of some of its most productive laborers. In addition to rural communes and unprecedented grain yields, the leap also called for rapid urban industrialization. On August 19, 1958, a series of *People's Daily* articles about the leap in Tianjin put it this way: "In this great era when 'one day equals twenty years,' neighborhood residents are following the road from socialism to communism, ever leaping forward" by living and working collectively. Housewives banded together to produce electric wires, and office workers set up sideline industries.[3] Urban residents, however, could not reach utopia without help from the countryside. Recently promulgated household registration regulations restricting rural-to-urban migration were ignored as city factories and workshops scrambled to hire workers. According to official counts, Tianjin's population swelled as rural people moved into the city during the leap.

The dramatic increase in temporary residents during the leap (not counted in Table 3.1) is especially striking. New industrial contract laborers were often given temporary *hukou* permits. The increase in temporary urban *hukou* holders in 1958 and 1959 was particularly significant:

- 1956: 74,000
- 1957: 102,000
- 1958: 232,000
- 1959: 168,000
- 1960: 73,000[4]

Other new arrivals did not have urban *hukou* at all, because city factories were in such a rush to hire peasant labor in 1958. One Tianjin government bulletin criticized factory managers who clamored, "We want them from villages, we want peasants," and who complained that "city people are

[3] The Tuesday issue of *People's Daily* featured five articles about Tianjin's leap: two on the front page and three on page 7. The quote is from the concluding sentence of a long article on page 7 about residents of a laneway getting organized; RMRB, August 19, 1958, 1, 7.

[4] Li Jingneng, *Zhongguo renkou, Tianjin fence*, 182.

TABLE 3.1. *Population Moving in and out of Tianjin's Urban Districts, 1956–1963*

	Moved In	Moved Out	Net Change
1956	221,038	161,046	59,992
1957	168,968	83,823	85,145
1958	136,937	102,647	34,290
1959	132,070	57,112	74,958
1960	118,186	64,859	53,327
1961	42,476	91,232	−48,759
1962	25,910	107,483	−81,573
1963	28,329	29,349	−1,020

Source: Tianjin shi dang'anguan, *Jindai yilai Tianjin chengshihua jincheng shilu*, 715.

useless" when it came to the leap's exhausting urban construction projects and production blitzes. The bulletin acknowledged that all city enterprises needed more labor because of the "new situation" brought about by the leap, but in line with earlier efforts to restrict migration in 1955 and 1957, it ordered officials to limit hires from villages.[5]

The leap's emphasis on warp-speed industrial development swept aside bureaucratic obstacles to migration and hiring, and many rural people were eager to take advantage of the free-for-all. Rumors of jobs in Tianjin that paid three yuan per day attracted potential workers from counties surrounding Tianjin, and some village officials even wrote letters of introduction for job-seeking migrants.[6] An internal report notes that 195,000 villagers from the twelve rural counties under Tianjin's jurisdiction in 1958 had received official permission to transfer to urban jobs – a full 6.6 percent of the total labor power in Tianjin's hinterland. Almost as many people left their villages without state approval: 127,506 in 1958, including 13.2 percent of the labor force in Cangxian county south of Tianjin. One major problem, the report continues, was that urban factories recruited workers in villages without permission from city labor officials: "The peasants do not move their *hukou* or grain card, they simply leave and the work unit then writes to the commune asking it to cancel the peasant's *hukou*."[7]

[5] *Tianjin shizheng zhoubao* 17 (April 28, 1958): 11–13.

[6] For rumors about high-paying jobs, see NBCK 2561 (August 20, 1958): 11; for letters of introduction from rural cadres, see RMRB, August 28, 1958, 6.

[7] *Tianjin shizheng zhoubao* 14 (April 6, 1959): 9–10.

What kind of work were these new employees doing? Evidence suggests that new arrivals in Tianjin in 1958 and 1959 did not quickly become regular workers in major urban industries. Rather, many rural migrants to Tianjin during the leap obtained temporary positions in small workshops, generally on the outskirts of the city. They were paid less than their counterparts in larger urban factories.[8]

Of the fifteen factories under the aegis of Tianjin's Hexi District Handicraft Industry Bureau in 1960, nine were situated within the city, and six were on the outskirts (Hexi, south of the city center and home to the former German concession, was one of the least densely populated of Tianjin's urban districts). The already well-established city enterprises included machine-equipment, printing, carpet, metals, and cooking utensil factories, and they employed a total of 1,984 workers. Although the number of workers at the city factories increased significantly after the leap began in 1958, most of the new employees were from within Tianjin, not from outside villages. After 1958, the nine factories within the city limits hired 728 urban residents, but only fifty-four villagers. Coveted factory jobs within Tianjin proper were out of reach for many rural people during the leap.

While Hexi's urban enterprises were already in operation when the leap began, most of the suburban workshops and factories were established during the big industrial push of 1958. The six suburban factories included a small brewery, an agricultural machinery plant, and brick and cement factories. Of the 634 workers hired at the district's six suburban enterprises since 1958, 304 were classified as "agricultural population," and 302 as "idle population" (*xiansan renkou*) from the suburbs.[9] At the brick factory, almost all of the laborers came from the suburbs, while the cement plant mainly employed people from rural Hebei and Shandong whom police had detained in Tianjin because they were part of the "blindly flowing population." But during the leap, city industry needed them. Instead of being sent home as they would have been during the "return to village" blitzes of 1955 and 1957, Tianjin's PSB sent them to make cement in the suburbs in early 1959.[10] One man named Li had been exiled from Tianjin to Xinjiang for the crime of protecting a counterrevolutionary in 1949. In 1958, Li returned to Tianjin to visit his mother

[8] Andrew Walder explains the role of temporary urban workers in *Communist Neo-Traditionalism*, 48–54.

[9] HDA, 17–1–15C, 1.

[10] HDA, 17–1–18C, 1, 24.

but failed to report back to his labor reform unit. Instead, he worked at odd jobs until police officers arrested him and assigned him to the cement factory.[11]

Cement workers like Li were not granted Tianjin *hukou* or regular positions. Their employment status remained temporary. Without official residence permits, their presence in the Tianjin area was semi-legal at best. For a time during the leap, increased production trumped the household registration system, and people moved around in search of the best deal. During the first half of 1960, workers in a suburban cement factory demanded better wages and urban *hukou*. When their appeals were met with silence, 19 of the plant's 171 workers left to pursue better opportunities. Ten workers went to find work in the northeast, five got better paying jobs at a nearby chemical plant (1.5 yuan a day versus the 1 yuan they had been making), and four disappeared without a trace.[12] While rural migrants were excluded from the best city jobs during the leap, those dissatisfied with low pay and instability in marginal enterprises did have room to maneuver.

Famine in Tianjin's Hinterland: The View from the City

Wage-paying jobs drew people from villages to Tianjin during the leap. This drain on the agricultural labor force contributed to worsening conditions in the countryside, which in turn compelled more peasants to flee villages. Grain deficits became a serious problem in the Tianjin region as early as August 1958. According to an internal report, in the counties surrounding Tianjin, "some places that lacked grain could not get it in a timely fashion, the supply system is chaotic, and some counties decided to make the peasants eat their remaining wheat seeds." As a result, five counties near Tianjin had only 58 percent of the seeds required for planting winter wheat.[13] For many villagers, complaining about food shortages was not a safe option. As Felix Wemheuer has shown, talking about hunger in the countryside was considered an "ideological problem" during the Socialist Education Movement of 1957 (a rural extension of the Anti-Rightist Movement), when people who spoke out about grain problems came under attack as potential regime enemies.[14] It made sense,

[11] HDA, 17–1–15C, 32.

[12] HDA, 17–1–18C, 36, 45.

[13] NBCK 2561 (August 20, 1958): 11.

[14] Felix Wemheuer, "'The Grain Problem Is an Ideological Problem': Discourses of Hunger in the 1957 Socialist Education Campaign," in *Eating Bitterness: New Perspectives*

then, for villagers to flee quietly. As the situation in rural Hebei became even more desperate in 1959 and 1960, many more villagers fled to the city. Their first priority was to find food. Malnourished beggars on the streets and visiting relatives who stayed for longer than usual were signals to city residents that something was horribly wrong in the countryside.

Starving peasants strained China's railway system during the crisis. A classified report sent to top central leaders in June 1960 reported that during the first quarter of the year, more than 176,000 "blindly flowing peasants" had taken trains without paying for tickets. Most of the fare-jumpers were from Shandong, Hebei, and Henan, and they were heading for the northeast, northwest, or to large cities. Peasants also regularly looted freight trains, according to a report that portrayed hungry farmers as uncouth hooligans rather than as disaster victims: "They eat anything that seems edible and steal whatever they can, and even willfully destroy and stomp on goods, urinate and defecate on things, and use high-grade women's socks as toilet paper."[15] Some famine refugees who managed to board trains ended up in Tianjin. During the first ten days of January 1961, city authorities at the Tianjin train station detained almost three thousand passengers arriving from the northeast, Shandong, and Henan. Most had edema, a swelling condition caused by malnutrition, and many were so weak that they fainted as they stepped off the trains. Fourteen of those who fainted never woke up.[16]

Tianjin residents who saw sick and dying beggars on the streets or who sheltered hungry rural relatives knew about the massive disaster in the countryside. Claims of ignorance by officials like Sidney Rittenberg, an American member of the Chinese Communist Party who worked at the national Broadcast Administration in Beijing ("Because the worst devastation was in the countryside, far from our view, most of us in the city knew nothing about it") certainly did not apply to most people in Tianjin.[17] By mid-1959, Tianjin residents had an idea of the scale

on China's Great Leap Forward and Famine, ed. Kimberley Ens Manning and Felix Wemheuer (Vancouver: University of British Columbia Press, 2011), 107–29.

[15] NBCK 3077 (June 20, 1960): 11–12.

[16] HPA, 855–6–2232Y, 6.

[17] Sidney Rittenberg and Amanda Bennett, *The Man Who Stayed Behind* (Durham, NC: Duke University Press, 2001), 248. William Hinton revives such claims of ignorance in his posthumously published *Through a Glass Darkly: U.S. Views of the Chinese Revolution* (New York: Monthly Review Press, 2006), 241–43. For more on the famine denials of foreigners living in China during the early 1960s, see Anne-Marie Brady, *Making the Foreign Serve China: Managing Foreigners in the People's Republic* (Lanham, MD: Rowman & Littlefield, 2003), 117–20.

and causes of rural problems. An internal report noted that quite a few people in Tianjin were critical of key aspects of the Great Leap Forward, including communization and the massive nationwide push to forge steel. The report charged that some city dwellers "cried out about the peasants' hardship, exaggerating the degree of grain shortage in villages. Some cadres and employees requested decreasing the urban standard of living and increasing peasants' food and oil supplies." This generous idea was not rewarded, but was instead written up by informers and reported as a "thought problem." A year later, food supplies dwindled so low that decreased urban grain rations would become a necessity. According to the same report, other city residents, rather than blaming the leap agenda, accused bad village officials of causing food shortages: "the peasants do not have enough to eat because [village cadres] practice fraud and give coercive orders."[18] Whether they faulted leap policies or criticized village leadership, Tianjin residents knew about the growing crisis, and they were aware of its multiple causes.

In study sessions, residents who had bad class labels were asked for their opinions about the leap. At one such meeting in December 1959 in Tianjin's Chentangzhuang neighborhood, a "bad element" named Wang offered his explanation of the leap's failures. "Ever since the people's communes became totally screwed up," Wang said, "all villagers are unenthusiastic about work, the fields are desolate, and production has been affected. Villagers have no income, all they get is a little bit of grain. Villagers in the suburbs do not work because they think that even if they work a lot they will only get two corn buns."[19] Wang was correct about failed harvests and that the initial euphoria of the leap was followed by disillusionment with the unmet promises of the commune system. But he was overly optimistic in assuming that peasants were guaranteed at least two buns a day.

Famine in Tianjin's hinterland was not as bad as it was in Anhui and Henan provinces, where entire villages were virtually wiped off the map. But for many, the difference between Tianjin and its hinterland during the famine was the difference between life and death. City residents also went hungry, fell ill, and suffered the psychological effects of food shortages, but they still received regular – albeit diminished – grain rations. Rural people had no safety net, and urban leaders considered them more expendable than city dwellers. That top policy makers rushed to save

[18] NBCK 2817 (July 8, 1959): 9–10.
[19] HDA, 43-2-23C, 11.

city people while villagers starved was the clearest proof of the socialist command economy's antirural bias.

Tianjin's top authorities were not necessarily callous, but they were overwhelmed with problems. Their first priority was protecting vital urban industries and the well-being of city residents, not rural counties that had only recently been dumped into their laps. Over the course of 1958, bureaucratic reshuffling presented a host of new challenges to such Tianjin leaders as first party secretary Wan Xiaotang. Early in the year, Tianjin lost its status as a special municipality and became subordinate to Hebei province, prompting a fierce battle for resources between the city and province. Tianjin became the provincial capital, and rather than answering directly to party center as they had before, city leaders now had to deal with another layer of bureaucracy. As early as 1954, Hebei provincial party secretary Lin Tie had been pushing for Tianjin to become a part of the province. He was rebuffed, but saw another opening in 1956 when Mao advocated increasing local authority and independence from party center in "On the Ten Major Relationships." Lin Tie spoke with Mao and then formally applied to take control of Tianjin. The State Council approved the measure on February 6, 1958, and Tianjin became Hebei's provincial capital on April 25, 1958.[20]

At the time, Tianjin's industrial output was almost double that of the rest of Hebei province. The provincial authorities who moved their offices to the new provincial capital in 1958 saw Tianjin as a cow that might nourish the rest of relatively destitute Hebei. Tianjin officials worried about what the change meant to their city's status. One said, "We used to be one of three big cities," referring to Beijing, Shanghai, and Tianjin, "Now we have gone down a level." Officials in the city's Bureau of Industry saw threats to their budget, saying, "Industrial investment will now become difficult. Hebei provincial leaders will consider problems on the basis of all of Hebei. They will not be as generous as party center was."[21] Such concerns were quickly proven correct. Central economic planners in Beijing still allotted more resources to Tianjin than to Hebei, but because provincial authorities had the final say in how to allocate Tianjin's part of the plan, they appropriated funds and materials for other projects. Tianjin leaders complained to Premier Zhou Enlai that the slow dismembering of their cow was making it difficult to meet yearly

[20] Xie Yan, "Tianjin shi gaiwei Hebei sheng shengxia shi" [Tianjin becoming a provincial-level city under Hebei province], unpublished article, n.d. [2008?], 1.

[21] NBCK 2420 (February 13, 1959): 14–15.

production targets, and in January 1959, party center required Hebei number crunchers to wall off Tianjin's resources from the rest of the province's budget.[22]

The headache of being subordinate to the province was aggravated in late 1958 when, following the leap's "bigger is better" mantra, the rural areas under Tianjin's control drastically expanded. In 1957, Tianjin leaders were responsible only for suburban villages immediately surrounding the city. In 1958, Tianjin prefecture (which had been headquartered in Yangliuqing and was directly subordinate to Hebei, not Tianjin) merged with Cangzhou prefecture and was then completely dissolved and put under the jurisdiction of Tianjin municipality. Tianjin leaders now had to manage twelve rural "super counties" (formed in 1958 by merging thirty counties into larger entities) with a combined population of 7,832,226. The rural population under Tianjin's control now dwarfed the number of people living in the city itself (3,500,690 in 1958).[23] According to one scholar, Hebei provincial leaders felt that the counties were "too poor" and hoped that Tianjin could help them.[24] In 1960, two more counties were added to Tianjin's portfolio, and the land under the city's control spanned the area between the Great Wall at Huangyaguan in the north and the boundary with Shandong province in the south. By the time these rural areas were transferred to Tianjin's control at the end of 1958, leap policies had already pushed them to the brink of disaster. Tianjin's leaders, who had spent the past ten years in the city, were unable to shift course in 1959. They were ill-equipped to handle the famine. They knew what was happening, but were not sure what to do about it.

As hunger worsened in rural Hebei during 1959 and 1960, Tianjin leaders received regular reports on the extent of the disaster. They also went on inspection tours of villages. Tianjin vice mayor Niu Yong and municipal Grain Bureau director Liu Pichang traveled to counties in the Cangzhou area in mid-1959 and were shocked by what they saw. Commune cafeterias served watery gruel, vegetable stalks, and leaves. Liu turned to Niu Yong and asked, "Is this okay?" The vice mayor shook his head and laughed nervously but said nothing. Later, Niu directed Liu to

[22] Wan Xiaotang jinian wenji bianjizu, ed., *Wan Xiaotang jinian wenji* [Collected writings commemorating Wan Xiaotang] (Tianjin: Tianjin renmin chubanshe, 2001), 20.

[23] Hebei sheng minzheng ting, *Hebei sheng xingzheng quhua biangeng ziliao, 1949–1984* [Changes in the administrative divisions of Hebei province, 1949–1984] (n.p., 1985), 80.

[24] Xie Yan, "Tianjin shi gaiwei Hebei sheng shengxia shi," 4.

MAP 2. Tianjin Municipality, 1960

lend wheat bran and dried yams to the afflicted areas, which the grain official did without obtaining permission from the national Grain Bureau or other Tianjin vice mayors. The Grain Bureau reported this lapse in protocol to Zhou Enlai, who ordered Tianjin and Hebei leaders to stop lending food without prior approval.[25]

In addition to reminiscences by officials like Liu Pichang, archival data and other internal documents confirm that municipal and provincial leaders in Tianjin knew full well that peasants were starving. Top officials in Tianjin received detailed reports of rural looting, starvation-related illnesses, and deaths throughout 1959, 1960, and 1961. Nine times over the course of three days in late 1960, farmers looted granaries in Shengfang, directly west of Tianjin.[26] In December 1960, when more than two hundred peasants besieged a rice warehouse in Tianjin's south suburbs, one looter was shot and killed by a militia guard.[27] In other parts of Hebei, including villages in the Tianjin region, commune organizations had completely collapsed and instances of people abandoning and selling children were "occurring often."[28] In January 1961, Tianjin leaders learned that 217,286 people suffered from edema during the previous year in the fourteen rural counties surrounding the city. More than two thousand had died from the condition, the report noted. Also in 1960, more than twenty-eight thousand people had been poisoned from eating dirt, seeds, or other non-edible items (we do not know how many died, but during two weeks in April, almost nineteen hundred people suffered poisoning in Wuqing county and twenty-one of them perished).[29]

City leaders dispatched work teams to investigate the perilous situation in villages. In February 1961, a newly formed task force called the Tianjin Village Livelihood Office (Nongcun renmin shenghuo bangongshi) sent investigators to Shigezhuang commune in Renqiu county. The work team's summary report began: "The main problems are that most

[25] Liu Pichang, "Chentong de huiyi" [Painful memories], *Tianjin wenshi ziliao xuanji* 79 (1998): 114.

[26] NBCK 3155 (December 28, 1960): 14–15.

[27] Guo Fengqi, ed., *Tianjin tong zhi: gongan zhi* [Tianjin gazetteer: Public security gazetteer] (Tianjin: Tianjin renmin chubanshe, 2001), 43.

[28] NBCK 3052 (May 8, 1960): 5–7.

[29] HPA, 878–2–45C, 32–33. On Wuqing, see Guo Fengqi, *Tianjin tong zhi: gongan zhi*, 42. According to another account, of the more than ten thousand peasants poisoned in Baxian, Baodi, and Wuqing counties in spring 1960, forty died. See Xie Yan, "Wan Xiaotang dailing Tianjin ren jieliang duhuang" [Wan Xiaotang led the people of Tianjin in conserving grain and getting through famine], unpublished article, August 1, 2008, 1.

cafeterias are doing poorly and the masses' lives are awful. The situation of illnesses and deaths is extremely serious." Villagers were so exhausted that instead of drawing well water they drank standing water from fetid pits. "Deaths are increasing by the month," the report continued. In November 1960, ninety commune members had died. In December, 190 more perished; and in January 1961, 251 died. Rural cadres hoarded grain and beat or fined villagers who tried to steal it. The work team in Shigezhuang discovered more than 700 cases of people being tied up and beaten; 10 people had been beaten to death.[30]

Wan Xiaotang, Tianjin's top leader, read such reports and even traveled to villages himself, but he was overwhelmed by the scale of the disaster. The tragedy pained Wan, who had been born and raised in a Shandong village, but even more frustrating was his impotence in the face of calamity. Wan went to Wuqiao county in February 1960, where he saw haggard villagers crying by freshly-dug grave mounds. In October, he traveled to Cangxian. There, an ill-advised policy to plant paddy rice on dry alkaline soil had doomed the fall harvest. "Do the peasants know how to plant, or do we know how to plant?" Wan asked, referring to officials who made disastrous agricultural decisions during the leap. "We cannot have this type of lunacy ever again," he said. An increasingly fatalistic Wan seemed resigned to the inevitable: people would starve to death in villages. "We cannot just suck crops out of the ground," he said over a meager meal with Cangxian county leaders. "It looks as if things will only get worse from now on."[31] In speeches to county leaders in November 1960 and April 1961, Wan told cadres that the solution was to explain the situation to the masses and to replace non-existent staples with "food substitutes" (*gua cai dai*).[32] This was a last ditch measure that came too late for many villagers.

Tianjin Gets Priority

Wan Xiaotang was defeated by the magnitude of the famine in the countryside. Yet he took drastic measures to help Tianjin when hunger

[30] HPA, 878–2–45C, 58, 60. Recent research confirms that many deaths during the famine were caused not by starvation but by state violence and terror. See Dikötter, *Mao's Great Famine*, and Ralph A. Thaxton, *Catastrophe and Contention in Rural China: Mao's Great Leap Forward Famine and the Origins of Righteous Resistance in Da Fo Village* (New York: Cambridge University Press, 2008).

[31] Wan Xiaotang jinian wenji bianjizu, *Wan Xiaotang jinian wenji*, 47.

[32] Ibid., 274–76, 288–90.

threatened the city. In January 1959, Tianjin leaders realized that food shortages might affect the ability of city residents to enjoy the traditional Chinese New Year dumpling meal. Wan Xiaotang sent grain director Liu Pichang to Shandong and Anhui to request assistance. Liu remembered, "We knew that these provinces also had difficulties, but if leaders [like us] showed up personally, it might help." Shandong officials agreed to provide Tianjin with tons of such dumpling ingredients as wheat, beans, cabbage, onions, and ginger. In the Shandong provincial capital of Jinan, Liu bumped into his counterpart from Beijing, who was also there to procure dumpling supplies. Liu took a stroll through the city's main vegetable market. The only items for sale in the Jinan market were spicy peppers and onions. Liu realized that Shandong was worse off than Tianjin was, but he worked to ensure that Tianjin residents would enjoy their holiday dumplings.[33]

Tianjin leaders, all of whom lived and worked in the city themselves, did their utmost to protect urban residents. Wan Xiaotang received daily reports from the city's grain bureau, foodstuffs bureau, and transport bureau detailing the exact amounts of grain being transferred into, sold, and stored in Tianjin. Wan then regularly called the offices of Premier Zhou Enlai and Central Finance Minister Li Xiannian to report on Tianjin's grain supply and to request assistance.[34] Central leaders based in Beijing took Wan Xiaotang's calls seriously and scrambled to prevent starvation in China's largest cities, even as peasants were dying in the countryside.

In July 1960, Liu Pichang attended a meeting convened by central finance minister Li Xiannian about how to guarantee adequate grain rations for China's three largest showcase cities: Beijing, Tianjin, and Shanghai. Even though Tianjin had lost its status as a special municipality directly under party center in 1958, during the worst food shortages of 1960 and 1961 central economic officials personally coordinated grain transfers to the three cities and also to Liaoning province, an important industrial base in northeast China. On July 5, 1960, Li Xiannian and Tan Zhenlin reported to Mao that Beijing, Tianjin, Shanghai, and Liaoning were running out of grain as soon as it was transferred in from outside provinces, and that if the situation continued, "there might be chaos." One week later, on July 13, Li Xiannian told Zhou Enlai that "the current

33 Liu Pichang, "Chentong de huiyi," 115.

34 Xie Yan, "Wan Xiaotang dailing Tianjin ren jieliang duhuang," 2.

amount of grain stored in Beijing and Tianjin is only enough to supply the cities for four days," while Shanghai had enough for two days and Liaoning for six days. Li said, "If we do not speed up the transport of grain to supplement these warehouses, there will be chaos."[35]

Liu Pichang remembered that at the time, a mountainous region in northern Sichuan province was the only place in China that had surplus grain that could be transferred to coastal urban centers. Liu traveled to Sichuan as Tianjin's representative and spent a month supervising the grain transfer, which required local women to carry sacks of grain down winding mountain paths until they reached passable roads. Trucks then transported the grain to train stations or Yangzi river ports for the journey to Tianjin.[36] This infusion, however, was not enough to keep urban grain rations at pre-leap levels. On September 7, 1960, grain standards for all city residents were slashed nationwide.[37]

Even after this belt-tightening, in late 1960 Tianjin vice mayor and finance and trade director Song Jingyi informed Wan Xiaotang that the city only had a three-day supply of grain left and that if the next scheduled food shipment failed to arrive on time, "there would be chaos." Wan sent Song to Beijing to report to central leaders about the imminent threat.[38] It was only at this point, when the food supplies of major cities like Tianjin reached crisis levels in December 1960, that central leaders arranged for foreign grain imports from Australia and Canada. Mao approved importing grain on December 12, 1960, and the first shipment from Australia arrived at the Tianjin port in February 1961.[39] By the end of June, more than 2.3 million tons of foreign grain had been imported, and according to Li Xiannian's biographers it went first to "Beijing, Tianjin, Shanghai, Liaoning, and major disaster areas."[40] Top leaders in Beijing

35 *Li Xiannian zhuan* bianxie zu, ed., *Li Xiannian zhuan, 1949–1992* [Biography of Li Xiannian, 1949–1992] (Beijing: Zhongyang wenxian chubanshe, 2009), 1:473–74.

36 Xie Yan, "Wan Xiaotang dailing Tianjin ren jieliang duhuang," 3; Liu Pichang, "Chentong de huiyi," 115–16. Liu's story seems especially remarkable because Sichuan was one of China's hardest-hit provinces during the famine. Liu's claim of a grain transfer from Sichuan to Tianjin in 1960 highlights the primacy of coastal cities over inland rural areas. On the severity of the famine in Sichuan, see Cao Shuji, *Da jihuang* [Great famine] (Hong Kong: Time International, 2005), 193–214; and Dikötter, *Mao's Great Famine*, 309–12.

37 ZYWX, vol. 13 (Beijing: Zhongyang wenxian chubanshe, 1996), 565–70.

38 Wan Xiaotang jinian wenji bianjizu, *Wan Xiaotang jinian wenji*, 170.

39 *Li Xiannian zhuan* bianxie zu, *Li Xiannian zhuan*, 1:482–83. See also Dikötter, *Mao's Great Famine*, 108–15.

40 *Li Xiannian zhuan* bianxie zu, *Li Xiannian zhuan*, 1:483.

and Tianjin had been receiving reports about starvation in villages for well over a year, and they had even personally visited famine-stricken rural areas. Yet they waited until China's largest cities were threatened to take drastic anti-famine measures.

Imports in late 1960 may have saved city residents from starvation, but food was still in short supply. In 1961, Tianjin again clashed with Hebei over scarce resources. On the eve of the central party work meeting in Lushan in August 1961, Wan Xiaotang called Tianjin's top economic planner Li Zhongyuan, who would be attending as part of the Hebei delegation. After it became subordinate to Hebei in 1958, Tianjin was not allowed to send its own delegations to central meetings. Just one month earlier, Tianjin's rural portfolio had been reduced to five nearby counties from the fourteen that had been added in 1958 and 1960. Apparently Hebei leaders, aware that Tianjin was keeping relief grain for the city and not for the surrounding countryside, saw that their plan for the city to lift the rural counties out of poverty had not worked out. The municipality's more manageable size must have come as a relief to city leaders who had been unable to handle rural problems during the leap. In 1961, Wan Xiaotang and Li Zhongyuan continued to prioritize the city.

Wan told Li to make sure central leaders knew that Tianjin's winter grain supply was tenuous. Wan's goal was to secure an increase in the total amount of grain allocated to Tianjin. In Lushan, Li Zhongyuan asked Hebei leaders Liu Zihou and Wu Yuannong to report Tianjin's difficulties to central leaders, but the next day, the provincial leaders did not mention Tianjin. When Li asked about this omission, Hebei officials justified their decision, saying that compared with other areas, Tianjin's situation was not so bad. City leaders had seen with their own eyes that rural Hebei was much worse off than Tianjin. Even though the Hebei officials were correct, Li's job was to lobby on behalf of the city, not the countryside.

Upset, Li Zhongyuan called Wan Xiaotang and asked him to come to Lushan, but Wan demurred because Hebei leaders had left him off the list of meeting participants in the first place and his presence would have violated protocol. Wan told Li that it was up to him to inform central leaders about Tianjin's problems. Li finally got his chance during his previously scheduled address about light industry. Noticing that Premier Zhou Enlai and finance minister Li Xiannian were in the room, Li departed from his original talking points. He played up Tianjin's supply shortage and requested more beans. After the meeting, Li learned that his impromptu plea displeased Hebei officials, but he did not care because he had achieved his goal. "Party center took measures and helped to solve some of Tianjin's difficulties," Li remembered.[41]

Wan Xiaotang and Li Zhongyuan knew that central leaders were terrified of the prospect of urban starvation. So they made an end run around Hebei provincial leaders and took their request directly to party center. The gambit succeeded, and Tianjin was guaranteed enough grain to make it through winter 1961. We have now seen evidence that urban leaders acted helpless when faced with widespread rural starvation, but they moved quickly and decisively when urban food supplies dwindled. Why the difference? Did top city officials view the lives of rural people as somehow less valuable than urbanites? The different treatment afforded to urban and rural China during the famine can be attributed to a number of factors. Most important, Maoist paeans to peasant virtue notwithstanding, the socialist planned economy consistently prioritized urban heavy industry. The party's top-down administrative hierarchy also gave cities the upper hand in political turf battles. In addition, officials at every point in the chain of command were reluctant to admit and report mistakes and problems. Such problems were easier to hide in China's relatively remote countryside.

China's coastal cities were showcases of socialist industry. By comparison, rural areas were invisible to the outside world. With very few exceptions, foreign residents, including journalists, diplomats, teachers, and students, were barred from leaving urban areas. During the Mao era, signs reading "no foreigners allowed beyond this point" were posted on major roads leading out of Chinese cities. If the worst of the famine and accompanying "chaos" were confined to the countryside, officials could attempt to perpetuate the lie that there was no mass starvation in China, and could claim that whatever hunger existed had been caused by natural disaster. Numerous internal reports and firsthand visits by city leaders contradicted this lie. So did the deteriorating situation in cities. Hunger, malnutrition, and anxiety about grain supplies became widespread in Tianjin.

Hunger in Tianjin

Food became much scarcer in 1959. Rationing began then. There were many discussions about who would get how much. It was decided by how much people ate as a rule. I didn't eat much then, so I had one of the lowest rations. I had

[41] Wan Xiaotang jinian wenji bianjizu, *Wan Xiaotang jinian wenji*, 39–40.

about twenty-six catties a month, eight ounces of grain a day (mostly cornmeal). There were not many vegetables. We began pickling parts of the veggies we used to throw away. There [were] only a few ounces of oil a month, maybe two ounces a month. Very little sugar. Coal was also scarce. Once food is scarce, everything is scarce. Each region had its own quota depending upon how much food was available. It was better for us in the big cities than in the countryside.[42]

– Nini Liu, Tianjin Water Works employee

As Nini Liu's remembrance suggests, people in Tianjin knew that they were better off than villagers, but that did not mean that life was easy during the famine years. Many Tianjin residents showed symptoms of edema. Pressing the flesh on coworkers' and neighbors' arms and comparing how long the depression in the skin lasted (a telltale sign of malnutrition) became a common pastime in Tianjin offices, alleyways, and schoolyards. Tianjin's leaders received weekly top-secret reports of new edema sufferers in the city. Between February 24 and 28, 1961, leaders learned of 4,871 new cases. This contributed to a total of 673,430 cases since reporting began, meaning that more than one fifth of Tianjin's urban population was malnourished.[43]

Wan Xiaotang not only read reports about urban hunger, he also conducted personal spot-checks. On the way home from his office one evening in 1960, Wan noticed that the lights were still on at PSB headquarters, where he had served as director during the 1950s. He stopped in and asked the staff why they were still working. He then instructed all the workers to roll up their pant cuffs and to press on their bare legs. No one's skin bounced back: they all had edema. The next day Wan ordered the grain bureau to increase daily rations for public security cadres because they were working late and needed extra meals.[44]

Not everyone in Tianjin was fortunate enough to benefit from Wan Xiaotang's personal intervention. After grain rations were cut in autumn 1960, families struggled to make ends meet. Wei Rongchun, still working as a factory supervisor and union official in Tianjin in late 1959 and early 1960, remembered that of the thirty cadres in his work unit, he was the

42 Nini Liu was the daughter of F. C. Liu and Grace Divine Liu, a Tennessee native who lived in Tianjin for four decades. Cooper and Liu, *Grace: An American Woman in China*, 284.

43 HPA, 878–2–45C, 57. It is unclear when the tally started. Writer Xie Yan puts the number even higher, at around 900,000 edema sufferers in Tianjin by late 1960; Xie Yan, "Wan Xiaotang dailing Tianjin ren jieliang duhuang," 2.

44 Wan Xiaotang jinian wenji bianjizu, *Wan Xiaotang jinian wenji*, 160.

only one who did not have edema. Even in normal times he did not eat much, but it also helped that he had a special deal with a waitress at the Masses' Restaurant in Tianjin. Wei went there after meetings and became friendly with waitress number four, frequently praising her service and good attitude. She rewarded him by providing extra sesame flatcakes and soup in exchange for a bit of money under the table. This arrangement lasted for about a year, but Wei never learned her name ("it would have been improper to ask," he said). One day the waitress was gone, and Wei inquired about her. She had been promoted because of her excellent service. "Her promotion meant hardship for me," Wei said.

In a survey of 161 households in a central Tianjin neighborhood conducted by the city's Policy Research Office at the end of 1960, about 60 percent had enough food to get through twenty-seven or twenty-eight days of the month, while 21 percent could make it through January 25, 1961, but only by watering down their meals. Seven other families were missing a week's worth of grain.[45] Some people quietly suffered, but others made noise. When the Chentangzhuang neighborhood in Tianjin's Hexi district cut the rations of its 1,634 residents by a total of 5,500 kilograms, people reacted furiously and fought for more grain, either by protesting or by altering and counterfeiting ration tickets. When residents heard about the reduction, they threatened to stage sit-ins at the neighborhood police station, or told local officials: "You might as well just shoot me in the head."[46]

Some Tianjin residents were understandably perplexed when ration reductions were accompanied by propaganda about the purportedly plentiful agricultural harvest of fall 1960. Urbanites with a "capitalist" class label asked: "If it is a bumper crop, then why are things getting more and more scarce?" and "Since it is a bumper crop, then increase [our rations] by one or two kilos. Why do we need to economize?" One Tianjin man assailed the euphemisms used by the regime to mask the extent of the crisis. "There is not enough grain to eat in villages and the hungry are fleeing to the northeast," he said. "In the past that was called 'fleeing a famine' (*taohuang*); now it is called 'blindly flowing' (*mangliu*), is it not the same?" Black humor was another way to handle the crisis. An engineer who was politically suspect because he had lived in Japan remarked, "In the future each year is going to get worse and worse, we will have to

[45] *Hebei jianshe* [Hebei construction] 521 (January 10, 1961): 28.
[46] HDA, 43-2-23C, 103.

import vegetables, and even the air will be rationed." He added that he wanted to go back to Japan.[47]

Throughout Tianjin, residents responded to food shortages by refusing to work. Some workers agreed to accept less grain only on the condition that they could follow the "five don'ts" (*wu bu gan*): "one, no meetings; two, no night shift; three, don't do urgent assignments (*tuji renwu*); four, don't do heavy work; five, don't take part in social activities." In October 1960, nine party members requested to withdraw from the party because they could not bring themselves to volunteer for reduced grain rations. Bi Yuanzhen at the Tianjin Number Two Cotton Spinning Plant quit the party, saying, "I eat a lot, I can't cut [my rations]."[48]

Frantic rumors spread about what might come next. Some people said that the value of grain tickets had been slashed in half, or that old people and children were only allowed to eat "eight treasures noodles," not grain. Some warned that "in three months, the great war will start." One wit put the famine in comparative perspective, saying, "One-third of the people in the Soviet Union starved to death when they went down the socialist road." Others were more hopeful: "America has sent two boats with rice and flour to lend to us, in twenty days life will get better."[49]

Tianjin residents smuggled food between city and countryside in order to help both themselves and their rural relatives. At first, in 1958, people sent grain out of Tianjin. On one day in May, city officials set up twenty-six checkpoints on the roads and waterways leading out of the city and discovered 1,800 instances of people carrying grain out of Tianjin, including women strapping grain to their bellies and pretending to be pregnant, and shipments of sealed coffins full of smuggled food.[50] Later, when conditions worsened in the city, urban work units and individuals sought out food in relatively well-off villages. In early 1959, Tianjin factories and elementary schools sent cadres to suburban villages to buy vegetables. The Tianjin city government ordered work units to stop this practice: "Because the cabbage on the market is often delayed and of poor

47 NBCK 3109 (September 14, 1960): 9–10.
48 NBCK 3129 (November 2, 1960): 9.
49 Ibid. On the politics of rumors during the Mao period, see S. A. Smith, "Talking Toads and Chinless Ghosts: The Politics of 'Superstitious' Rumors in the People's Republic of China, 1961–1965," *American Historical Review* 111 (2006): 405–27; and S. A. Smith, "Fear and Rumour in the People's Republic of China in the 1950s," *Cultural and Social History* 5 (2008): 269–88.
50 *Tianjin shizheng zhoubao* 24 (June 16, 1958): 14.

quality, when city residents see cadres carrying vegetables home they all ask about it. This has negative effects."[51]

City people without connections could rely only on the overstretched urban food supply network. Tensions mounted at neighborhood grain shops, where harried shop workers squabbled with hungry customers. In June 1962, when one Tianjin woman named Wang purchased dried yam chips (a common substitute food at the time), she forgot to get her ration booklet back from a female clerk named Su. When Wang returned, Su refused to give back the booklet, saying, "I have the authority, and this is the way it is going to be." The two women then began to curse and spit at each other. Other people waiting in line took Wang's side and threatened to beat the rude clerk. The grain shop manager had to apologize and hold off the angry crowd until police officers arrived to defuse the situation.[52]

Crime and the Black Market

Security officials had their hands full during the famine years in Tianjin. In addition to disputes caused by frayed nerves at neighborhood grain shops, urban theft was on the rise. Criminal behavior ranged from pilfering to armed robbery. In late 1961, nine of the twenty-six employees at a neighborhood nursery stole food that was intended for the children. One woman took food fifty-eight times; she was finally caught when the nursery's chef discovered her stealthily pouring cooking oil into her own container. Another woman stashed twelve pieces of the children's fish in her lunch box. The nursery workers' behavior was criticized as evidence of "corrosive bourgeois ideology," and they were disciplined by their work unit.[53]

Police did not get involved when nursery workers stole food from children, but they took notice when a thief broke into the home of one of Tianjin's top leaders. In 1960, public security officers informed Tianjin party secretary Zhang Huaisan that they had caught a burglar stealing flour from his home. They asked Zhang how to handle the matter. The party secretary was magnanimous. "People do not have anything to eat," Zhang said. "If this thief has any other illegal behavior, then deal with him according to the law. But if this grain is the only thing you have on him,

[51] *Tianjin shizheng zhoubao* 7 (February 16, 1959): 9.
[52] HDA, 1–6–15C, 27.
[53] Ibid., 45.

then forget it, let him take it."[54] Robbers sometimes got away with much more than a few bags of flour. In March 1962, thieves jumped over the gate of an electrical machinery factory in Tianjin's central Heping district. The intruders killed two employees who were on guard duty, cracked the factory safe, and escaped with ten thousand yuan and one thousand ration tickets for food and other goods. They were never caught.[55] Later in the year, a pistol-wielding man wearing a blue coat and a worker's hat walked into a bank on Dali Road in Tianjin's former British concession and demanded cash. When employees put up resistance, the bank robber killed one and wounded another before fleeing the scene.[56]

Many people engaged in illicit behavior stayed at small urban inns. In 1961, public security officials inspected residents of more than three hundred inns in Hebei's five largest cities, including Tianjin. Of the 1,200 "criminals" identified during the investigation, 1,059 were "speculators and profiteers," most of whom had rented long-term rooms at the inns, where they conducted black market trades.[57] During the famine, Tianjin's black markets swelled with goods, including food from rural areas that had weathered the famine without major losses.

Between January 1 and January 15, 1961, Tianjin officials counted almost eight thousand cases of illicit black market activity at thirteen different sites within the city. Of the cases, 22 percent involved people selling things they had produced themselves, 27 percent involved people who had transported items between city and countryside, and 33 percent involved "speculators" reselling goods at a profit.[58] One investigator counted more than eight hundred people selling goods at one Tianjin market on a single day in January, and estimated that two thousand people were milling about, looking at goods, and blocking traffic. "There are no goods that the black market does not have," the report claimed.[59]

Municipal cadres who patrolled the streets fought a losing battle against peddlers, according to Geng Chen, who was director of Tianjin's Finance and Trade Commission during the early 1960s. The crux of the problem was that the city's prohibition on private trade clashed with

[54] Zhang Huaisan jinian wenji bianjizu, ed., *Zhang Huaisan jinian wenji* [Collected writings commemorating Zhang Huaisan] (Tianjin: Tianjin renmin chubanshe, 1999), 296.
[55] Guo Fengqi, *Tianjin tong zhi: gongan zhi*, 44.
[56] Ibid., 461.
[57] Zhongyang gongan bu, *Gongan gongzuo jianbao* [Public security work bulletin] 52 (December 11, 1961): 4.
[58] NBCK 3173 (February 6, 1961): 5–6.
[59] NBCK 3167 (January 23, 1961): 10.

new central policies, including the Twelve-Article Emergency Directive of November 1960 and the Sixty Articles on Agriculture of March 1961. These measures aimed to ameliorate the rural famine by encouraging family plots and allowing limited markets in villages. Cities, perhaps fearing capitalistic "chaos," were slower to permit free trade. Peasants wondered why they were allowed to sell their own vegetables at home, but were harassed by city officials when they tried to sell cabbage in the city. On several occasions, peddlers punched and drove away Tianjin officials when the latter attempted to stamp out market activity on city streets.[60]

In 1962, Tianjin authorities finally decided to regulate behavior that they had failed to eradicate. Thirty-seven market sites were legalized in July 1962. By the end of the year, one-quarter of all pork and half of the fruit sold in Tianjin changed hands in peddlers' markets. The Finance and Trade Commission registered more than 7,000 people as peddlers, and of these 2,322 were "workers who had been downsized" (*bei jingjian de zhigong*), a full 32.1 percent of the total (most of the rest, 62.2 percent, were unemployed city residents). Top party theorist Chen Boda came to Tianjin on an inspection visit shortly after the markets were legalized. Chen, who had advocated doing away with money during the leap, toured the sites and was aghast at what looked suspiciously like capitalism. The average peddler earned 125 yuan per month, far more than the 50–70 yuan a state worker made. Some fishmongers made as much as 700 yuan. "Where have you lured the working class off to?" Chen demanded to know.[61] Geng Chen, who accompanied Chen Boda on the tour, might have been fired for telling him the truth: "downsizing" in the aftermath of the famine had driven the workers' class to the markets. The rustication of workers who had entered the city after 1958 was the final phase of Tianjin's leap, and is the focus of Chapter 4.

City, Countryside, and the Leap

People experienced the leap and its aftermath in diverse ways. One of the key variables that determined how people in China weathered the disaster was whether they were in a large city like Tianjin or in a rural commune like Shigezhuang in Renqiu county, where a Tianjin-based work team discovered horrifying starvation and violence in 1961. Certainly the famine

[60] Geng Chen, "Liushi niandai chuqi Tianjin shi kaifang tanfan shichang de qianqian houhou" [The whole story of opening peddlers' markets in Tianjin in the early 1960s], *Tianjin wenshi ziliao xuanji* 79 (1998): 119.

[61] Ibid., 123–25.

affected rural areas unevenly, and not everywhere was as unfortunate as Shigezhuang. But overall, city residents had much greater odds of surviving the leap. So did the thousands of migrants who entered cities during the industrialization frenzy of 1958 and 1959. People in Tianjin were not immune from hunger during the lean years, but municipal and central leaders – well aware of the apocalyptic scene in the countryside – went to extraordinary lengths to prevent urban starvation, even brushing off comments from Hebei provincial officials that the city was relatively well off.

It is ironic that a movement that aimed to dramatically improve living conditions in the countryside did more to poison rural-urban relations than any other event in the history of the People's Republic. The failure of Mao's utopian surge toward a more modern and equal future would have profound consequences for the relationship between city and countryside in the 1960s and 1970s. First, central economic officials blamed the disaster on a "lack of experience" that caused them to lose control of the mechanisms of state planning. Their answer was more planning and better control, including full implementation of a household registration system that restricted mobility and assigned individual grain rations throughout the 1960s and 1970s. Second, Mao Zedong himself argued that the disaster occurred because the "democratic revolution" (meaning the Communist Party's attempt to overthrow "feudal" forces and eliminate exploitation through land reform) had been left incomplete in rural areas. Mao called for a more thorough revolution in the countryside. These twin responses to the famine – more planning plus more revolution – prioritized cities while assaulting and dumping on villages.

4

The Great Downsizing of 1961–1963

For Wei Rongchun, it was time to go home.[1] It was late 1960 in Tianjin, and the twenty-seven-year-old factory worker and union chairman had been away from his family long enough. Wei was one of more than ten million city workers nationwide who returned to their home villages in the aftermath of the disastrous Great Leap famine. Several hundred thousand people left Tianjin for the countryside between 1961 and 1963.[2] But contrary to accounts that emphasize the "coercive" or "forced" nature of urban-rural migration during the Maoist period – particularly the massive rustication of the early 1960s – Wei Rongchun left Tianjin voluntarily.[3] He was the first in his belt-making factory to sign up to "support agriculture," and his boss was so taken aback that he tried to talk Wei out of

[1] Interviewee 1.

[2] Dangdai Zhongguo congshu bianjibu, *Dangdai Zhongguo de Tianjin*, 1:127, puts the number at 400,000, but other sources suggest that the number was lower. Population data report that 222,064 people moved out of Tianjin's urban core between 1961 and 1963, but because of continued immigration, the net reduction was only 131,349. Tianjin shi renkou pucha bangongshi, ed., *Tianjin shi renkou tongji ziliao huibian, 1949–1983* [Collected materials on Tianjin population statistics, 1949–1983] (Tianjin: Nankai daxue chubanshe, 1986), 254.

[3] Solinger refers to "coercive repatriation" and a "forced exodus" with "deportations" after 1960. Friedman, Pickowicz, and Selden call the downsizing a "forced population transfer." Persuading workers to return to their home villages sometimes involved coercive tactics and was obligatory for workers and family members who arrived in cities after 1958. Using such words as "coercive" and "forced," however, leaves out workers who returned home voluntarily like Wei Rongchun. Dorothy J. Solinger, *Contesting Citizenship in Urban China: Peasant Migrants, the State, and the Logic of the Market* (Berkeley: University of California Press, 1999), 39; Friedman, Pickowicz, and Selden, *Revolution, Resistance, and Reform in Village China*, 19.

leaving. His boss did not want to lose an employee with Wei's skills and know-how. "I am a party member, I should lead the way in responding to the party's call," Wei argued, referring to the August 10, 1960 central directive ordering the entire nation to "do agriculture and grain in a big way."[4] The matter was settled. Wei's application letter to return to his village in Baodi county, about fifty miles north of Tianjin, was approved, and his *hukou* changed from "non-agricultural" to "agricultural."

What Wei did not tell his disappointed boss was that his family needed him back in the village. Wei's father had recently hurt his leg in an accident, rendering him unable to do heavy farm work or shoulder buckets of water (a crucial daily task in north Chinese villages, where wells were often a long distance from homes). Wei also failed to mention that he had only seen his wife for a few days each year since they had married in the early 1950s. It was time to think about starting a family. Almost ten years after arriving in Tianjin, Wei returned home. His time as a city worker had changed him permanently, and his return would change his village for the better.

This chapter sheds light on the human consequences of an unstudied but crucial moment in the history of the People's Republic. Few people outside of China know much about the downsizing (*jingjian*) of the early 1960s, and aside from Tiejun Cheng's doctoral dissertation, few works in English mention the event.[5] This is partly because the Maoist regime, embarrassed by its retreat from the grandiose goals of the Great Leap Forward, prohibited newspaper and broadcast reports on downsizing. Policies specifying the numbers and categories of people who were supposed to return to villages were classified as secret and are still tightly guarded. The number and social impact of downsized workers were comparable to later groups of sent-down youth. But unlike educated youth sent to villages during the 1960s and 1970s, most downsized workers never had the opportunity to return to cities, complain about their treatment in villages, and write memoirs. Academic scholarship and popular culture in both China and the West have privileged the experiences of urban sent-down youth, obscuring equally important moments of rural-urban contact.

[4] ZYWX, vol. 13 (1996), 516–26.

[5] Cheng, "Dialectics of Control," 125–33. One notable book in Chinese on the massive urban-to-rural migration is Luo Pinghan, *Da qianxi: 1961–1963 nian de chengzhen renkou jingjian* [Great migration: The downsizing of urban population, 1961–1963] (Nanning: Guangxi renmin chubanshe, 2003).

More than twenty million rural people moved to Chinese cities during the feverish industrialization drive of the Great Leap Forward. Sending these migrants back to their villages in the early 1960s was an attempt to fix the imbalance between agriculture and industry that had contributed to food shortages and starvation. Contrary to what we might expect, given the guaranteed rations and benefits received by urban residents in the socialist planned economy, for some people cities were not necessarily more desirable places to live than villages in the aftermath of the leap. As famine conditions improved, new policies allowed family plots and rural commerce, and returning home to villages appeared attractive to some migrants.

When urban work units and neighborhood committees received orders to reduce the urban population in 1961, millions of people faced a vexing choice: follow party policy and return to the countryside, or fight to hold on to the benefits of city life, including salaried work, subsidized housing and health care, better educational opportunities, infrastructure, and entertainment options. Some people, such as Wei Rongchun, quickly volunteered to head for the countryside, even though they were not required to (only workers who had arrived in Tianjin after 1958 were subject to mandatory repatriation). Others took advantage of a full repertoire of protest techniques to negotiate or resist rustication, including sit-ins, arguments, petitions, and suicide attempts. Contrary to images of an inflexible, unyielding, and harsh Maoist state, such negotiation was sometimes successful, especially when it was framed in terms of family obligations and duties.

The leap and its aftermath marked the most high-stakes period of rural-urban interaction since the Communists had come to power in 1949. Downsizing was a series of intense negotiations between city and village people – city people who were mostly ex-villagers themselves, and former villagers who were on the verge of becoming ex-city people. This chapter will first trace central leaders' stuttering steps toward a return-to-village program, and will then explore the variety of individual and collective responses to the policy. I conclude by assessing the impact of returned workers on their home villages.

Orders from the Top: Explaining the Decision to Downsize

After several years of listening to sunny reports that ignored their worsening reality, people in Tianjin, including those originally from villages, were desperate for solutions that matched the magnitude of the leap disaster. Sweeping solutions became possible after summer 1960, when top leaders met in Beidaihe and discussed economic recovery options that would bring an end to the leap. The main challenges were to adjust agricultural organization and fix the imbalance between grain producers and grain consumers. Wang Man, head of the Hebei provincial labor bureau, understood the problem as follows: since 1958, untrammeled urban industrial development had drawn huge numbers of peasants into the cities. This meant that salary payments far outstripped original budget plans. More money was put into circulation to pay the new workers' salaries, leading to urban inflation and a decline in city living standards. At the same time, the new workers drained grain supplies, so peasants were forced to sell more grain to the state at low prices, causing shortages in the countryside. Too many workers on the job negatively affected productivity in factories, which led to declines in state revenues, and the depleted rural labor force was unable to increase agricultural yields. Wang Man did not mention falsified harvest reports and excess requisition of grain, two of the other root causes of the famine, but his interpretation reflects economic officials' sense of a major imbalance in the planned economy.[6]

The beginnings of a policy that would balance agriculture and industry appeared in the August 10, 1960, "do agriculture and grain in a big way" directive. This document was the only push that workers like Wei Rongchun needed to return to their villages. The first item of the directive, which appeared on the front page of *People's Daily* on August 25, 1960, was to "squeeze out all of the labor force that can be squeezed out, and replenish the agricultural front, primarily the grain production front."[7] The August 10 directive and others like it in late 1960 called for a shift in the labor force, but gave no sense of the scale of the proposed transfer and remained focused on the usual suspects who had been targeted for removal from large cities like Tianjin during the mid-1950s: temporary workers, people in odd jobs (*qinza renyuan*), and the "blindly flowing" population. It would take the endorsement of Mao Zedong for the movement to become targeted and massive.

Mao's stamp of approval at the end of 1960 initiated the downsizing policy that would take shape in the coming year. Mao finally came on

[6] Wang Man, *Liushiliu nian de huigu* [Recollections of sixty-six years] (Self-published memoir, n.d.), 330–31. I obtained this source in 2005 and estimate that it was published in the late 1990s or early 2000s.

[7] ZYWX, vol. 13, 517.

board in late October, directing all provinces to redirect as many industrial workers as possible to agriculture.[8] At a central work meeting on December 30, 1960, the chairman was much more specific and determined. "It will be one hell of a mess if the 26 million newly added people do not go back [to villages]," he said, speaking of the rural migrants who had flooded cities during the leap. "Pushing them back down is difficult, but they definitely must be pushed back down."[9] It is worth noting the hierarchy implicit in Mao's language: villages were subordinate places to go "back down" to.

After Mao spoke, the removal of millions of rural migrants from Chinese cities was much closer to becoming reality, but those who would be affected by his order had little idea what was about to hit them. "Do agriculture and grain in a big way" propaganda provided few clues about what the slogan would mean in practice. An oral propaganda outline drawn up for cadres in Hebei province began, "The current situation is an excellent situation." This preposterous opening would immediately signal to listeners that the party was still out of touch with reality. "Agriculture is the base of the national economy, and grain is the base of the base," the outline continued. "Why is this? Because people need to eat every day, three meals a day. Eating two meals a day feels a bit awkward, and eating only one is just plain unbearable."[10] Here, finally, was a public admission from the party that the current situation, although still "excellent," was untenable.

The outline's claim that agricultural labor was the most glorious kind of work did provide hope for some. Some rural cadres who propagandized the outline in speeches actually disparaged industry, warming the heart of at least one peasant in Wuqing county, directly northwest of Tianjin. "Why the heck is the working class 'elder brother,' anyway?" the man asked, referring to the longstanding practice of newspapers referring to city workers as "elder brothers" (*gongren lao dage*) and peasants as "younger brothers" (*nongmin xiongdi*). "I have not understood this for a long time," he continued. "Everyone's got to eat, it is impossible to do without agriculture, it is great that agriculture is the base now!"[11] Overly optimistic, the man thought that "doing agriculture in a big way" meant that peasants would finally be treated on par with city workers. He failed

[8] Roderick MacFarquhar, *The Origins of the Cultural Revolution: Vol. 2: The Great Leap Forward, 1958–1960* (New York: Columbia University Press, 1983), 324.

[9] Jin Chongji and Chen Qun, *Chen Yun zhuan*, 2:1238.

[10] HPA, 864–1–236Y, 21–23.

[11] NBCK 3130 (November 4, 1960): 12.

to realize that the purpose of recovery was to return the economy to a pre-leap status quo where villagers sacrificed to support urban industry.

The Wuqing peasant was not alone in misinterpreting pro-agriculture propaganda. Grassroots officials giving speeches about the new policy told peasants that their lives would soon be the same as, or even better than, those of city people. Young cadres in Cangxian, Wuqiao, and Wuqing counties urged villagers who had spent time in Tianjin to speak about the bitterness of city life. One said, "In the city, workers not only get dirty and tired when they work, but they have to sleep outside in the courtyard when it is cold. When you compare the two, the city is like hell and our home is like heaven." The purpose of this story, which accurately reflected the lives of some city laborers (especially temporary migrant workers), was to keep young villagers at home working the fields. Yet the remark was highlighted in a report to city leaders as an example of "talking irresponsibly."[12] It was politically incorrect to disparage cities.

Other village cadres faced criticism for changing the phrase "reform the backward appearance of villages in three years" to "eliminate the difference between city and countryside in three years." By the end of 1960, it was no longer acceptable to speak of eliminating the rural-urban gap. In the aftermath of the leap, bland bromides about overcoming "backwardness" subsumed egalitarian revolutionary goals. When a cadre in Wuqing county tried to dissuade village youths from going to Tianjin, telling them, "hold on for two or three more years, by then city and countryside will be the same," he was censured for "recklessly making vows." It was hopelessly unrealistic for him to predict that "they live in fancy foreign buildings in the city but we will live in them too, the air here will be better than in the city, and maybe city people will come running out to our village!"[13] This Wuqing cadre had failed to realize that the utopian dream of equal wealth for city and village had died. With the leap's tragic failure, Mao had lost hope in rural China's potential for revolutionary change.[14] After 1960, the best case scenario reverted to "reforming" the countryside's "backward appearance."

[12] Ibid.

[13] Ibid., 12–13.

[14] Instead, he saw the countryside as a haven for counterrevolutionaries who had to be attacked. On November 15, 1960, responding to reports of widespread famine and political terror, Mao Zedong said that in many districts, "bad people are in charge, beating and killing people. Grain production has dropped and people do not have enough to eat. The democratic revolution is still incomplete, and feudal forces are causing great trouble"; MWG, vol. 9 (1996), 349.

The appearance of many villages would certainly change with an influx of returned workers, but how to pull off the transfer was still up in the air during the first half of 1961. Even though Mao had explicitly approved the idea at the end of December 1960, apparently some members of the party's central committee were opposed to sending millions of city workers to villages all at once because of the immense difficulty of the task.[15] By the time the central committee met on May 31, 1961, advocates of large-scale downsizing had won out.

At the central committee's work meeting, President Liu Shaoqi and economic czar Chen Yun argued that the only choice left was to reduce China's "non-agricultural population." Liu spoke frankly, saying that, in squeezing peasants for grain, the party was acting like a landlord. He also admitted that the party's top leaders had assumed an urban identity, placing them in opposition to rural people. "Currently city people – that means us – are competing with peasants over rice, meat, oil, and eggs to eat," Liu said: "We bought up many things, and the peasants are unhappy. If it keeps up like this, a sharp conflict will arise in the worker-peasant alliance."[16] Liu was not advocating an amendment of the worker-led alliance, but he had learned from the urban shortages of 1960 that the well-being of city people was threatened if the party squeezed peasants too hard.

Rural China could not support such a large nonagricultural population, Liu argued. He allowed that some workers might have difficulty understanding why they were being cut, but held that they would warm to the idea of returning to villages when they heard about official approval of family plots and the resurgence of sideline production. "When the situation in villages gets better, it will be easy to mobilize workers to return," Liu said.

15 Roderick MacFarquhar, *The Origins of the Cultural Revolution: Vol. 3: The Coming of the Cataclysm, 1961–1966* (New York: Columbia University Press, 1997), 32.

16 Renmin chubanshe ziliao shi, *Pipan ziliao: Zhongguo Heluxiaofu Liu Shaoqi fangeming xiuzhengzhuyi yanlun ji*, 1958.6–1967.7 [Materials for criticism: collection of counter-revolutionary revisionist utterances by China's Khruschev Liu Shaoqi, June 1958–July 1967] (Beijing: Renmin chubanshe ziliao shi, 1967), 176.

The text of Liu's speech in the above source differs from the version in ZYWX, vol. 14 (1997), 357, where Liu's explicit references to city people as "us" (*chengliren, ye jiu shi women*) and goods being bought up by "us" (*bei women shougou qilai*) are omitted. The latter source also changes "worker-peasant alliance" (*gongnong lianmeng*) to "between workers and peasants" (*gongnong zhi jian*). Based on central leaders' hands-on involvement in its production, I believe the 1967 text is more accurate (for evidence of Mao, Zhou Enlai, Lin Biao, Chen Boda, and Jiang Qing's involvement in overseeing the production of Liu Shaoqi's collected "utterances," see MWG, vol. 12 [1998], 422–23).

At the same meeting, Chen Yun agreed that family plots were critical to ensuring that people in both cities and villages had enough to eat. Chen addressed critics of rustication who said that returned workers would have to eat no matter where they were. He estimated that each returned worker would, on average, need seventy-five kilograms fewer of state grain annually (thanks to harvests from private plots plus savings in grain processing and transport). This meant that a return of twenty million workers would save the state 1.5 million tons of grain.[17]

Both Chen Yun and Liu Shaoqi stressed that downsizing would be difficult and that problems, even protests, were sure to arise. But according to Chen, the only other option – increased requisition of villagers' grain – was a non-starter. Villagers had already been pushed past the breaking point during the leap. The great downsizing was officially under way. At the May 31, 1961, work meeting, party leaders proposed a nine-point program specifying how to reduce the urban population.[18] The document, officially released by party center on June 16, ordered a reduction of more than twenty million urban people over the course of three years: ten million in 1961, at least eight million in 1962, and the rest in the first half of 1963. All "black people and black households" (meaning those without urban *hukou*) living in large and medium-sized cities were to be investigated.[19] Each province, city, and urban district set numerical targets. On June 16, the Tianjin party committee met and decided to cut the urban population by three hundred thousand by 1963. A year later, Tianjin's overall target jumped to four hundred thousand.[20]

City authorities now knew how many people to remove, but many confusing logistical questions remained unanswered. Who was supposed to leave the cities? What about their family members? Would people who were downsized receive any compensation? Should rightists, capitalists, and other political outcasts be handled differently from other downsized workers? Similarly, villages needed guidance on how to house, feed, and assign farm work to the influx of returned workers. Over the course of 1961 and 1962, a series of directives addressed these issues.[21]

[17] ZYWX, vol. 14, 374. See also MacFarquhar, *Origins of the Cultural Revolution: Vol. 3*, 32.

[18] Jin Chongji and Chen Qun, *Chen Yun zhuan*, 2:1242.

[19] ZYWX, vol. 14, 412–13.

[20] MacFarquhar, *Origins of the Cultural Revolution: Vol. 3*, 33. See also Zheng Zhiying, ed., *Tianjin shi sishiwu nian dashiji* [Forty-five year chronology of Tianjin] (Tianjin: Tianjin renmin chubanshe, 1995), 202; and Wan Xiaotang jinian wenji bianjizu, *Wan Xiaotang jinian wenji*, 333.

[21] An April 25, 1962, order from the Hebei Provincial Downsizing Small Group mandated that people labeled as counterrevolutionaries, landlords, rich peasants, and bad elements

A June 28, 1961, circular tackled the most pressing question of who had to leave. All new workers who had come from villages since January 1958 had to return home, unless they had become "production backbones" or skilled experts in urban workplaces. Workers who had started their jobs before the end of 1957 should return to villages only if they were genuinely willing to do so. Generally, people who were "originally" urban residents would not be sent away. These provisions targeted rural migrants who had moved to cities during the leap. Downsized workers would receive severance packages according to the time they had spent on the job, and they would receive stipends for their journey home. The funds were to be paid by the workers' original work units.[22]

Wei Rongchun volunteered to leave his position at the belt factory and return to his village before any of these guidelines had been issued. Because he started work in Tianjin in 1951, he would not have been targeted for mandatory downsizing, but he jumped to volunteer. When he offered to leave, there was no discussion of compensation. He wanted to go home for family reasons and did not need financial incentives. After he had been living in the village for several months, his factory called the commune headquarters and left a message telling Wei to come to Tianjin to collect his severance payment. Wei did not want to make the trip and did not realize how much money was involved. He told the factory to send the funds. He was pleasantly surprised when he received a lump sum equivalent to thirteen months of his salary.[23]

All details about downsizing plans, quotas, and policies, including severance packages like Wei's, were kept secret from the public. Internal orders prohibited newspaper or radio reports on the program, and limited propaganda to discussions within work units.[24] When factories and residential committees received orders to begin cutting in mid-1961, their first task was to determine how many people in each work unit or neighborhood met the conditions for mandatory rustication. After a head count, "persuasion" began in small group and one-on-one

could be downsized but their severance payments were set at half the amount of regular returned workers. But on July 7, the State Council ruled that capitalist-class businesspeople should not be sent to villages during the downsizing. Hebei sheng laodong ju, ed., *Jingjian zhigong daiyu wenjian huibian (1961–1966)* [Collected documents on the treatment of downsized employees, 1961–1966] (n.p., 1966), 20, 83–84.

22 ZYWX, vol. 14, 505–7.

23 Interviewee 1.

24 In the Hebei Provincial Archive, I found a gag order issued by *People's Daily* and the New China News Agency on March 22, 1962, but judging by the content of newspapers in 1960 and 1961, downsizing reports had been prohibited since the beginning of the movement. HPA, 864–1–269Y, 56.

meetings. Officials struggled to explain the downsizing to targeted workers and families.

A few Tianjin factories and an urban district party office were criticized for publicly using secret abbreviations, such as "begin the double-cut movement" (meaning cut population and cut grain rations). Propagandists were instructed to stick to such well-worn euphemisms as "support agriculture" and were prohibited from saying "cut" or "shrink," which made people feel like they were being fired.[25] Whatever it was called, salaried workers knew that "supporting agriculture" meant becoming an unpaid farmer.

One propaganda outline issued by Hebei provincial authorities suggested ways to make "return to village" candidates feel better. Villagers who had come to the city during the leap, "whether they were hired according to rules and procedures or whether they came to cities on their own," were to be thanked for their contributions to industry. They should feel grateful for the "ideological awakening" and new technical skills they had gained under the tutelage of the urban proletariat, but now the nation needed them to make even greater contributions on the agricultural front.[26] Even propaganda admitted that cities were superior to villages. How would workers respond to this line of argument?

Waffling

Many factors came into play as people decided how to handle downsizing. How a factory or neighborhood committee approached return-to-village targets often colored responses: harsh or confusing orders spurred resistance, while reasoned persuasion might lead to grudging acceptance. Much more important was each individual's personal circumstances. For almost everyone involved, the stakes were extremely high, touching on such considerations as finances, family, housing, and pride. For some, being pushed out of Tianjin meant losing a job and a major source of guaranteed income. This prospect was devastating. But for others, in the recently relaxed economic atmosphere, downsizing offered opportunities to make money through trade or sideline production. Some returned villagers were proud to use the skills and connections they had gained in the city to help with rural collective projects. But many felt ashamed at having to leave positions of genuine responsibility, and feared that fellow villagers would see them as failures.

[25] NBCK 3252 (August 4, 1961): 9.
[26] HPA, 864–1–257Y, 7.

Villagers definitely saw Wang Kaiwen as a loser. Wang, born in 1933, grew up in Tianjin.[27] His family was originally from Duliu, a small market town in Jinghai county directly southwest of Tianjin. Well known for its special vinegar, Duliu was larger than the average Jinghai village, but most of its residents were farmers with agricultural *hukou*. Wang began working in Tianjin's Hexi district government office in 1951, delivering documents and handling other odd jobs. In mid-1961, Wang caught a respiratory illness and was recuperating at home in Tianjin. In July, two cadres from the Hexi personnel department visited Wang and convinced him to return to Duliu. Government offices were under pressure to reduce nonessential staff, and while Wang was not a recent arrival to Tianjin, he was an obvious target. He was an "odd-job man" (*qinza renyuan*, a category targeted for removal), and he was sick and gullible. He wanted to please his bosses and did not consider the long-term implications of answering the party's call to support agriculture. One of the cadres told Wang that the assignment in Duliu would last for ten months. He was lying.

Wang followed directions and submitted his first application letter to return to Duliu on July 15, 1961. His letter is a revealing example of how a relatively uneducated city employee (Wang had only attended two years of elementary school) distilled propaganda about rural China. In shaky handwriting, Wang wrote, "I will lead the way in rebuilding my home village.... I will change the appearance of my home village along with the dear country people." Wang had absorbed messages about the need to reform and remake villages. Villages were also home to tough heroes steeped in "excellent revolutionary tradition," Wang wrote. Clearly differentiating himself from the rural people he was about to join, Wang pledged to learn from the "arduous, diligent, courageous, and excellent work style of the peasants." Wang praised Duliu villagers, but he certainly did not consider himself one of them.

Nor did Wang's parents want him to become a peasant. Wang's father, a worker at the Tianjin Construction Bureau, opposed his son's decision to go to Duliu. Wang was already twenty-eight and had no marriage prospects. His parents knew that if he was in the countryside with no salary and no urban *hukou*, it would be even more difficult to find a suitable partner. But his downsizing had already been set in motion. The Hexi district government and party committee approved Wang's application on July 25, 1961, and sent his file to Jinghai county's newly

[27] Information about Wang is from a thick dossier about his case in HDA, 32–2–47C, and interviewee 6.

established "Office to Shrink Non-agricultural Population and Support Agricultural Production."[28] Wang began having second thoughts. Before he was scheduled to leave, he told his superiors that he had changed his mind; he did not want to go to Duliu after all. His parents disapproved, he said, and his respiratory problems were flaring up.

The cadres in charge of getting Wang to leave Tianjin told him he had "thought problems," but decided not to push him. Because he had started working at the district government well before 1958, they could not force him to leave. According to a Hexi personnel office report, one month later Wang changed his mind again. He sought out district leaders and requested to be sent to Duliu, guaranteed in writing that he was ready to go, and pledged that this time there would not be any more problems. But Wang's troubles had just begun.

Wang had probably done the math after hearing about how severance packages were calculated for returnees. He figured that he could pocket a large sum of cash and relax in the village for a while before returning to Tianjin, which was only a few hours away by bicycle. On August 27, 1961, he went to Duliu accompanied by two Hexi district cadres carrying paperwork to transfer Wang's *hukou* to the rural town. When he deposited 450 yuan of his 508 yuan severance payment (equivalent to ten months of his salary) in the Duliu bank, the Hexi officials told him, "you are not allowed to spend it irresponsibly." On his first night in Duliu, Wang stayed at his uncle's house. It would take him until 1990 to undo what had happened that day.

Wang's behavior after arriving in Duliu was less than exemplary. But the main reason for his dissatisfaction was that his superiors had deluded him. Wang was led to believe that his stay in the village would be temporary and that he would be treated as a "sent-down cadre" (*xiafang ganbu*), not as a regular commune member. He thought that as an employee of a city district, be would be considered an official and would be in a position of superiority in Duliu.

Pushing and Pulling

Leaders of factories and offices were under considerable pressure to meet rustication quotas, and had little guidance on how to carry out the complicated task. While some work units made threats or lied in order to force non-essential employees to leave, others did not want to get rid of

[28] This office would later change its name to the Jinghai county "Downsizing Office."

any workers. Downsizing was extremely stressful for grassroots cadres charged with convincing workers to leave Tianjin.

According to an internal report from early August 1961, some Tianjin work units neglected to inform workers that returning to villages was voluntary if they had started work before 1958. Factories also took advantage of downsizing to jettison undesirable employees. They targeted old and sick workers, people with bad family backgrounds, and workers who "acted up," skipped work, lacked technical skills, or were "not needed for production."[29] It was not surprising that factories would interpret downsizing as an opportunity to increase efficiency, in effect using rural China as a dumping ground. Just as rural China had borne the brunt of the famine, it also had to assume the costs of the post-leap recovery.

Factories valued young, skilled workers who had arrived in Tianjin during the leap more than older workers who were not subject to downsizing. Enterprises pushed hard to keep their most productive employees, prioritizing the economic success of the work unit over restoring the national balance between agriculture and industry. In 1962, the Tianjin Construction Materials Company was in a bind. More than 90 percent of the company's 3,470 employees were from villages. If the company followed national downsizing policy, it would be decimated. Some workers, similar to Wei Rongchun, heard about the chance to return home and immediately volunteered to leave Tianjin. Leaders of the company pressured the volunteers to withdraw their applications by organizing youth league "backbones" and "activists" to "mobilize" people *not* to return to villages. The factory was using classic mass movement tactics to undermine the party's latest campaign. The strategy worked: workers withdrew their application letters and unpacked their bags.[30] Tianjin authorities responded to the problem by ordering work units to stop obstructing their employees from voluntarily returning to villages.[31] Negotiations about downsizing occurred at multiple levels of Tianjin society: workplace leaders haggled with their superiors, just as downsizing targets themselves did.

Tianjin city leaders also criticized factories that were overly vigorous or slipshod in trying to get rid of workers. Some factories simply posted lists or announced the names of those who had to return to villages at meetings without explaining the policy or its rationale. After the director

[29] NBCK 3252 (August 4, 1961): 9.
[30] HPA, 859–2–12C, 62b.
[31] HPA, 859–2–13C, 118a.

of the Heping District Mechanized Embroidery Collective read out the names of twenty-five people targeted for downsizing, he said, "If you do not have any complaints, then go to the personnel department to do the paperwork. If you do have complaints, I will wait and we can talk after the meeting." Only one worker headed to the personnel department. The other twenty-four surrounded the director and pleaded with him for six hours.[32]

When workers tapped for downsizing expressed reluctance to leave Tianjin, some factories threatened them and even locked them up. At the Beiyang Cotton Mill, six of the ten downsizing targets in one workshop had already departed by July 1962, but the other four refused to leave. The workshop party secretary became impatient and confined each of the four to private rooms. "Because of your unclear understanding of returning to villages," he said, "we have brought you here to improve your ideology." Two cadres were assigned to hector each hesitant worker full-time. The workers were prohibited from talking to one another and could only leave the use the toilet or get a drink of water.

One of the detained workers, named Pang, had migrated to Tianjin in 1950 and joined the party in 1958. In 1959 he was honored as a model worker and was awarded with a vacation at the Beidaihe beach resort. But as the famine hit and anxieties rose in Tianjin, Pang suffered from stomach problems and sold goods on the black market. In his private room, cadres glared at Pang, slapped the table, and forced him to sit up straight. Pang said in his defense that conditions in his home village were rough and that he would be unable to feed his wife and four children there. As tensions escalated, Pang finally said, "I would rather die here than go." A cadre named Liu said menacingly, "even if you die you will still have to go. When are you going to die? When will you get into a coffin? I will buy a wreath for you."[33] After Pang reported this treatment to higher levels of the city bureaucracy, his bosses were criticized. But negotiation only went so far. Eventually, Pang was convinced to leave Tianjin.

Tianjin workers from rural backgrounds did not respond meekly to threats, lies, and struggle sessions. Workers protested loudly and organized to resist the prospect of being removed from the city. Resistance to downsizing took many forms, from grumbling and complaining to posting big-character posters, writing petitions, and stealing factory property.

[32] HPA, 859–2–12C, 39.
[33] HDA, 1–6–15C, 63–64.

Some return-to-village targets went home for a few days, then immediately came back to Tianjin. Others were so despondent at the prospect of losing urban benefits that they attempted suicide. These types of problems were exactly what economic czar Chen Yun feared when he outlined the downsizing program in mid-1961.

Suicide

By the end of October 1961, downsizing work wrapped up for the year. Chen Yun said that he felt great relief when he heard reports that ten million people had already been transferred from cities to villages. "In the beginning, when we decided to cut people from cities, I was afraid that a lot of suicide-type situations would occur and that there would be many difficulties," Chen said.[34] The downsizing of 1961 had gone more smoothly than Chen had expected for several reasons. First, people who were genuinely willing to return home left quickly when the party made them a decent offer. Also, in 1961 the leap crisis was still so acute that citizens recognized the need for drastic measures. By 1962, economic conditions had improved enough that it would be difficult to convince city residents that an additional eight million people nationwide had to return to villages. Most of the "situations" that Chen Yun dreaded occurred in 1962, not 1961.

In July 1962, the Hebei provincial downsizing office reported that "suicide incidents are occurring repeatedly in several regions." During May and June, twenty-four people had attempted suicide in seven Hebei regions because of downsizing, and eleven had died. Seven had tried to kill themselves in Tianjin.[35] A woman named Li came to Tianjin from her home village in 1958 to work at a hat-making factory. In March 1962, factory management convinced her to resign because of a long illness that kept her from working. When she heard that the factory was sending workers back to their villages, she was afraid that she would be forced to leave Tianjin. Li hanged herself on the morning of May 8. Another woman, Liu, had been hired at a Tianjin health clinic. On May 4, when she was "mobilized" to return to her village, she apparently agreed to leave the city, but before her departure she became despondent and overdosed on sleeping pills. She was revived at the hospital.[36]

[34] Jin Chongji and Chen Qun, *Chen Yun zhuan*, 2:1243.
[35] HPA, 859–2–12C, 38.
[36] HPA, 859–2–10C, 71.

Complaining, Petitioning, and Pilfering

Suicide was an extreme reaction to the prospect of job loss and displacement. Grumbling, complaining, or simply ignoring orders to leave Tianjin were more common types of resistance. In spite of *hukou* and ration restrictions, people voted with their feet. Twenty-four of the sixty-six people sent back to villages from Tianjin's Number Four Coal Briquette Factory returned to Tianjin after spending a short time at home.[37] They were presumably able to get their jobs back or find other work. People who refused to leave Tianjin echoed a common refrain: "The city has four good things: fixed work hours, monthly wages, set grain rations, and guaranteed supply."[38] Many migrants thought that village life could not compare with the guaranteed benefits of urban residence.

It was easy to see through euphemisms about "cutting" or "reducing." Wags commented that cutting people (*jianren*) was the same as being unemployed (*shiye*, a social condition the Communists had purportedly eliminated in the early 1950s). "Whether you make dumplings or buns with pork filling, the taste is the same," residents complained. Others used official rhetoric to poke fun at the party. Grassroots cadres sarcastically debated whether the current situation could be classified as an economic crisis. "An economic crisis in capitalist countries is when so many goods are produced that they cannot be sold and they have to be thrown into the ocean or destroyed," a Tianjin cadre said. "Right now our country does not produce much and people cannot buy what they want," he reasoned, "so it does not count as an economic crisis."[39]

Complaints and satire were a good way to blow off steam, but were not effective strategies for return-to-village targets who hoped to stay in Tianjin. Organizing to make demands or petitioning to higher levels was risky for people being downsized, but it occasionally worked. Some targets explicitly referred to their legal rights, arguing that "mobilizing us to return to villages and not letting us live in the city means that there is no freedom of residence. This is a violation of the constitution."[40] This claim was technically correct, for China's 1954 constitution guaranteed freedom of movement. But petitioners would not get very far with this line of argument. When Minister of Security Luo Ruiqing explained new

[37] NBCK 3252 (August 4, 1961): 8–9.
[38] HPA, 859–2–11C, 73a.
[39] Ibid., 73a–73b.
[40] Ibid., 73a.

household registration laws in early 1958, he called freedom of residence a "guided freedom" subordinate to the needs of socialist construction.[41] Persistent petitioners who repeatedly made demands risked being classified as "unreasonably causing trouble" (*wuli qunao*), as we shall see in the case of Wang Kaiwen, the unmarried man who was duped back to Duliu. Such a label in one's personal file meant that future petitions were likely to be ignored, denied, or used as grounds for arrest and detention. But the threat of petitioning could be a potent weapon for aggrieved return-to-village targets, because factory managers feared attracting attention from higher levels about problems and unruly behavior.

In 1958, twenty-one workers' relatives were hired as temporary loaders at the Tianjin train station freight depot. During the downsizing of 1961, they were "not successfully cut" because the workers simply refused to leave their jobs. In May 1962, management tried again and told the loaders they were being let go. In response, they organized, demanded answers, and sought a better deal. The workers pointed out that they had only signed a one-year contract, but had been working for longer than that and earned the same salary as permanent employees. They wondered why they were being fired when a leading cadre's wife had received a permanent job. Finally, the loaders demanded continued grain ration stipends and said that a severance payment of one and a half months of salary was unreasonably low. After talks between management and the downsized loaders reached an impasse, thirteen loaders went to the State Council in Beijing to plead the group's case.[42] Recognizing that they would have to leave their jobs, the workers tried to gain a more favorable settlement. When that failed, they played their ultimate trump card by petitioning in the capital.

In some factories, workers were in a much stronger bargaining position than management. In mid-1962, leaders at a radio factory in Tianjin were so afraid that return-to-village targets would refuse to leave that they caved in to virtually every demand. When workers saw that factory management would satisfy every request, their conditions for returning to villages spiraled out of control. Soon the workers began taking whatever they wanted from the factory, including bicycles and radio components, as management watched helplessly. A worker named Hao outfitted a radio repair shop in his home village with pilfered factory machinery; the

[41] Zhang Qingwu, "Basic Facts on the Household Registration System in China," *Chinese Economic Studies* 22, no. 1 (1988): 100.

[42] HPA, 859–2–10C, 72. We do not know the result of the loaders' petition.

shop reportedly made monthly profits of more than one thousand yuan, at least ten times more than Hao's monthly salary at the radio factory.[43] Workers ensured that they would not be returning to villages empty-handed by taking advantage of official fears of resistance and petitions.

Even if the radio factory workers and rail freight loaders managed to make downsizing a better deal, most still lost their jobs and urban *hukou*. Bargaining and petitioning were usually ineffective for workers who wanted to hold on to their city jobs, benefits, and legal residency. But there was another way to stay in Tianjin. Officials looked much more favorably upon individual requests for exemption from downsizing based on family considerations. Resilient family ties sometimes proved stronger than the "great wall" dividing urban and rural China.

Playing the Family Card

As we have seen, Wei Rongchun volunteered to return home because of family obligations. The opposite also occurred. Migrants in Tianjin who, according to policy, were required to return to villages, received special consideration because of family problems or duties. For some individuals, deciding how to handle the downsizing of the early 1960s hinged more on fulfilling domestic obligations than on weighing urban benefits against rural difficulties. Neighborhood officials responsible for deciding who had to leave Tianjin often responded humanely to emotional appeals about family situations, contravening policy and propaganda about downsizing. People who pleaded that the difficulty of rural labor compared unfavorably with the conveniences of city life were criticized for having thought problems. But authorities considered domestic issues legitimate reasons to stay in the city. Eradicating the traditional family was not even close to becoming a reality in early 1960s Tianjin.[44] Instead, policy implementation on the ground often valued family unity. Exemptions based on special family circumstances were the main reason that Tianjin had difficulty fulfilling its downsizing quota.

The relaxation of migration controls during the leap allowed families and couples to reunite in the city. During the downsizing effort, neighborhood residential committees tried to convince family dependents to

[43] HPA, 859–2–12C, 39–40.

[44] Joseph Esherick argues that Chinese family ties became stronger, not weaker, during the turbulence of the 1960s and 1970s; Joseph W. Esherick, *Ancestral Leaves: A Family Journey through Chinese History* (Berkeley: University of California Press, 2010), 295.

leave Tianjin. As "do agriculture in a big way" propaganda heated up in fall 1960, propagandists anticipated that recently arrived migrants would refuse to leave Tianjin for family reasons. They preemptively – and unsuccessfully – attempted to forestall this eventuality through a barrage of propaganda celebrating return-to-village models.[45]

In October 1960, *Tianjin Evening News* ran a series of articles praising village wives who separated from their city husbands, a city mother-in-law who encouraged her daughter-in-law to return to her village, and a woman who made her elderly rural mother go home. Zhang Shufen came to the city in 1958 and got married to a Tianjin man. She did a bit of housework every day and enjoyed strolling around and relaxing with her husband on his days off. One day Zhang suddenly realized that if China's "village population all acted like me and ran to the city with nothing to do, unwilling to do agricultural labor, village labor power would shrink, and agriculture and socialism would not develop." Supported by her family and neighbors, Zhang returned to her home village. The article did not discuss the effect of this separation on Zhang's marriage. When another Tianjin wife decided to separate from her husband to support agriculture, her husband and mother-in-law supposedly said, "only by building up the great family of 600 million [Chinese] people can our small family be harmonious."[46] The message was that the big socialist "family" trumped the nuclear family.

Not all readers – city cadres included – accepted this argument. In December 1960, family members who had recently left Tianjin came back to get through the winter. A twenty-one-year-old rural woman named Ji came to Tianjin and married a city worker in 1958. She went home to Renqiu county with her one-year-old baby in November 1960, but returned to Tianjin a month later. "I have a baby so I cannot work in my hometown and nobody in the village provided for me, so I came back to Tianjin," she said. Ji's local police station in Tianjin granted her and at least thirty-eight other neighborhood people in similar situations temporary *hukou* and grain rations for three months. Those who had "flowed back" (*daoliu*) from villages were to be told that returning to villages was glorious, but decisions on their cases would be postponed until spring.[47] At the local level, some officials handled appeals flexibly and humanely.

[45] The propaganda blitz took place before the official downsizing policy (and the accompanying media ban) went into effect in mid-1961.

[46] TJWB, October 6, 1960, 2.

[47] HDA, 43-2-23C, 112.

In spring 1961, the original issues that led family members to flow back to Tianjin had not disappeared. Neighborhood committees and police stations argued about how to handle rural relatives. Mrs. Wang, née Yang, a sixty-four-year-old from Fengrun county in Hebei, came to stay with her son and daughter-in-law in Tianjin in 1960.[48] In August she was mobilized to return home because her husband was still in Fengrun. He was sick and Wang needed to care for him, so she left. In October, Wang came back to Tianjin. Because her *hukou* registration was still rural, she was not entitled to any grain rations in Tianjin. Food was short in the Wang household and tensions ran high. Wang and her daughter-in-law's quarrelling finally ceased when Wang was granted a temporary three-month urban *hukou* and grain provisions.

When his mother's short-term *hukou* was on the verge of expiring, Wang's son, a cadre at the Tianjin Number Four Cotton Mill, took action to keep her in the city. The file on Wang's case in the Hexi District Archive includes three letters written in early 1961. The first was from her village, explaining that she was old, had stomach problems, and nobody could take care of her. The second, from the union office at her son's factory, ostensibly "clarified" the family's situation. The union pointed out that both Wang's son and his wife worked during the day, and suggested that the elderly Wang could help look after the couple's two young children.

The final letter, written by Wang's son on February 26, 1961, stressed family obligations (children should take care of their parents; grandparents should help look after grandchildren) that would strike a chord with Tianjin neighborhood officials and police officers:

> Dear leading comrades of the return-to-village office and police station:
>
> My mother, Mrs. Wang, née Yang, is sixty-four years old and has a stomach illness. In 1960, when she was mobilized to return to her village, my wife sent her *hukou* out with her. My mother gave birth to me and six brothers. Five of us live in Tianjin, one lives in Harbin, and one is at the Great Northern Wilderness State Farm in Heilongjiang. My father lives in our home village but has no labor power and relies on us brothers to support him.
>
> Because my mother has no labor power, if she were to return home she could not work and would be no help to agriculture. The commune and village have already confirmed this. But three of us brothers belong to working couples and each of us has two or three children at home who need supervision. I therefore request that you show consideration for my work and for my mother's illness. I request that you investigate and allow my mother to stay in Tianjin.

[48] Ibid., 173–81.

After reading this letter, Chengtangzhuang neighborhood cadres and police officers disagreed about what to do with Wang. "Little Li," the official in charge of return-to-village work, was still angry that back in July 1960, Wang's daughter-in-law did not mention Wang's husband in Fengrun. To Little Li, it was crucial to know that the husband was in the village, presumably able to support Wang. He wanted to send her back.

Little Li's colleagues at the police station acknowledged his opinion, but requested that the neighborhood party committee consider Wang's extenuating circumstances: not only was she old and unhealthy, but her husband was also rather elderly, and most of her children worked in Tianjin. On March 10, 1961, five days after Little Li and the police station issued conflicting opinions, the neighborhood party committee agreed to give Wang a permanent urban *hukou* because she was quite elderly, her commune did not want her back, and "after returning she would increase the burden on her village." This appeared to be the final word, but on March 14, the Hexi District Public Security Bureau concurred with Little Li, overruled the neighborhood office, and ordered local officials to continue to mobilize Wang to return to Fengrun, because her husband could support her there. We can infer that if she had been widowed, there would have been no debate and she could have stayed legally in Tianjin.

The file ends on March 14, 1961, so we do not know if this second round of pressuring Wang to leave the city was successful. But it is clear that local cadres and police officers charged with handling return-to-village cases sympathized with family-based claims. As downsizing peaked in 1961 and 1962, hundreds of family members who had arrived in Tianjin since 1958 received exemptions. In August 1962, cadres from the Number Four Road residential committee in Hexi district identified 293 return-to-village targets, but immediately disqualified 97 Tianjin wives whose only rural relatives were in their *niangjia* (a married woman's parents' home). "Owing to customs and habits, generally do not mobilize a woman back to her *niangjia*," the report read. It would have been shameful for a married woman to return alone to her parents' home. Eighteen others in the neighborhood were granted exemptions because they "truly cannot get along with" or had "disharmonious" relations with rural relatives. For grassroots urban cadres, customs and family squabbles were valid reasons for return-to-village targets to remain in Tianjin. This was not what Chen Yun had in mind when he drew up downsizing regulations in the first half of 1961, but the practical, humane quality of family-based exemptions probably helped limit the disturbances that kept Chen up at night.

Other downsizing targets who did not immediately receive family exemptions could still convince local officials to leave them alone. A twenty-nine-year-old worker named Li at the Hexi district cooking utensil factory successfully persuaded leaders that she should be allowed to stay in Tianjin because she had three children, including an infant, and was pregnant again. One of Li's colleagues also gained an exemption because her husband was sick at home and she needed to take care of him. Another woman worker at the Hexi printing press had come to Tianjin in 1958, apparently because her acrimonious relationship with her rural mother-in-law had given her a mental disorder. According to the Hexi Daily Use Articles Company, her mental state was still abnormal and she was therefore not required to return to her village.[49]

Claiming special status because of family problems or obligations was the best way to avoid being sent back to villages. But there were definite limits to what authorities considered acceptable excuses. Caring for children and sick relatives was valid; love and spousal unity were not. In mid-1962, an internal bulletin reported that Tianjin employees were rushing to get married in an attempt to sidestep downsizing. When work units tried to dissuade couples from having quick weddings, people complained, "this is not freedom of marriage, this is not following the marriage law."[50] Even if the marriages proceeded successfully, in many cases they would not have prevented spouses with rural backgrounds from having to return to villages. Guidelines from 1961 anticipated that "doing agriculture in a big way" might cause separated spouses to consider divorce. The party's suggestion was for couples to return to villages together, or to sacrifice togetherness for the cause of socialist construction. "Awakened youths should correctly view the question of falling in love," the guidelines suggested.[51]

Back in Duliu, Wang Kaiwen began to wonder whether he would ever find love. Maybe his parents were right that volunteering to support agriculture would hurt his chances of finding a girlfriend. He began to mention his bachelor status in his petition letters to Tianjin officials. Still stuck in Duliu in 1964, he wrapped up two separate written pleas by pointedly noting that he had not yet married. With this in mind, he hoped that city authorities would favorably consider his request to return to Tianjin. They did not. As we have seen, for local cadres to consider

[49] HDA, 17-1-15C, 21–23.
[50] HPA, 859-2-11C, 3.
[51] HPA, 864-1-257Y, 12.

exempting people from downsizing, family problems or obligations had to involve irreconcilable disputes or young, elderly, or sick relations in need of care. Wang's prolonged bachelorhood did not qualify him for special consideration. Even though he had been misled about the terms of downsizing, Wang had initially volunteered to go to Duliu and his fervent application letter remained on file. Others who were allowed to stay in Tianjin had consistently requested family exemptions from the very beginning of the process.

Why did Wang Kaiwen do whatever he could to escape Duliu? How do we explain the discrepancy between discontented Wang and happy Wei Rongchun, who used the skills and connections he gained in Tianjin to help his village throughout the 1960s, 1970s, and 1980s? To understand the diversity of ways in which returned workers changed rural China – and how villages affected returned workers – we must travel to the villages themselves.

Downsized Workers in Villages

How a returned worker fared in rural China depended on his or her resources in and out of the village, including family and professional networks. Technical skills and a willingness to work hard also helped them get along. Finally, returned workers' sense of self-identity – rural or urban, peasant or worker, cadre or commune member – was key in determining their success in villages. Those who clung to an urban identity or thought of themselves as superior cadres earned the resentment of villagers. People who assumed rural identities had an easier time fitting in.

Much hinged on the economic conditions and social geography of each particular village. Places with serious grain shortages or jealous village officials were less welcoming, while a solid economic base and forward-thinking cadres made for an easier integration. When people like Wang Kaiwen behaved badly, refused to work, and repeatedly complained to higher levels, it was not surprising that some villagers considered returnees an unwelcome burden.

Wang was allowed to relax in Duliu for two days in August 1961 before being assigned to collective work. His first task was to help with the fall harvest, but he only worked for half a day and then disappeared. Wang's production team searched all over for him to no avail. He eventually reappeared, and the next day he was told to watch over the crops, but he refused to go. On a third occasion, Wang worked a half day and then rode his bicycle back to Tianjin. According to an investigative report by the Hexi district personnel office from October 7, 1961, villagers often heard Wang requesting a leadership position and complaining, "I am a sent-down cadre, where do they get off assigning me work?" The report noted that Wang's behavior and requests seemed bizarre to villagers, who "mistakenly thought that his mental state was abnormal."[52] In May 2005, Duliu residents still remembered Wang not by his given name, but as "Crazy Wang" (Wang *shenjing*).[53]

Wang had no memory of living in Duliu as a child, had no friends there, and clearly felt that he was a city person, not a peasant.[54] Wang's aunt became frustrated with his behavior and told him to settle down. She testified to city cadres in 1964: "Right after he arrived, I said, 'can you do farm work? Can you handle this kind of life?' My nephew said, 'Fine, attack my enthusiasm.'" After Wang had run away to Tianjin several times, his aunt admonished him. "I advised him to work hard, build a base, settle down and establish himself," but he did not listen.[55] After Wang's cousin got married, there was no room for Wang at his aunt's house anymore. He stayed in brigade housing for a short while and finally began living with his parents in Tianjin full-time, busily appealing his case and only going to Duliu twice a month to pick up grain rations. He had already spent all of his downsizing severance.

Duliu cadres did not miss Wang. The village party secretary told me that Wang "is not a real peasant, he is a city person" (*bu shi zhenzheng de nongmin, ta shi chengshi de ren*). "Tianjin people cannot do farm work," he said. "The city government should take care of him."[56] Wang considered himself an urbanite, and so did villagers in Duliu. To them, Wang was a city person, and therefore the city's problem. Considering Wang's behavior in Duliu and his jobless, *hukou*-less status as a perpetual petitioner in Tianjin, it was no surprise that Wang had no luck with love. "Wang never got married," an elderly man sitting under a tree in Duliu told me in 2005. "If you do not work and do not have much of an income, how can you get married? Even in the village it's that way. A bare stick! (*guanggun*)."[57]

[52] HDA, 3-2-47C, 13.
[53] Interviewees 7, 8, 9.
[54] When we met, he told me that China must rely on its "peasant little brothers," clearly differentiating himself from them.
[55] HDA, 3-2-47C, 10.
[56] Interviewee 7.
[57] Interviewee 10. "Bare stick" means bachelor, but also "loafer" or "ruffian." The man sitting under the tree seemed to imply both meanings.

By May 1963, Wang's petitions to various government agencies were labeled as "unreasonably causing trouble" and he was accused of trading on the black market. He kept petitioning but the response was always the same: he had volunteered to go to Duliu in the first place, his behavior had been bad, and he needed to "settle down" (*anxin*) to collective farm work. Every once in a while he managed to squeeze a stipend out of a government agency because of his health problems, but his requests to return to Tianjin continued to be rebuffed.

Wang's *hukou* was finally moved back to Tianjin in 1990, and his monthly welfare funds were transferred to Tianjin in 2002 (before that he still went to Duliu every month to collect a stipend). In 2005, Wang was still riding his bicycle to visit various government offices in Tianjin, and occasionally traveling to Beijing to petition for a reconsideration of his case. He wanted his years of "agricultural work" in Duliu to be figured into a monthly pension as a government worker. Peasants have never received pensions in the People's Republic, but Wang wants credit for doing farm work.

There is a precedent in the reform era for former political outcasts to receive compensation for time spent in villages during the 1960s and 70s (discussed in Chapter 6), but not for downsized workers. When I met Wang, he explained his grievance:

> When the government and party order you to do something, what can you do, can you oppose it? No, you must follow orders. So I went to support the agricultural front. I made a mistake, and the party also made a mistake. It should accept this and correct the mistake, but it never has. When Deng Xiaoping took power he immediately redressed the mishandled cases of the five bad elements and rightists, and stopped the class theory system, but because I was not in that category my problem was never solved. At least call me retired, or let me do some work for the country.

Wang's case has dragged on for forty-five years. Unlike the mistreatment of class enemies during the Cultural Revolution, which was condemned by China's reform-era leadership, the downsizing of the early 1960s is still considered a legitimate and correct response to the excessively "leftist" leap.[58]

[58] People who were victims of revolutionary excesses received recognition and even compensation for their suffering, while those like Wang who were traumatized by the modernization side of the revolutionary modernization coin were ignored. For recent positive assessments of downsizing, see Wu and Zheng, *Jiejue "san nong" wenti zhi lu*, 511; and *Dang de wenxian* bianji bu, ed., *Gongheguo zhongda juece he shijian shushi* [Stating the

Wang's downsizing experience went poorly for a number of reasons. He felt tricked into agreeing to go to Duliu, but his written application doomed his chances of returning to Tianjin. Wang considered himself a city person, not a peasant. He had no friends or strong social networks in the village. He had never done farm work in his life and did not want to start at the age of twenty-eight. Village cadres thought he was a burden and the average villager called him crazy. While Wang may have been an extreme problem case, other workers who lacked networks, skills, or rural identities had similarly difficult experiences in villages.

Villagers did not welcome returnees who ate more grain than they produced. In October 1961, Wuqing county officials said that if any more people returned to villages, they would not be getting any grain at all.[59] Rural authorities were unwilling to further cut villagers' meager diets in order to accommodate downsized workers. Even if villages and communes were able to provide food and housing to returned workers, the returnees often faced discrimination or snide remarks from rural residents and cadres. Common comments included: "these returned people all fell through the sieve" (meaning that they were of lower quality), "let's see if they run away again," "with more people, work points will decrease," and "the people who are coming are all mischievous and noisy, we don't want them."[60] Even Wei Rongchun, who said he was generally happy with his experience, remembered some village residents who gossiped that the returned workers had come back because they had failed or made mistakes in the city.

Wei did not let such talk bother him. He knew that in his case, it was not true. But a few misbehaving apples almost spoiled the bunch. Other returnees in Baodi acted more like Wang Kaiwen, squandering their severance payments (or even lending the cash to others at high interest) and trading on the black market. Returned workers were spotted in Baodi and Jiaohe counties selling steamed buns, sheep, rabbits, chickens, ducks, ceramics, glassware, cigarettes, window screens, and clothing at high prices.[61]

While some downsized workers made money as peddlers, others like Wei Rongchun worked hard in their home villages. Wei's nuanced sense of

truth about major policy decisions in the People's Republic] (Beijing: Renmin chubanshe, 2005), 205.

59 HPA, 859–2–7C, 23b.

60 For the first two comments, HPA, 864–1–269Y, 175; for the latter, HPA, 859–2–2C, 124b. Under the socialist planned economy, villagers earned work points and factory workers earned cash wages.

61 NBCK 3389 (June 29, 1962): 7–8.

identity helped him fit in. When I asked him whether he considered himself a worker or a peasant, he said, "It is difficult to say. Am I a worker who lives in a village? But I also lived in the city for a long time." Wei did not call himself a peasant. He thought of himself as a rural person who had been shaped by his time as a worker in Tianjin. After overcoming his initial fears and difficulties in Tianjin during the 1950s, Wei was comfortable and confident in both city and countryside. This dual identity, plus Wei's network of family and friends in the countryside, made him a successful returned worker.

Although Wei's main reason for volunteering to go back home was to fulfill his family obligations, his wife and father were not entirely happy to have him back. After Wei left the room for a moment during one of our interviews, Wei's wife, who had barely seen him since their wedding in the early 1950s, told me, "I was not willing for him to come back." The urban salary he sent back to her every month was worth more than his daily presence in their village home. Wei's father, unwilling to admit the seriousness of his leg injury, also told Wei to keep his city job because his salary was paying for his younger brother's university education in Beijing. "My dad said he could handle things on his own," Wei said. But Wei knew better.

As soon as he got back home, Wei became a normal peasant, doing collective farm labor and earning work points. But thanks to the foresight of their village party secretary, Wei and other returned workers were able to contribute in other ways. During the famine, village party secretary Hu Yishun had sent his family, including his sixteen-year-old son Hu Penghua (who would later play a key role in the rise of neighboring Xiaojinzhuang as a model village, described in Chapter 8), to the Miyun reservoir cafeteria, where one daughter worked and procured free food for the others. But he had also gotten a taste of the benefits rural industry could bring to his village. When the leap started, Hu Yishun was in charge of establishing a farm tool repair factory at the nearby commune headquarters. In 1958, commune headquarters had electricity, but most villages did not. Hu was convinced that the village needed electricity in order to establish its own small workshops. In their spare time, villagers used river reeds to weave baskets for sale. The village spent the proceeds on electrification.

Electrical materials and components, including steel cables and ceramic insulators, were extremely hard to come by in the early 1960s. Hu knew that if he waited for central planners to allocate the goods, it could take years for electricity to arrive. In 1962, Hu called together Wei Rongchun, other returned workers, and a villager who had served in the army. One former coal mine worker's assignment was to ride a three-wheeled bicycle cart to Tangshan. He used his connections at the mines to purchase enough ceramic insulators to fill his cart.

Wei Rongchun's job was to accompany the ex-soldier to a county south of Beijing, where an army buddy helped them obtain a truckload of steel cables. On the journey back to Baodi, the truck broke down in Wuqing county. The men had skipped lunch that day, and as darkness fell, they were increasingly cold and hungry. They walked to the nearest commune office. When they got to the door, the jumpy cadre on duty grabbed the pistol on his desk, on guard against strangers in the night. Wei, thinking quickly, remembered that his friend at the belt factory in Tianjin, the factory's vice-party secretary, was from a Wuqing village. "Don't be scared," Wei called out, saying that he was a friend of a certain vice-party secretary Liu. Wei's friend happened to be the gun-toting cadre's older brother, and the situation was immediately defused. Any friend of Liu's was a friend of the village official. He fed the men, found a new battery for the truck, and sent them on their way. Factory and army connections turned out to be vital in obtaining materials – and in getting them home safely.

Wei Rongchun's village was the first in the area to get electricity. Homes and lanes were illuminated at night, but more important, electricity made efficient irrigation possible and supported small village factories. In 1962, soon after electricity came, Hu and Wei worked together to establish a rice and flour processing workshop. Proceeds from the workshop could be invested in agricultural advances. Three villagers went to Tianjin to buy the processing machine. The brigade opened a cotton fluffing workshop in 1964 and a small-scale gunnysack factory in 1967. Before 1967, all gunnysacks in the area were produced by a neighboring village. They used footlooms and could finish about twenty sacks in a day. Wei Rongchun went to Tianjin and looked up an old comrade at his factory. The men had a meal and some drinks, and Wei used village funds to purchase two Toyota-made electric looms. The looms produced more than one hundred sacks daily.

Wei's city connections and his skills in operating textile machinery paid off for his village in the four decades after he voluntarily left his city job. He recognizes this. "You could say that after I returned to the village I made some contributions," he said. "Yes, I used the technical skills I had learned in the city, but more important, I got in touch with my friends from my time in the city." He had a few regrets about leaving

Tianjin. In the city, he had more authority, earned more money, and living conditions were better. But returning home seemed like the right thing to do.

Downsizing's Unintended Consequences

Party leaders saw downsizing as the only way to right the imbalance between industry and agriculture. An implicit admission that the socialist economy had gone horribly awry, the policy was not publicized as it unfolded. Mao Zedong, in a self-congratulatory mood, was amazed that the party had been able to rusticate people in the aftermath of the famine. "We have 20 million people at our beck and call," he said. "What political party other than the ruling CCP could have done it?"[62] The party indeed deserved organizational credit for the downsizing, but Mao was patting himself on the back for calling a tow truck after smashing his car into a tree. Downsizing was not a revolutionary policy. It was an attempt to patch up the crippled socialist economy, to restore grain production to pre-1958 levels so that urban industry could continue to exploit artificially cheap raw materials from rural China. Whatever positive impact skilled, connected workers had on village industrialization in the 1960s, 1970s, and 1980s was an unintended consequence of the program. Downsizing policy and propaganda never referred to the urban-rural transfer of technology as a goal. Rather, the aim was to stabilize and increase grain supplies after the terrible famine. Returned workers themselves and savvy village cadres, not party center, deserve credit for innovations in collective industry.

In addition, Mao's claim of moving twenty million people is difficult to verify. Sources differ on the total number of people cut from cities between 1961 and 1963. On the high side, Wu Li and Zheng Yougui claim that 29.4 million workers were downsized, but because of new urban employment assignments for high school graduates and other new city hires, the net reduction in employees was 17.51 million.[63] Luo Pinghan, basing his numbers on a 1963 central report wrapping up downsizing work, estimates that 19.4 million people were downsized, while others put the number at 15.97 million.[64] Given the incentives for local cadres

[62] MacFarquhar, *Origins of the Cultural Revolution: Vol. 2*, 335.

[63] Wu and Zheng, *Jiejue "san nong" wenti zhi lu*, 510.

[64] Luo Pinghan, *Da qianxi*, 257. For the text of the 1963 central report, see ZYWX, vol. 16 (1997), 550–55.

to meet quotas by inflating figures, I suspect that the lower number is more accurate.

Tianjin did not come close to meeting its downsizing target. As late as May 1962, Tianjin party secretary Wan Xiaotang was still exhorting city officials to downsize 220,000 employees and shrink the city population by 400,000 in the coming year. He was frustrated. Wan noted that insufficiently vigilant *hukou* control was allowing almost as many people to enter Tianjin as were cut. Population data show that 222,064 people moved out of Tianjin's urban core between 1961 and 1963, but because of continued immigration, the net reduction was only 131,349.[65] The 1961–1963 outflow from Tianjin to rural villages would be surpassed by the 371,904 people who left the city during the three-year period between 1968 and 1970, when urban sent-down youths and political outcasts made up the bulk of the migrants.

Many downsized workers contributed more to villages than these later waves of city people. At best, returnees were like Wei Rongchun, the creative and technical impetus behind each successive wave of his village's industrial development after 1963. Every time central policy allowed or encouraged collective enterprises, downsized workers were front and center, using their urban ties to obtain scarce supplies, to secure outsourcing contracts from city factories, and to teach successive generations of village youths technical skills. Able to move comfortably in villages and cities, they led rural delegations to Tianjin and were the first to greet urban work teams arriving in villages.

At worst, the returnees were pests, black marketeers, a burden on rural grain supplies, and a headache for village cadres. As the various levels and generations of cadres who have had to deal with Wang Kaiwen can attest, these troublemakers also represented a formidable legacy of downsizing. Wang's case shows that the party has never come to terms with the long-term effects of the lives that it shoved off course in the early 1960s. Between the extremes of Wang and Wei, millions of returnees lived rural lives devoted to farm work and family. Sometimes regretful at having had their urban benefits, salaries, conveniences, and independence taken away, the returnees were perhaps more aware of rural-urban difference than anyone else in Mao's China.

[65] Tianjin shi renkou pucha bangongshi, *Tianjin shi renkou tongji ziliao huibian, 1949–1983*, 254. This net decrease is 30,943 higher than the one used by Li Jingneng, *Zhongguo renkou, Tianjin fence*, 89, cited in MacFarquhar, *Origins of the Cultural Revolution: Vol. 3*, 34.

In Chapter 5, we turn to two groups that were comparatively ignorant about the realities of rural life when they arrived in Tianjin-area villages in the mid-1960s: the first major wave of sent-down youth, and urban work teams conducting the Four Cleanups movement. Villagers who knew that the disaster of the early 1960s had urban origins were understandably suspicious of uninvited guests from the city. The urbanites came to address problems that had emerged in the aftermath of the famine, but their impact was much less benign than the downsized workers who preceded them.

5

The Four Cleanups and Urban Youth in Tianjin's Hinterland

On an inspection visit to villages outside of Tianjin in 1960, top party theorist Chen Boda approached a group of peasants. Eager to make conversation, the editor of *Red Flag* greeted them: "Are you fishing?" The anglers responded in the affirmative, but demurred when Chen, ever alert to signs of illicit market activity, asked if they planned to sell the fish. "It seemed that they did not want to have anything to do with us," Chen recalled as he recounted the story four years later.[1] But after Chen asked about local crops, the group warmed to him and chatted as they walked toward Tuozidi, a village of five hundred people. Chen was in Xiaozhan, a marshy area between Tianjin and the Bohai gulf.

The most well-known person from Tuozidi was Jiang Deyu, a rice specialist and national labor model who had visited the Soviet Union and met with Chairman Mao Zedong. But when the peasants brought up "labor model Jiang," Chen Boda had no idea who they were talking about. One local jumped at the opportunity to complain to a top party leader. "Aren't we supposed to emphasize class struggle now? We think that labor model Jiang is a landlord, or at least a rich peasant," Chen recalled the peasants telling him. "He has cheated our Xiaozhan." Chen asked Tianjin leaders to investigate Jiang, who was stripped of his honors and kicked out of the party in 1962. Chen was impressed with his seemingly successful foray into rural work. "Why was it that I went for

[1] Chen told the story to staff members of *Red Flag* and the Marxism-Leninism Research Academy who were preparing to join work teams in the Four Cleanups movement. Chen Boda, "Xiaxiang wenti" [On going to villages], reproduced by Hebei shengwei siqing bangongshi, October 4, 1964, HPA, 855-19-1045C, 39-40.

only two hours and I learned about the matter, but many local comrades had been there for more than ten years and did not know about it? Why were the masses willing to tell me this, but not willing to tell others?" The key, Chen reckoned, was his attitude. "The masses check you out and see if they can bare their heart to you," he said. "I am a very stupid person, and have very little experience in working with the masses, but no matter how bad you are, as long as your attitude is correct, you can quickly discover problems."

Chen's experience in suburban Tianjin led him to return to Xiaozhan in March 1964 during the Four Cleanups movement, much to the regret of many local people. Chen rapidly uncovered other problems during the movement, which aimed to clean up politics, economy, ideology, and organization. Chen charged that class enemies had not only hidden their true identities, they had usurped village leadership and enjoyed protection from higher-ups. His claims led to a witch-hunt that implicated thousands of villagers, killed tens of people, and tortured and imprisoned many others in Tianjin's south suburbs. Beyond Tianjin, the "Xiaozhan experience" was promoted as a successful "power seizure" in a central document circulated nationwide in October 1964.[2]

Many rural people who knew that urbanites had weathered the leap famine at their expense did not welcome intrusive Four Cleanups work teams. Just when many villages were finally recovering from the leap disaster, self-righteous city people attacked the very practices that were making rural people's lives tolerable – freer trade, keeping grain in villages rather than giving it to the state, and private family plots. In assaulting the petty corruption and political "errors" that had arisen during the leap and its aftermath, the Four Cleanups movement exacerbated rural-urban tensions and ended up alienating cities from villages almost as much as the famine had.

At the same time that tens of thousands of officials, university graduates, and students from Tianjin went to the countryside on work teams to carry out the Four Cleanups, thousands of Tianjin teenagers moved to villages as "sent-down youth." This chapter focuses on these concurrent waves of city transplants between 1963 and 1966. Unlike the downsized workers who preceded them, many Four Cleanups work team members

[2] For the full text of the report, see ZGSX, 482–518. According to Bo Yibo, the report was responsible for pushing the Four Cleanups in a more radical direction, causing the downfall of countless rural cadres across China. Bo Yibo, *Ruogan zhongda juece*, 2:1123–24.

and sent-down youth had never spent time in villages before. The Four Cleanups were meant to expose hidden class enemies and punish corrupt rural cadres. Work team members were also supposed to follow the "three togethers" (live, eat, and work) and learn from poor and lower-middle peasants. Propaganda urged sent-down youth to transform "backward" (*luohou*) and "poor and blank" (*yi qiong er bai*) villages, but also to reform themselves through rural labor and class struggle.

These dual messages – villages as backward and corrupt but also as revolutionary crucibles worthy of humble study – jockeyed for position in the minds of city people sent to the countryside in the mid-1960s. The gap between what work team members and sent-down youth were told to expect in villages and what they actually saw and experienced was jarring. Rural poverty, even in the relatively well-off area surrounding Tianjin, shocked and disillusioned urban people. Friction escalated between peasants and the city transplants who occupied their homes. Conflict and violence were built into the Four Cleanups, were encouraged by leaders like Chen Boda, and foreshadowed the violence and bloodshed of the Cultural Revolution. In contrast, battles between urban youth and rural residents were the unintended consequence of a policy that tried to ameliorate post-leap employment pressures in Tianjin by dumping troublemaking teenagers into villages.[3]

This chapter will discuss the goals and methods of the Four Cleanups and sent-down youth programs, and will explore the contradictions between policy, propaganda, and reality. The two programs unfolded simultaneously and featured clashing approaches to the countryside. These approaches reflected the tension between revolution and modernization that was built into the Maoist project. One sought to address Mao's fears that the revolution was dying by unleashing an attack on hidden rural "class enemies." The other pushed youth to leave cities in order to reduce urban unemployment while attempting to convince them that they could reform "backward" villages. Unmoored from their city families and neighborhoods, sent-down youth had far less power in villages than Four Cleanups work teams, who retained ties to urban offices that could issue orders to politically subordinate rural cadres. Both groups' presence ended up deepening the gap between city and countryside. Urbanites' confrontational approach was more to blame for this than were villagers themselves, who struggled to deal with the uninvited guests.

[3] Thomas P. Bernstein, *Up to the Mountains and Down to the Villages: The Transfer of Youth from Urban to Rural China* (New Haven: Yale University Press, 1977), addresses the entire history of the transfer program.

Attacking Rural Wealth

Xiaozhan, like much of the area southeast of Tianjin, used to be underwater. After the sea retreated, reedy marshland was gradually populated by migrants from north China. Many villages did not appear on the map until two developments during the late Qing: first, the discovery that the wetlands were perfect for paddy rice cultivation; and second, the establishment of Yuan Shikai's Beiyang military training camp.[4] After the army's arrival, Xiaozhan township, eighteen miles from Tianjin's city center, developed quickly, and by 1964 had a population of eleven thousand. Its proximity to urban Tianjin oriented the region's rice, vegetables, and handicrafts (primarily woven reed products) toward the city. When Chen Boda visited Xiaozhan, the region's political and economic fortunes were still closely tied to Tianjin.

The Four Cleanups in Tianjin's outskirts began with little hint of the turmoil to come. In January 1964, Tianjin established test points in the south suburbs: one in Xiaozhan commune and another in Beizhakou commune, three miles northwest of Xiaozhan township. Work teams sent to the south suburbs included city and suburban cadres and recent university graduates. Their initial findings were unremarkable. The class composition of the area was complicated, owing to the motley mix of migrants who had settled its villages over the past seventy to eighty years. Land reform in 1951 had been mild, which allowed class enemies to falsely claim poor peasant status; some had wormed their way into leadership positions. But the overall achievements of the region were noteworthy, most cadres were good, and those who had committed mistakes should not be struggled against excessively.[5] At this point, it appeared that Xiaozhan's Four Cleanups would be "brief and uneventful," much like in Hebei's Raoyang county, where rural leaders used the movement to reward friends by giving them politically valuable "poor peasant" class labels and to punish rivals with damning "rich peasant" and "landlord" labels.[6]

The Four Cleanups, also known as the Socialist Education Movement, was Mao's response to problems that had spun out of control during and

[4] Xie Yan, "Chen Boda zuo'e zai Xiaozhan" [Chen Boda does evil in Xiaozhan], *Tianjin shi zhi* 6 (2004): 15.

[5] Xie Yan, "Chen Boda zuo'e," 16; Liu Jinfeng, *Zhengrong suiyue: Liu Jinfeng huiyilu* [Extraordinary years: Liu Jinfeng's memoirs] (Tianjin: Tianjin renmin chubanshe, 2000), 220.

[6] Friedman, Pickowicz, and Selden, *Revolution, Resistance, and Reform*, 54, 61.

after the Great Leap famine – corrupt village cadres who wined and dined at state expense, or who underreported harvest numbers in order to reduce the amount of grain requisitioned by the state. Black market trading, profit-making rural sidelines, and private agricultural plots may have been necessary survival strategies during the three hard years, but were harbingers of "revisionism," meaning a betrayal of Marxist principles. There was also the trumped-up fear that class enemies who had avoided detection during land reform had assumed positions of power, continuing to exploit poor peasants. To Mao, these were all dangerous signs that China's countryside was experiencing a capitalist restoration. This was a dark vision of rural China, and Mao wanted to attack it in a "war of annihilation" (*xiaomie zhan*) carried out by Four Cleanups work teams.[7]

Mao's lieutenant Chen Boda entered the battlefield in March 1964, when he returned to Xiaozhan. Chen, described by Michael Schoenhals as Mao's "senior perception management advisor,"[8] was a city-based author and propagandist, but he had written about agriculture and knew that the chairman saw the countryside as an important ideological battleground. By expanding his political activities to Tianjin's hinterland, Chen was "working toward" what he thought Mao wanted.[9]

The Four Cleanups movement varied tremendously depending on where and when it was carried out. The shifting viewpoints and alliances of top central leaders pushed the cleanups through many permutations between 1963 and 1966, first focusing on cadre corruption, then stressing class struggle.[10] Because the campaign proceeded in phases, certain counties completed one version of the movement, then had to go through

7 ZGSX, 506. The best overview of the Four Cleanups is still Richard Baum, *Prelude to Revolution: Mao, the Party, and the Peasant Question, 1962–66* (New York: Columbia University Press, 1975). For an excellent case study, see Chan, Madsen, and Unger, *Chen Village*.

8 Michael Schoenhals, "The Global War On Terrorism as Meta-Narrative: An Alternative Reading of Recent Chinese History," *Sungkyun Journal of East Asian Studies* 8, no. 2 (2008): 185.

9 MacFarquhar and Schoenhals apply British historian Ian Kershaw's idea of "working toward the *führer*" to Mao; Kershaw, *Hitler*, 2 vols. (London: Allen Lane, 1998, 2000). Mao was deliberately vague in expressing himself to his subordinates, forcing them to guess at his intentions and sometimes going beyond what Mao himself had imagined. This was a recipe for radicalism. Roderick MacFarquhar and Michael Schoenhals, *Mao's Last Revolution* (Cambridge, MA: Belknap Press of Harvard University Press, 2006), 48.

10 See Baum, *Prelude to Revolution*, and Baum and Frederick C. Teiwes, *Ssu-Ch'ing: The Socialist Education Movement of 1962–1966* (Berkeley: Center for Chinese Studies, University of California, 1968).

another after policy changed. Other counties were barely affected at all. Some Four Cleanups work teams consisted of officials from the county and commune levels, while others, like those in the Tianjin suburbs, were dominated by city people. When powerful officials from urban centers like Tianjin and Beijing became involved in the rural movement, they felt pressure to take charge and show results.

The first sign that Xiaozhan's Four Cleanups might become eventful was the appearance of Zhou Yang, deputy director of the central propaganda department. Zhou went to the Tianjin region in late February to visit sent-down youth, but thanks to a few words from Chairman Mao, Zhou changed his itinerary. Mao, upset that writers and artists were not serving workers and peasants, ordered Zhou to spend time at the grassroots. "If he's unwilling to go, then order the army to force him to go down," Mao told Chen Boda. Ostensibly out of concern for Zhou Yang's health, Chen and Tianjin officials arranged for Zhou to stay somewhere close to the city. They settled on Xiyouying, a village of 1,100 people in Beizhakou commune.[11]

Zhou Yang stayed in one of the nicest houses in Xiyouying, the home of female village party secretary and labor model Zhang Fengqin and her husband. Zhou and others in his entourage did not reveal their official positions, saying they were writers hoping to "experience life."[12] Village life confused Zhou Yang. Some villagers told Zhou that his host, who had been featured just weeks earlier in a laudatory *Tianjin Daily* profile about her honest words and deeds, was actually no good.[13] When Tianjin propaganda chief Wang Kangzhi visited Zhou to see how he was doing, Zhou said, "The more I learn about problems here, the more complicated they get. I'm like a doctor who can only inquire about a patient's condition but cannot write a prescription."[14] Enter Chen Boda, who would not hesitate to issue prescriptions. Chen's earlier discovery of labor model Jiang Deyu's purported problems, combined with his awareness of Mao's concerns about revisionism and class struggle, encouraged him to take charge of Xiaozhan's Four Cleanups.

On March 5, 1964, Liu Jinfeng, who had served as party secretary of Tianjin's south suburbs since 1953, accompanied Chen Boda to

[11] Chen Xiaonong, comp., *Chen Boda zuihou koushu huiyi* [Chen Boda's final oral memoir] (Hong Kong: Yangguang huanqiu chuban Xianggang youxian gongsi, 2005), 248.

[12] Wang Kangzhi jinian wenji bianjizu, ed., *Wang Kangzhi jinian wenji* [Collected writings commemorating Wang Kangzhi] (Tianjin renmin chubanshe, 2001), 124.

[13] TJRB, February 2, 1964, 2.

[14] Wang Kangzhi jinian wenji bianjizu, *Wang Kangzhi jinian wenji*, 124.

Xiyouying. As their car neared the village, Chen ordered the driver to stop. Chen wanted to walk the final half kilometer to the village. He thought that entering the village in a car would distance them from the masses. After hearing a report from the Four Cleanups work team stationed in Xiyouying, Chen visited Zhang Fengqin's house. Chen took note of the three new outbuildings in Zhang's compound, saw hefty bags of rice stacked up inside, and fixated on something he had never noticed in villages before: double-paned glass windows. After twenty minutes, Chen had seen enough. He told Zhou Yang to move to a poor peasant's house. Chen then reported his findings to the work team. "Zhang Fengqin does not seem like a poor peasant, her family is richer than all other villagers. She got rich after becoming party secretary," Chen said. "The double-paned glass exposed Zhang Fengqin. She's a poor peasant who's not really poor, a labor model who does not labor, she's become a politician." Something had to be done, Chen told the work team. "You can tell with just one look that she's the enemy. You take care of this, we can't have mistakes here," he ordered.[15] When he returned to Tianjin, he told city officials that Zhang should be removed from her leadership positions.

The work team jumped into action and assembled evidence of Zhang's crimes, which included illegally profiting from seven village factories established during the early 1960s, falsifying harvest reports in order to keep excess grain for the village, and hiding her true class identity, which was allegedly "rich peasant element" (*funong fenzi*).[16] These accusations distressed Liu Jinfeng, who had spent years promoting Zhang Fengqin as a star female village leader. Zhang had organized Xiyouying's first mutual aid society and cooperative in the 1950s. Now she was being attacked because her house did not conform to what Chen Boda thought a village cadre's home should look like. Liu Jinfeng saw rural prosperity not as a crime, but as evidence of his successful stewardship of the suburbs.[17]

Underreporting grain yields and investing in profitable sidelines were common rural survival strategies after the Great Leap famine.[18] These

[15] Liu Jinfeng, *Zhengrong suiyue*, 204–5; Wang Hui, "Wo suo zhidao de 'Xiaozhan siqing'" [What I know about "Xiaozhan's Four Cleanups"], *Tianjin wenshi ziliao xuanji* 102 (2004): 207.

[16] ZGSX, 488–89, 503.

[17] Liu Jinfeng, *Zhengrong suiyue*, 213.

[18] Gao Wangling, *Renmin gongshe shiqi Zhongguo nongmin "fan xingwei" diaocha* [An investigation into Chinese peasants' "counteraction" during the commune period] (Beijing: Zhongguo dangshi chubanshe, 2006). See also Dali L. Yang, *Calamity and*

practices were also likely to earn village leaders popular support, while cadres who insisted on handing everything over to the state faced grumbling. Ironically, a *Tianjin Daily* profile had praised "honest" Zhang Fengqin for saying, "however much we harvest, that is what we will report," and chastised villagers who complained that Zhang's honesty put the village at a disadvantage. But it turned out that Zhang had been dishonest, to her village's advantage. Xiyouying had kept thirty-five hundred kilograms of extra grain for itself. The village reportedly earned four hundred thousand yuan in "sudden huge profits" from sideline industry during the early 1960s, and even rented a long-term room at a Tianjin hotel in order to make business deals in the city.[19] For leaders like Mao and Chen Boda, the post-leap recovery looked suspiciously like capitalism.

Zhang Fengqin was not the only village leader to thrive economically after the leap. Other communities that took advantage of their proximity to Tianjin did especially well. One village in Huanghua county, directly south of Tianjin on the Bohai gulf, stationed five cadres in Tianjin to trade seafood for city-made goods. When the village leader negotiated a deal with a Tianjin shoe factory, he stayed at a top city hotel and went shopping for an alarm clock, a handbag, and a fur-lined cap. During the Four Cleanups, work teams condemned these dealings.[20] Villagers' lives may have been improving in 1963 and 1964, but the means to this end – increased trade and the subversion of the state grain monopoly – were a painful repudiation of Mao's revolutionary vision.

Work team members followed Chen Boda's example and searched for evidence of excessive prosperity. Former members of work teams told me that their first task in villages was to look for the biggest, nicest houses. Those families would be struggle targets, and work teams were instructed to remain aloof from them. Likewise, small, run-down hovels were markers of political reliability. Candidates for membership in newly formed poor peasants' representative associations (an organization of activists meant to assist work teams and eventually replace cadres overthrown during the Four Cleanups) came from these households.[21] Internal

Reform in China: State, Rural Society, and Institutional Change since the Great Leap Famine (Stanford: Stanford University Press, 1996).

[19] ZGSX, 488, 503.

[20] Zhonggong Hebei shengwei *Hebei siqing tongxun* bianjibu, ed., *Hebei nongcun jieji douzheng dianxing cailiao* [Representative materials on class struggle in Hebei villages], vol. 2 (April 1966), 83.

[21] Interviewee 11, interviewee 12. On the poor peasant associations, see ZYWX, vol. 18 (1998), 580–83.

documents also mentioned eyeballing villagers' homes, but warned that this might lead to errors. One work team member admitted:

> I thought that whoever's home is poorest and filthiest was automatically a poor and lower-middle peasant. Wang Guiyin's home is the dirtiest and his son is a poor peasant association representative, so I thought that he could become an activist. But the masses said that his origins were unclear. I went to the police station to check his file and to my great surprise, he was a landlord who had been struggled against.[22]

The lesson learned was that while appearances were important markers, class enemies could be hidden anywhere. Material realities often contradicted villagers' official class labels, in part because receiving a landlord or rich peasant label during land reform often led to discrimination and poverty.

According to this logic, Zhang Fengqin's home should have alerted propaganda chief Zhou Yang that his host's "poor peasant" status was spurious. But Zhou's mind was elsewhere. His original purpose in traveling to Tianjin was not to live in a village himself, but to mobilize the city's young people to emulate model sent-down youth. Zhou's statements about why city teenagers should transform themselves into peasants formed the basis of a propaganda blitz in spring 1964. His message was almost the polar opposite of Chen Boda's simultaneous battle against excessive village wealth during the Four Cleanups. In order to attract urban youth to the countryside, Zhou had to avoid linking poverty to political virtue.

"The First Generation of Intellectuals to Become Peasants"

Zhou Yang's stay in Xiyouying was sandwiched between visits with sent-down youth in the Tianjin area. In February and again in early May 1964, Zhou visited nationally famous model youth Hou Jun and Xing Yanzi in Baodi county.[23] In the early 1960s, the two young women had chosen to become peasants instead of seeking city jobs and university educations (Hou in Beijing, where her family lived; Xing in Tianjin, where her father was a factory official). Also in February 1964, Zhou spent a week in

[22] *Jinjiao siqing jianbao* [Tianjin suburbs Four Cleanups bulletin] 14 (December 1, 1965): 11.

[23] Baodi xian zhi bianxiu weiyuanhui, ed., *Baodi xian zhi* [Baodi county gazetteer] (Tianjin: Tianjin shehui kexueyuan chubanshe, 1995), 58; Zheng Zhiying, *Tianjin shi sishiwu nian dashiji*, 246.

Jinghai county, where he dropped in on model youth Wang Peizhen.[24] Wang, a 1957 graduate of Tianjin's Number Seven Girls' Middle School, became famous after marrying an illiterate peasant and settling in his village in 1959.[25] On March 5, Zhou Yang addressed Hou, Wang, Xing, and other "advanced educated youth" who had traveled to Tianjin for the occasion. Zhou's rambling remarks fueled a propaganda drive that accompanied the city's transfer of teenagers to villages in 1964.[26] In April alone, twenty-three hundred teenagers moved to Baodi villages, ostensibly permanently.[27] By the end of the year, more than fourteen thousand youths had been sent from Tianjin to Hebei villages or to more distant frontier encampments.[28]

While Chen Boda obsessed about rampant wealth in villages, Zhou Yang worried about the "poor and blank" and "backward" condition of China's countryside. The best way to improve villages, Zhou argued, was not through combative work teams, but by sending urban educated youth to "laborize" (*laodonghua*) themselves and to "intellectualize" (*zhishihua*) peasants. "The main target of socialist education is peasants," Zhou said, "500 million peasants are uneducated. Who's going to go and disseminate? We could send work teams, but where do we have that many people? It's mainly going to rely on the power of educated youths." Zhou saw the long-term settlement of urban youths in villages – and not outside work teams – as the most effective way to transform China's countryside. He exhorted youths to teach villagers the basics of reading, writing, and arithmetic. "In this way, village culture, science, and education will be

[24] Jinghai xian zhi bianxiu weiyuanhui, ed., *Jinghai xian zhi* [Jinghai county gazetteer] (Tianjin: Tianjin shehui kexueyuan chubanshe, 1995), 23.

[25] Liu Xiaomeng et al., *Zhongguo zhiqing shidian* [Chinese educated youth encyclopedia] (Chengdu: Sichuan renmin chubanshe, 1995), 716.

[26] A transcript of Zhou Yang's speech, including the interjections of Tianjin party secretary Wan Xiaotang, mayor Hu Zhaoheng, and Wang Peizhen, can be found in HPA, 864-2-296Y, 10–15. This document, *Zhou Yang yijiuliuwu nian san yue wu ri zai jiejian xiaxiang zhishi qingnian xianjin renwu de jianghua jilu* [Transcript of Zhou Yang's talk upon meeting advanced educated youth sent down to villages on March 5, 1965] is misdated. The propaganda outline based on the talks and Zheng Zhiying's chronology confirm that Zhou spoke in March 1964, not in 1965. See Zhonggong Tianjin shiwei xuanchan bu, *Guanyu dongyuan he zuzhi chengshi zhishi qingnian canjia nongcun shehuizhuyi jianshe de xuanchuan tigang* [Propaganda outline on mobilizing and organizing urban educated youth to participate in village socialist construction], March 22, 1964, TMA, X281-96Y, 1–4; and Zheng Zhiying, *Tianjin shi sishiwu nian dashiji*, 244. The heading for this section comes from Hu Zhaoheng's interjection at Zhou Yang's March 5, 1964 speech.

[27] NBCK 3624 (May 26, 1964): 7.

[28] Zheng Zhiying, *Tianjin shi sishiwu nian dashiji*, 258.

built up, and the appearance of villages will change bit by bit because of you," Zhou said. "Transform traditions, go about it little by little. This will remold yourselves and remold villages."[29]

As divergent as Zhou Yang's approach seemed from Chen Boda's, each man had good reason to believe that he was following Mao's wishes. In June 1964, Mao mentioned Xiaozhan as evidence that revisionism had already appeared in China.[30] Through the end of the year, Mao supported Chen's version of class struggle in Xiaozhan. Yet the Four Cleanups' "war of annihilation" was concurrent with the first systematic, large-scale transfer of urban youth to the countryside in 1964. To promote the sent-down youth program, Zhou Yang repeated verbatim Mao's comments from the 1950s about the "poor and blank" countryside, which was a "vast universe" where educated youth could "make great contributions." The gap between a happy realm for sent-down youth and the Four Cleanups' dark war against excessive rural wealth could be measured by what had transpired between 1958 and 1964. After the leap's crushing failure, China's population was no longer a "sheet of white paper" on which "beautiful things" could be written and painted, as Mao had put it in 1958.[31] The paper had been sullied.

Why, then, was Zhou Yang promoting a pre-leap script about rural China in 1964 when the times apparently called for a "war" to punish village officials for their alleged transgressions during the famine? Practical concerns about how to handle increasing numbers of unemployed, trouble-making urban youth drove the 1964 rustication program. Behind Zhou's platitudes were thousands of idle teenagers who had few job prospects in Tianjin.

According to a March 30, 1964, directive from Tianjin's municipal government, the main group targeted to go to villages were youths holding long-term urban *hukou* who "were unable to advance in school or be employed."[32] While some documents referred to this group as "educated youths" (*zhishi qingnian*), others used the euphemism "society youths" (*shehui qingnian*), meaning aimless young people unattached to schools

[29] HPA, 864–2–296Y, 13.

[30] Bo Yibo, *Ruogan zhongda juece*, 2:1116.

[31] On April 15, 1958, Mao wrote, "Aside from other characteristics, the most striking characteristic of China's population of 600 million is that it is poor and blank. This may seem like a bad thing, but actually it is a good thing." He then called the population a "sheet of white paper"; MWG, vol. 7 (1992), 177–78. Mao's statement about the "vast universe" where young intellectuals could "make great contributions" (*da you zuo wei*) was in response to a report in December 1955. Liu Xiaomeng, *Zhongguo zhiqing shidian*, 5.

[32] TMA, X281–96Y, 9.

or work units. They had dropped out of school or failed entrance exams and could not find jobs, either because of rebellious behavior, poor grades, or bad class labels.[33]

Xue Meng quit high school in the early 1960s. In spring 1964, when he was eighteen years old, he signed up to join the movement to send urban youths to the countryside. On April 25, 1964, he left Tianjin for a Baodi village. Xue volunteered because it seemed like a revolutionary thing to do, but more important, as a high school dropout, he had little hope of finding city work. "If I would have received a job assignment in Tianjin, I would have stayed," Xue admitted.[34] Ameliorating urban unemployment was one of the central – and often unstated – goals of the sent-down youth program.[35] While newspapers stressed the revolutionary value of urban youth remolding themselves and transforming villages, internal documents confirmed that urban job shortages in the wake of post-leap retrenchment were also a central motivation. One oral propaganda outline was explicit:

> Perhaps some parents think, "Tianjin is such a large industrial city, can we not solve city youths' employment problems?" We cannot. Industrial development depends on technical improvement and mechanization, not on building new factories and adding new employees. Because of this, the number of employees our industrial and other construction enterprises can absorb is very limited.[36]

Propaganda arguing that contributing to rural development was better than sitting idle in the city targeted parents who hoped to keep their children in Tianjin. Much of the resistance to the sent-down youth program came from family members. In April 1964, when a sixteen-year-old Tianjin girl named Wang volunteered to go to a village, her mother made her a big meal of eggs and dumplings, saying, "villages are so bitter, don't go!" The mother wanted Wang to stay at home and help with housework. When Wang was not swayed by big meals, her family tied her up while she was sleeping and hid her pants so that she could not leave the house. Wang dictated an S.O.S. note to her niece, which the younger girl then delivered to the local street committee cadres who were in charge of mobilizing jobless youth.[37]

[33] Chinese scholars have called these youths "cast-offs" from the lower strata of urban society; Liu Xiaomeng, *Zhongguo zhiqing shidian*, 14, 61.

[34] Interviewee 13.

[35] Bernstein, *Up to the Mountains and Down to the Villages*, 33.

[36] TMA, X281–96Y, 3b.

[37] *Hexi qu jianbao* [Hexi district bulletin] 125 (May 4, 1964): 1–2, HDA, 1–6–21C. This internally circulated newsletter featuring reports of problems in the Hexi district of Tianjin was read by top district officials.

In another case, a Tianjin factory official beat his son when the unemployed seventeen-year-old signed up to go to a village. The cadre said, "If you go, I'll break your leg," and tried to make good on this threat when his son returned from a send-off ceremony with a bouquet of flowers and a certificate approving the boy's transfer to Baodi. The father made the teen return the certificate, and then beat him with a belt for an hour until the strap broke into three pieces. Mangled belt in hand, the boy limped off to the local Communist Youth League office and reported the abuse.[38]

According to one internal report, the longer parents had spent in villages, the more likely they were to obstruct their children from leaving Tianjin. For parents who had left the countryside so that their children could enjoy the benefits of urban life, the sent-down youth program seemed like downward mobility. Tianjin parents from village backgrounds had a clear understanding of the rural-urban divide. They feared that their children could not handle farm work, that they were too young to be on their own, that nobody would care for them if they fell ill, that they would not earn money to support the family, and that they would permanently lose their urban *hukou* and guaranteed rations. One parent said of the prospect of a child moving to the countryside, "I spent half my life in a village. It's bitter and exhausting. I really don't know about this."[39] Some Tianjin youth ignored their families' warnings about village life. The bitterness that their parents and grandparents spoke of had changed, had it not? Mao said that the countryside was a vast universe where they could make great contributions. It was galling for the teens to discover that their parents had been right.

"We felt cheated," Xue Meng said. "The propaganda said that there were employment problems in the city so we should come to the countryside. We did, and then the people who refused to go to villages were rewarded with jobs several months later. As soon as we left, there were lots of jobs in the city." When faced with a choice between sitting idle in the city or being revolutionary in a village, many Tianjin youths had chosen the latter option. A new wave of city hirings in mid-1964 revealed that there had been a third possibility. The news that their friends in the city were getting jobs was made worse by the realization that village life was indeed bitter. A December 1964 provincial report on problems in Baodi and other counties noted that most sent-down youth lacked sufficient grain, winter clothes, and blankets, and that adequate housing

[38] *Hexi qu jianbao* 124 (April 25, 1964): 1–2, HDA, 1–6–21C.
[39] *Hexi qu jianbao* 111 (March 21, 1964): 3, HDA, 1–6–21C.

was in short supply. Urban youths including Xue Meng received monthly allowances and packages of extra food from their parents to supplement their meager village diets.

Propaganda had mentioned the need to transform rural poverty, but youth who had never been to villages before did not know what to expect. They were more receptive to messages about how Jixian county north of Baodi had "mountains filled with flowers and fruit, and plains full of rice and grain" (as one urban cadre had promised sent-down youth at a mobilization meeting) than to vague warnings about enduring hardship.[40] One Tianjin youth complained, "You cheated us into coming by giving us red flowers and showing us movies."[41]

In 1964, sent-down youth were not the only urbanites to discover that rural reality defied expectations. Members of Four Cleanups work teams, many of whom were only several years older than the sent-down youth, learned lessons about village poverty that conflicted with encomiums about fighting a war of annihilation against class enemies and corrupt rural cadres. Chen Boda exhorted city people to get close to the masses by following the three togethers. But the closer they got to the masses, the more skeptical some work team members became about a capitalist restoration in the countryside.

The Three Togethers

After successfully taking down Zhang Fengqin in Xiyouying, Chen Boda continued his search for problems in the Tianjin suburbs. In spring 1964, Chen visited Xiaozhan again. He returned to Tuozidi, where farmers had complained about labor model Jiang Deyu four years earlier. It was rainy, but Chen again insisted on walking into the village. He took off his shoes and socks, slipping and sliding through the mud. For lunch, villagers had prepared a substantial meal with several dishes, steamed buns, and rice. When Chen saw the food he refused to "eat big and drink big," one of the main crimes village officials were accused of during the Four Cleanups. Chen said he would have a corn bun, so his village hosts rushed to make some. When the buns were ready, Chen divided one up and passed pieces around before taking two bites and declaring the meal finished. Chen then said that even though Jiang Deyu had been cashiered in 1962, he was still in charge behind the scenes in Tuozidi. Jiang would also have to become a struggle target during the Four Cleanups, Chen said.[42] After

[40] HPA, 907–7–85Y, 23.
[41] *Hexi qu jianbao* 176 (July 4, 1964): 5, HDA, 1–6–21C.
[42] Liu Jinfeng, *Zhengrong suiyue*, 206–7.

Tuozidi, Chen's next stop was Xiaozhan township, where he decided that township party secretary Zhang Yulun was actually a class enemy from a "bandit family."

Chen thought that he had found a good formula for getting close to the masses and discovering problems in the suburbs. This was his modified version of the three togethers. Chen stayed in a colonial-style guesthouse in Tianjin's former British concession, where he enjoyed privately screened films (including one about the life of Beethoven),[43] and he did not do farm work, but when he went to the countryside he portrayed himself as down-to-earth. First, walk into villages, even if your feet get muddy. Second, be seen eating simple food. Chen had learned the latter lesson during his 1960 visit to Xiaozhan, when he insisted on eating a humble vegetable bun. In late 1964, he told a group of writers and editors preparing to join Four Cleanups work teams that his attention to appearances had paid off. "Recently I went back there and two peasants pointed at me from afar and said, 'that old man wearing glasses came here in 1960 and ate a vegetable bun. Now he's back.' All I did was eat once and the common people remembered it," Chen said with misplaced pride.[44]

After 1964, people in Xiaozhan would remember Chen's accusations during the Four Cleanups more than his bun chewing. Wang Hui, director of the Tianjin municipal party committee's general office, was instrumental in publicizing Chen's charges. Wang spent two weeks in Xiaozhan drafting the report that was circulated nationwide about the region's Four Cleanups. He later regretted his involvement. "This was the most important document from Tianjin that party center had circulated since liberation. It was also the document with the worst impact," he wrote in 2004.[45] Even though his final report adhered to Chen Boda's orders, outlining the massive corruption, sexual misconduct, and evil deeds of "class aliens" Zhang, Jiang, and Zhang, Wang Hui's impression of suburban village life differed from Chen Boda's. This is because Wang, unlike Chen, stayed in Xiyouying for an extended period of time. Wang followed the three togethers in a peasant home. "There was not even a basic latrine pit in the yard," he wrote, "so going to the toilet was very difficult." In retrospect, Wang found it ironic that he and other work team

[43] "I like to watch films about bourgeois life in the eighteenth and nineteenth centuries, no less than I like reading old Chinese books," Chen told Tianjin mayor Hu Zhaoheng. Quan Yanchi, *Tianjin shizhang* [Tianjin mayor] (Beijing: Zhonggong zhongyang dangxiao chubanshe, 1993), 83.

[44] Chen Boda, "Xiaxiang wenti," HPA, 855–19–1045C, 40.

[45] Wang Hui, "Wo suo zhidao," 197.

members normally lived in nice buildings equipped with bathrooms, but were struggling against grassroots rural cadres living in mud huts. "Their small-scale farming lives were extremely far from a capitalist restoration," he wrote.[46]

Throughout rural China in 1964 and 1965, members of Four Cleanups work teams had experiences that clashed with the goals of the movement. Chen Boda stressed the need to overthrow hidden class enemies and corrupt village officials who had enriched themselves. But work team members from cities were far more impressed by widespread poverty than by examples of rural wealth. Mao sent his doctor, Li Zhisui, to participate in the Four Cleanups in Jiangxi province, where "after sixteen years of revolution, it seemed to me that China had not progressed at all. The standard of living was terrible."[47] Closer to Tianjin, in Baxian west of the city, work team members "were unclear on why after more than ten years of being liberated the poor and lower-middle peasants could still be so impoverished," according to an internal report. The local diet consisted solely of boiled carrots, a family of five shared one dirty quilt and two bowls, and daughters were sold or married off as child brides. Work team members thought these conditions were "incomprehensible, and did not link them to cadres' four unclean problems."[48] They followed orders to struggle against enemies and temper themselves in the revolutionary crucible of the countryside, but also privately took note of economic reality.

Testimonials about how to overcome revulsion at the dirtier aspects of village life became a popular genre in internal publications like *Hebei Four Cleanups Newsletter* and *Tianjin Suburbs Four Cleanups Bulletin*. Work team members usually concluded articles with an obligatory sentence or two acknowledging that their own bourgeois ideology was the filthiest thing of all. But the bulk of the texts aimed for shock value and reinforced the idea of rural inferiority. One woman work team member described an elderly female villager with a putrefying open neck wound who spit rancid globs on the floor and then cooked steamed buns in a dirty face-washing basin. The young woman forced herself to take a few bites of the bun, ran outside, and vomited. On her next visit, she inhaled smelling salts before entering the home. After examining her thought, she

[46] Wang Hui, "Wo suo zhidao," 206–7.

[47] Li Zhisui, *The Private Life of Chairman Mao: The Memoirs of Mao's Personal Physician* (New York: Random House, 1994), 429.

[48] *Hebei siqing tongxun* [Hebei Four Cleanups newsletter], November–December 1964, HPA, D651.7 15:1.

apologized for offending her host and the two women became friendly, but the disgusting parts of the testimonial overwhelm its happy ending.[49] Other work team members wrote about snot-nosed village children who urinated or defecated in bed. The city visitors eventually controlled their disgust and helped to clean up the mess, but readers could be forgiven for thinking, "gross," instead of "I, too, need to reform my bourgeois ideology."

Four Cleanups work team members from Tianjin may have been disgusted by village life, but they knew that eventually the movement would end and they would be able to return to the comforts of city jobs and schools. They were well aware that their performance in the movement could affect opportunities for career advancement. Enthusiastically following the three togethers was a ritual meant to impress work team colleagues and peasants alike. One thirty-year-old Tianjin woman named Yang did not mention rural filth in her personal diary about her time on a Four Cleanups work team in the Hengshui area of Hebei in 1964 and 1965, although she commented on the hardships of farm work and the "extremely obvious selfish mentality" of peasants who seemed overly concerned about grain distribution.[50] Yang dwelled more on her superiors and fellow work team members than on village life or the details of the Four Cleanups. She saw her stint in the village as a hoop to jump through in order to advance her career.

In between diary entries about going to the county town for a shower and wondering when the movement would ever end, Yang complained that her efforts to follow the three togethers were not being recognized by her superiors. In July 1965, she was outraged at a formal review of her performance. The language used on her evaluation form especially galled Yang. "Ai! I work myself to death day and night but I didn't even get the word 'enthusiastic,' instead I only got 'hard working,'" Yang wrote. She wore an old cotton jacket to show her closeness to the peasants, but nobody believed that it was really hers, "so in my evaluation I got a 'simple lifestyle' but no 'arduous.'" For Yang, the three togethers were more about appearances than about uniting with villagers. How the Four Cleanups might affect her professional development was her paramount concern. In this regard, she was not alone.

Work team members in the Xiaozhan region also wanted to show their superiors that they were enthusiastic about the Four Cleanups. In

[49] *Hebei siqing tongxun*, November–December 1964, HPA, D651.7 15:1.
[50] Personal diary, AC.

Xiaozhan, Chen Boda's involvement raised the stakes. Work team members who wanted to seem revolutionary could not afford to ignore the orders of a central leader who seemed so certain about ominous plots. While Yang worried about what others thought about her jacket, work team members in Xiaozhan competed to ferret out as many hidden class enemies as possible. Their zealousness spiraled into violence.

Xiaozhan's Shocks

After Chen Boda identified evil ringleaders in the Tianjin suburbs, work teams compiled materials on the three "counterrevolutionary cliques" centered around female labor model Zhang Fengqin, rice specialist Jiang Deyu, and township leader Zhang Yulun. Each clique included about eighty people, who were criticized at mass meetings. Anyone with ties to the counterrevolutionaries also came under suspicion: one official source reports that 2,711 people in the south suburbs were implicated in "mistaken cases" during the Four Cleanups.[51]

Tianjin leaders helped to push the movement in a violent direction by endorsing Chen Boda's verdict on the cliques' three ringleaders. By the end of April 1964, Zhang Fengqin was kicked out of the party and her husband was arrested. Jiang Deyu and Zhang Yulun were detained later in the year. Once the cliques had been identified and their leaders punished, family, friends, and others who had connections to the counterrevolutionaries became fair game for inhumane treatment.

Work team members and villagers beat and tortured suspected counterrevolutionaries in Xiaozhan. According to an official source, there were twenty-nine "abnormal deaths" during Xiaozhan's Four Cleanups.[52] One former member of a work team there told me that the dead included beating and suicide victims.[53] Chen Boda blithely encouraged the violence after someone told him about a beating in Xiaozhan. "The masses want to beat him, they have the revolutionary spirit," Chen said. "First, they are not beating a good person. Second, they did not beat him to death."[54]

[51] Tianjin shi Jinnan qu difang zhi bianxiu weihuanhui, ed., *Jinnan qu zhi* [Jinnan district gazetteer] (Tianjin: Tianjin shehui kexueyuan chubanshe, 1999), 425.

[52] Tianjin shi nongcun hezuo zhi fazhan shi bianji bangongshi, ed., *Tianjin shi nongcun hezuo zhi fazhan jianshi, 1949–1987* [Concise history of the Tianjin village cooperative system, 1949–1987] (Tianjin: Tianjin shi nongye hezuo zhi fazhan shi bianji bangongshi, 1989), 324.

[53] Interviewee 11.

[54] Liu Jinfeng, *Zhengrong suiyue*, 230–31.

Violence occurred on stage at meetings and also during interrogations. At one session, Zhang Fengqin was subjected to the "swing the coal briquette" torture. One person grabbed her by the hair, another took her legs, and they swung her around violently. Zhang's hair was torn from her head and two of her front teeth were knocked out.[55] She tried to hang herself at home, but two female work team members stationed in her house stopped her.[56]

Other rural officials in the Tianjin region heard about the carnage in Xiaozhan and were terrified. In October 1965, work team members reported that "because of Xiaozhan's shocks," cadres were afraid of getting killed: "People say, 'as long as I have a breath in my body after the movement is over, it will be okay.'"[57] Some could not take the pressure. A rash of suicides swept through villages when a new wave of work teams entered Hebei villages in autumn 1965. In October alone, thirty-six suicides in the Tangshan region were attributed to the Four Cleanups. In the province as a whole, 533 people had killed themselves during the movement, including 73 in the Tianjin region and 2 within the municipality.[58] Even though internal reports urged caution and deplored the deaths, leaders including Gu Yunting (Tianjin's party secretary in charge of agriculture and the suburban Four Cleanups) emphasized harsh struggle well into early 1966. In a speech to work team political officers, Gu spoke approvingly of the treatment used against Zhang Yulun in Xiaozhan, who "was struggled against so hard that his sweat soaked the ground."[59]

Sex and the Four Cleanups

Accusations about almost any perceived transgression – economic, political, or personal – led to humiliation and violent punishment. Some of the harshest criticism and treatment were reserved for alleged sexual improprieties. In the official report about the "Xiaozhan experience" circulated nationwide, both Zhang Fengqin and Zhang Yulun were singled out for having had illicit sexual relations (Zhang Fengqin with a

[55] Ibid., 231.
[56] ZGSX, 510; Zhonggong Tianjin shiwei bangongting, "Chen Boda tongzhi jianghua jiyao" [Summary of comrade Chen Boda's remarks], November 24, 1964, HPA, 855–19–1045C, 50.
[57] *Jinjiao siqing jianbao* 1 (October 25, 1965): 7.
[58] *Hebei nongcun siqing jianxun* [Hebei village Four Cleanups news in brief] 40 (November 21, 1965): 1–3.
[59] *Hebei nongcun siqing jianxun* 98 (May 6, 1966): 3–4.

Xiyouying vice brigade leader, Zhang Yulun with the "concubine" of a "landlord-capitalist").[60] After the charges against the two village leaders were publicized, work team members investigated the sexual histories of lesser targets, sometimes viciously. When one female cadre in a village a mile away from Xiyouying denied charges that she had slept with her village party secretary, work team interrogators stripped her naked and forced icicles into her vagina.[61]

In such cases, work team members justified their brutality by arguing that adultery and seduction were nefarious tools that class enemies used to corrupt upright officials. Yet members of work teams themselves were not immune from sexual entanglements. Disciplinary guidelines drawn up for Four Cleanups work teams required that members not engage in "chaotic sexual relations" or form romantic attachments with other team members or villagers.[62] Some people from Tianjin, released from the routines of city jobs and classrooms, had difficulty following these rules. In November 1964, Hebei governor Liu Zihou criticized Gu Yunting for allowing two suburban work teams to fall apart because of sexual improprieties.[63] Work team members were not supposed to add a fourth "together" to their interactions with villagers.

One team sent to Hangou in Tianjin's north suburbs was totally out of control. Two leading officials on the work team had sex with one another in multiple peasant homes. This angered villagers. When one local man learned that his young daughter had walked in on the two in flagrante, he called them "contemptible creatures." Two other work team members flirted or slept with village women, and a third snuck out of Hangou to pursue an adulterous affair with a woman from his work unit in Tianjin. According to an internal report, the work team's sexual misconduct undermined its ability to clean up village problems, and was responsible for the "premature death" of the Four Cleanups in Hangou.[64]

While the Hangou debacle was kept under wraps, another case of sexual misconduct in Tianjin's east suburbs received wider publicity.

[60] ZGSX, 511, 490.

[61] Liu Jinfeng, *Zhengrong suiyue*, 231.

[62] Zhonggong Tianjin shiwei jiaoqu siqing gongzuo zongtuan, *Shehuizhuyi jiaoyu xuexi wenjian* [Socialist education study documents] (Tianjin, January 1966), 239.

[63] Zhonggong Tianjin shiwei bangongting, *Zihou tongzhi zai tingqu Yunting tongzhi huibao Tianjin jiaoqu siqing yundong qingkuang he buzhi wenti shi de zhishi* [Comrade Zihou's orders upon hearing Comrade Yunting's report on the situation and problems with the Four Cleanups movement in the Tianjin suburbs] (November 13, 1964), HPA, 855-19-1111C, 42.

[64] *Hebei siqing tongxun* 3 (November 23, 1964): 1–2.

In the latter instance, the village woman involved suffered the brunt of the criticism. The two Tianjin work team members she had supposedly seduced were censured for giving in to temptation, but their weakness was presented as excusable. As the Tianjin journalist who publicized the case put it, "class enemies stealthily shot off a pink cannonball that exploded in the Four Cleanups work team, and some work team members fell wounded."[65] The message was that sex could be a dangerous weapon wielded by crafty villagers.

According to the lurid account circulated in Four Cleanups newsletters and featured in an exhibition about the "fruits of the Four Cleanups" on public display at Tiananmen Square in Beijing, a young female village accountant known as the "little fox" was to blame for the "pink cannonball."[66] Village cadres threatened by the Four Cleanups purportedly encouraged the little fox to entrap a recent university graduate from Tianjin. The graduate was in charge of documents related to the movement. After seducing him and gaining his trust, the little fox was able to read secret files and provide intelligence to her backers. But the relationship was discovered and the graduate had to cut off contact with the young woman. The next step in the plan was for the little fox to sleep with an older married man on the work team. Under the pretense of lending a literary magazine to the man, the little fox stroked his hand and they immediately fell into bed. After this coup, she was allowed to attend meetings of the work team party branch and to borrow internal documents from her new lover, all the while passing along classified information to village cadres.

The woman disputed this narrative. She denied that there was any political motive or spying involved. The relationship with the young graduate was "sincerely falling in love," she said. Before they were discovered, the two went on dates to Tianjin movie theaters and strolled in the city's riverside parks. Sex with the older married work team member, a cadre in the Tianjin planning commission who had a long history of sexual misconduct, was not consensual, the woman said. She claimed that he had forcibly humiliated her. After the work team interrogated the woman and tried to get her to confess to her plot, she mailed letters to party center and personally delivered protest petitions to the Tianjin party committee and municipal government, excoriating the "bandit team" as "bullies protected by the powerful."

[65] *Hebei nongcun jieji douzheng dianxing cailiao*, vol. 1 (February 1966), 191.

[66] The following paragraphs are based on *Hebei nongcun jieji douzheng dianxing cailiao*, vol. 1, 190–203; vol. 2, 216–24; and interviewee 14.

The work team turned up the pressure on the little fox by organizing a "struggle corps" of village activists against her. Finally, the team's political instructor humiliated her by broadcasting its version of events at a village-wide struggle meeting. After four days of criticism, she gave up, saying, "I admit defeat, without the help of the entire village I would not have reformed myself. I will write the party a letter of repentance and will not do any more plots." She was kicked out of the youth league and forced to do supervised labor. The two men were disciplined for having succumbed to seduction. The graduate had his youth league membership revoked and the old cadre was booted from the party. The "profound lesson" learned by the work team was that "we relaxed our political thought work and were cheated by the enemy's sexual entrapment."[67]

There is reason to doubt the veracity of the work team's story. It is likely that team leaders, wanting to avoid the criticism leveled at their lewd comrades in Hangou, sought to deflect blame by accusing the little fox of seduction and spying. It was the word of the work team against a village woman, and when villagers sensed which way the wind was blowing at struggle meetings, they turned against her. When the university graduate was finally allowed to enter the party in the 1980s, his colleagues discussed the matter and characterized it as "falling in love." There had been no plot.

There was, however, a power imbalance between urban work teams and villagers – especially female villagers – in Tianjin's suburbs. Their relationship was akin to that between colonizer and colonized, in that the work team members had free rein to make threats and commit assaults. They were not supposed to sleep around, but if they did, they only received slaps on the wrist. The little fox and other rural women in similar situations, including village party secretary Zhang Fengqin, were in the most subordinate position of all during the Four Cleanups. The little fox used all of the protest channels available to her, but was unable to successfully refute the work team's charges. As long as work teams remained stationed in villages, people who felt wronged by the Four Cleanups could only resist in symbolic ways. One villager complained about the hypocrisy of punishing sexual misconduct by yelling, "Lin Tie is the [Hebei] provincial party secretary and he still has a concubine." Another filled a work team's anonymous opinion box with excrement.[68] The most effective strategy

[67] *Hebei nongcun jieji douzheng dianxing cailiao*, vol. 1, 202.

[68] *Jinjiao siqing jianbao* 78 (May 24, 1966): 4; *Hebei nongcun siqing jianxun* 35 (November 7, 1965): 2.

was to simply wait until work teams declared the movement over and decamped from villages.

Villagers confronted with burdensome sent-down youth did not have the luxury of waiting for them to leave. As "new-style peasants," the urban youth were supposedly in the countryside for life. But villagers had more options at their disposal in handling sent-down youth than in dealing with politically powerful Four Cleanups work teams from the city. When battles broke out between peasants and relatively powerless urban youth, they were not so one-sided.

Confrontations

When Dongjia party secretary Hu Yishun learned that his village would host urban youth in 1964, he requested only male teenagers. He saw the transfer as a useful infusion of labor power and wanted men, not women. Eighteen young men arrived in Dongjia on April 25, 1964. Impressed by downsized worker Wei Rongchun's success in using his city connections to help bring electricity to Dongjia, Hu put Wei in charge of the newcomers. Hu figured that Wei's experience in Tianjin would give him authority with the city kids. He was right.

Most of the youth sent to Dongjia were middle-school dropouts. About half of them had had run-ins with the law. One problem child named Zhao had been sentenced to three years of labor reform but escaped before being sent to the village by Tianjin street committee cadres. Once in Dongjia, Zhao refused to work and cheated money from villagers in order to buy liquor. After only a month in the village, his misbehavior was reported to top national leaders in a classified report about "several problems requiring attention when mobilizing urban educated youth to go down to villages."[69]

Another young tough named Yu also tested Wei Rongchun's patience. Instead of working in the fields, Yu went out by himself and caught crickets. He took them to Tianjin and sold them to city people who kept the insects as pets. Apparently poverty motivated Yu's peddling. While the other youths in Dongjia received allowances and care packages from their families, Yu got nothing. When Wei Rongchun told Yu that his cricket peddling was unacceptable and that he had to stop going to Tianjin, Yu became angry and threatened to "waste" (*fei*) Wei.

[69] NBCK 3624 (May 26, 1964): 7.

The next night, Wei called all of the urban youth to a meeting. Before leaving his house, he put a large kitchen knife in his pocket. As the meeting began, Wei showed Yu the knife. "I hear you want to waste me," Wei said. "Well, here's your chance, go ahead." He put the knife on the table in front of Yu, loosened his collar, and pointed to his neck. "But you should know that Liu Guanghan is my master and if you kill me, you'll have killed his disciple," Wei added, referring to a famous secret society boss from Tianjin.

Wei was bluffing. He did not know any underworld bosses; he had only heard about them in Tianjin. But Wei's name-dropping unnerved Yu, who started backing away. Wei grabbed the knife and started toward Yu, saying, "fine, if you won't waste me, I'll waste you!" Yu turned and ran out of the building. After this confrontation, Yu stopped catching crickets and worked quietly in the village. Wei used his urban know-how to keep unruly sent-down youth in line. But other problems were not so easily solved, especially for village cadres who lacked Wei's urban street smarts.

Villagers quickly tired of the youths' antics. One report described about half of the 2,300 Tianjin youth sent to Baodi in April as having resolute ideology and laboring enthusiastically. The rest were less than enthusiastic, while about seventy teens had "evil ways" and soured the experience for everyone else.[70] The kid who bellowed auspicious songs at rural weddings and funerals and then demanded money for his services was harmless enough, and the hapless one who nearly burned down his host's house while trying to boil an egg could be forgiven. But forming gangs and brawling had led to injuries, and the pilfering of food and money was getting out of control. Urban youths crossed the line when they urinated out of their windows, peeped at village girls using the bathroom, spread rumors that certain young women were not virgins, and taught local boys to masturbate.[71]

Villagers began to fight back. One sent-down youth named Wang in Jixian north of Baodi had formed a gang of toughs that picked fights with locals. When another urban youth reported on Wang, Wang's gang bloodied the tattletale's eye. After Wang punched the village party secretary, who had tried to intervene, villagers trussed Wang up. Then one of Wang's mates tried to release him. Villagers tied up the friend and marched him to the nearest police station, pausing to beat him with a rifle stock when

[70] Ibid.

[71] *Hexi qu jianbao* 176 (July 4, 1964): 1–5, HDA, 1–6–21C.

he refused to cooperate.[72] For some village cadres, dealing with unruly sent-down youth was the most difficult task they had ever encountered. "I have been through countless political movements, but have never gotten a headache," one village cadre said. "Now my head really hurts!"[73]

Village and county officials demanded that Tianjin street committees stop sending city "rejects" (*feipin*).[74] But some urban districts continued to dispatch troublemakers to the countryside, and when Baodi officials traveled to Tianjin to complain, city cadres refused to show the visitors relevant files and offered vague assurances that everything would be fine.[75] Everything was not fine. Villagers' headaches would not subside until the outbreak of the Cultural Revolution, when many urban youths returned to the city to join the new movement or to complain about their hard lives in the countryside. After 1966, many of the youth who had settled in Dongjia village in 1964 were never heard from again.

Fallout

In Tianjin's south suburbs, practical problems emerged after Chen Boda and Four Cleanups work teams sacked and punished "bad" village cadres. As the fall harvest in Xiyouying came around, it became clear that the village's income had fallen drastically since the Four Cleanups had started and that peasants would receive less grain than they had under deposed village party secretary Zhang Fengqin's leadership. Unwilling to let his model flounder, Chen went into damage control mode. The first step was to invest funds in improving "village appearance" (*nongcun mianmao*). Chen diverted 250,000 yuan for building projects in Xiaozhan, and asked Tianjin economic planners to consider moving city factories there.[76] Even though village leaders' homes were too luxurious for Chen's tastes, apparently the area needed a makeover. It was standard practice for leaders to lavish state funds on model units. But architectural improvements would not solve the serious threat that a drop in local incomes posed to the credibility of Chen's model.

[72] *Hexi qu jianbao* 180 (July 14, 1964): 1, HDA, 1–6–21C.
[73] *Hexi qu jianbao* 176 (July 4, 1964): 6, HDA, 1–6–21C.
[74] TMA, X281–97Y, 14.
[75] NBCK 3624 (May 26, 1964): 8.
[76] Tianjin shi nongcun hezuo zhi fazhan shi bianji bangongshi, ed., *Tianjin shi nongcun hezuo zhi dianxing shiliao xuanbian: 1949–1987* [Selected representative historical materials on the Tianjin village cooperative system, 1949–1987] (Tianjin: Tianjin shi nongye hezuo zhi fazhan shi bianji bangongshi, 1988), 132; Li Zhongyuan, *Bashi shuwang* [Narrating the past at age eighty] (Tianjin: Tianjin renmin chubanshe, 1998), 205.

During the Four Cleanups in Xiyouying, the work team learned that Zhang Fengqin had kept five hundred mu of "black land" off the books.[77] Now that the land had been reported, Xiyouying was responsible for handing over more grain to the state. Also, following the Four Cleanups' attack on money making, the village's sideline income in 1964 plummeted by 44 percent.[78] Chen Boda was learning an important lesson about how rural leaders had managed to keep life bearable for villagers. He was frustrated that villagers supported "bad" cadres and hated "good" ones. "Bad cadres hid land and gave too much grain to the masses," he said in Tianjin in late November 1964. "With good cadres in charge, the hidden land is made public and the masses get less grain. This means that good cadres cannot continue on."[79] Now he understood why Zhang Fengqin enjoyed popular support. "Since the Four Cleanups movement, the burden on the masses has increased," he said. "If I were a common person in Xiyouying, I would also endorse Zhang Fengqin."[80]

It was unacceptable to Chen that Xiyouying owed more to the state after he had tried to clean up the village's problems. He ordered no requisitioning of grain from the "black land" for at least three years, and directed Tianjin officials to immediately distribute to villagers eighty-five thousand kilograms of grain that had already been collected and warehoused. When Tianjin's deputy propaganda director Fang Ji mentioned commune rules mandating that forms had to be filled out before grain could be given to villagers, cranky Chen went on a Mao-like tirade against bureaucracy:

> Why is the commune so bossy? This form, that form, burn them all! They've set up this complicated system that makes it impossible for us to get involved, then they can play tricks. Their crock of a system is hairsplitting and pretentious, they use it to frighten people. Why don't you take care of this! Your Four Cleanups work team is incompetent! This affects the masses' livelihood, it affects next year's production, but you do nothing about it! The commune is stirring up trouble by doing it this way! Let the masses discuss this and distribute grain however they want.[81]

[77] Zhonggong Tianjin shiwei bangongting, "Shiyi yue ershier ri wan Chen Boda tongzhi de tanhua jiyao" [Summary of comrade Chen Boda's remarks on the evening of November 22], December 2, 1964, HPA, 855–19–1045C, 83.

[78] Tianjin shi Jinnan qu difang zhi bianxiu weihuanhui, *Jinnan qu zhi*, 844.

[79] "Chen Boda tongzhi jianghua jiyao," HPA, 855–19–1045C, 53.

[80] "Shiyi yue ershier ri wan Chen Boda tongzhi de tanhua jiyao," HPA, 855–19–1045C, 83.

[81] "Chen Boda tongzhi jianghua jiyao," HPA, 855–19–1045C, 54.

Fang Ji made sure that the grain was dispensed right away, and also carried out Chen's orders that finance authorities forgive outstanding debts owed by Xiyouying villagers.

Chen Boda was discovering how difficult it was to be a village leader. He bent the rules to maximize villagers' incomes, much like Zhang Fengqin had in previous years. Chen's ability to manipulate events on the ground in the Tianjin suburbs changed along with the overall direction of the Four Cleanups. Mao's late 1964 critique of Liu Shaoqi's version of the movement also applied to Xiaozhan. The "twenty-three points," circulated on January 18, 1965, stressed uniting 95 percent of cadres and called for an end to "human wave tactics," stating, "we must not concentrate excessively large work teams within a single hsien [xian], commune, or brigade."[82] Chen Boda was chastened. Xiaozhan was a prime example of human wave tactics – more than five thousand people served on work teams there. And instead of uniting 95 percent of cadres, Chen had claimed that "more than 80 percent of grassroots power" in Xiaozhan was "not in our hands."[83]

After making a few conciliatory moves in January 1965, including releasing Zhang Fengqin's husband from jail and allowing Zhang to labor under supervision at home, Chen backed off from Xiaozhan's Four Cleanups.[84] The intensity of the movement diminished, and the last work teams left Xiaozhan in September 1965. This was small consolation to people classified as members of counterrevolutionary cliques, including Jiang Deyu and Zhang Yulun, who remained in jail until the 1970s.

When Tianjin cadres returned to check up on Xiaozhan in spring 1966, they found that the problems they had tried to stamp out had already reappeared. New village cadres who had taken office during the movement were stepping down and refusing to work; gambling and black market grain trades had reemerged.[85] Resentment simmered among those who had been targeted during the Four Cleanups. The wife of one "unclean" village cadre cornered the inspection team and told them that they could not leave until the furniture confiscated from her family in 1964 was

[82] Baum, *Prelude to Revolution*, 119, 122.

[83] Liu Jinfeng, *Zhengrong suiyue*, 208.

[84] Chen Boda, *Chen Boda yigao: yuzhong zishu ji qita* [Manuscripts by the late Chen Boda: Accounts from prison and more] ([Hohhot]: Nei Menggu renmin chubanshe, 1999), 58; HZDSJ, 196.

[85] *Hebei siqing tongxun* zengkan 15 (April 20, 1966): 26; *Jinjiao siqing jianbao* zengkan 15 (May 12, 1966): 4.

returned.[86] One former village party secretary became enraged when he ran into Four Cleanups activists at a public works project, yelling, "you fucking bastards, you relied on the influence of the movement to oppress people. Come on, let's go one-on-one, I'll get my knife and stab you."[87]

Chen Boda was imprisoned until a year before his death in 1989, but he remained reluctant to admit that he had done anything wrong in Xiaozhan. At a mass denunciation meeting in the southern suburbs in April 1974, officials excoriated Chen in absentia for having supposedly boasted, "On the whole, I did a good thing for the people of Tianjin by carrying out the Four Cleanups for a year in Xiaozhan. If it were in the past, the common people of Tianjin would build a temple and erect a monument to me."[88] Chen's later comments were less celebratory, but he still defended himself. When Chen read in the newspaper about Zhang Fengqin's post–Cultural Revolution rehabilitation, he had difficulty accepting that the Four Cleanups in Xiaozhan had been completely repudiated. What really disturbed Chen was that Zhang Fengqin and her husband were being compensated four thousand yuan by the collective for the money and property that had been seized from her in 1964. "Both of them are villagers, both are 'cadres,' and neither worked. Where could they have gotten so much money?" Chen wondered. "Just from this point, I think that the entire case was not necessarily a complete mistake."[89]

Chen was being disingenuous. He knew exactly how Zhang and her husband had made their money, and in 1964 he had admitted that if he were a villager, he would have supported their rule-bending ways. By the end of 1964, Chen was breaking the rules by handing out grain that should have gone to the state. In spite of his largesse, the people of Xiaozhan can be forgiven for not building a temple or monument to honor Chen and the work teams that did his bidding. Villagers were better served by the peculations of a Zhang Fengqin than by the disruptive presence of a central leader like Chen Boda.

[86] *Jinjiao siqing jianbao* 53 (March 5, 1965): 8.

[87] *Hebei siqing tongxun* zengkan 15 (April 20, 1966): 25.

[88] Zhonggong Tianjin shiwei pi-Lin zhengfeng bangongshi, "Nan jiao quwei zhaokai pipan dahui henpi Lin Biao fandang jituan zhuyao chengyuan Chen Boda de fangeming zuixing" [South suburbs party committee convenes a large-scale meeting to ruthlessly criticize the counterrevolutionary crimes of Chen Boda, important member of the Lin Biao anti-party clique] *Pi-Lin pi-Kong jianbao* 67 (April 17, 1974): 3, AC.

[89] Chen Boda, *Chen Boda yigao*, 58; see also Chen Xiaonong, *Chen Boda zuihou koushu huiyi*, 248.

Intrusive policies and visitors coming from Tianjin drove a wedge between city and countryside. Although the Four Cleanups and the sent-down youth movement of the mid-1960s contained sometimes clashing messages, both addressed problems that had emerged in the aftermath of the Great Leap famine, and both resulted in a more adversarial rural-urban relationship. Abandoned by cities during the famine, villagers focused on survival. A short time later, urban people came to punish them or to treat them as a safety valve for city unemployment pressures. As we shall see in the following chapter, uninvited visitors continued to appear in Tianjin-area villages in 1966 and 1967 as the Four Cleanups wound down and the Cultural Revolution exploded. What had happened during the leap also turned out to have life-shattering consequences for political outcasts from Tianjin who were exiled to villages at the outset of the Cultural Revolution. In 1964, urban people saw villages as battlegrounds where socialist China had to be saved from a capitalist restoration. By 1966, the countryside had become a virtual jail for city people accused of capitalist crimes.

6

Purifying the City

The Deportation of Political Outcasts during the Cultural Revolution

In November 1966, a thirty-six-year-old woman named Ding Yun was expelled from Tianjin, along with her husband and four sons. Officials in charge of the Cultural Revolution at a food shop in the city's former British concession, where Ding worked as a clerk, signed off on her expulsion. She was deported to her native place, a village in Hebei's Wanxian.[1] In the report calling for Ding's removal, Ding and her family were derided as the "dregs of society" (*shehui de zhazi*). "In order to protect order in the city," they had to be relocated to a village, where they could be supervised and reformed. "To have this type of person living in a large city under the current circumstances of war preparedness (*zhanbei*) has many disadvantages and few benefits," the report explained.[2]

What had Ding done wrong to render her unfit for urban residence? Her alleged crimes included stealing food on the job. As early as 1951, she had been caught giving cookies to her children. During the food shortages of the early 1960s, she colluded with co-workers to steal three sacks of grain. More serious was the allegation that Ding had falsely claimed "middle peasant" (*zhongnong*) class status and covered up her

[1] Wanxian is now called Shunping county. All materials about Ding are from a file on her case from the Heping District Vegetable Foodstuffs Company (Heping qu shucai fushipin gongsi), deportation file 74, AC.

[2] In 1964, Mao Zedong convinced other top leaders that in the face of threats from the Soviet Union and the United States, China had to prepare for war by developing a "third front" of heavy industry in the interior of China. See Chen Donglin, *Sanxian jianshe: beizhan shiqi de xibu kaifa* [Third front construction: The development of the west in the period of preparing for war] (Beijing: Zhonggong zhongyang dangxiao chubanshe, 2003).

father's landlord past. She also reportedly had sex with two classmates and a teacher in her village before migrating to Tianjin in 1951, and after moving to the city she had relationships with five men. Adding to the evidence against Ding was the misbehavior of her three youngest sons, who were purportedly "little hooligans" who stole food for their pet dog and cat, and who once commandeered a three-wheeled bicycle cart for a joyride across Tianjin.

During the first three years of the Cultural Revolution, Ding and her family repeatedly crossed the rural-urban divide. Their first stint back in her native village was short. After the leadership of her food shop was overthrown in January 1967, Ding returned to Tianjin, joined a rebel organization, and moved back into her home, which had been ransacked and sealed by red guards. But Ding was soon kicked out of the rebel group because of questions about her class background. Matters worsened for her in March, when party center ordered the redeportation of people who had returned to cities.[3] In May, a day before the deadline for Ding to leave Tianjin, she fled to Beijing, where she appealed to central authorities to reconsider her deportation. She stayed in Beijing as a petitioner until December 1967, when she returned to Tianjin. A faction sympathetic to Ding had gained the upper hand at her store, but by March 1968, the faction had lost and a Revolutionary Committee had been formed. She then fled to her home village on her own, lying low until a Revolutionary Committee was finally established there. No longer able to escape scrutiny in the countryside, Ding showed up at her workplace for the last time in September 1968, with her three sons in tow. She said that she was looking for a "way out" (*chulu*) and was willing to confess to her problems (*jiaodai wenti*).

Ding Yun never found a way out. She was immediately detained in a dormitory room and was repeatedly beaten and kicked during struggle meetings over the course of the next nine days. In her absence over the past summer, the Heping District Revolutionary Committee had labeled her a "bad element" and endorsed her redeportation. On September 26, 1968, Ding hanged herself in her makeshift cell. Her sons were found sitting in the room with her when her body was discovered. At the time, her suicide was blamed on "fear of punishment" (*weizui zisha*), an official

[3] *Zhonggong zhongyang zhuanfa Beijing shi gongan ju junshi guanzhi weiyuanhui san yue shiba ri bugao* [Party center circulates the Beijing Public Security Bureau's Military Control Committee's Bulletin of March 18], *Zhongfa* [1967] 101 (March 18, 1967), in WDGW.

designation that denied benefits to her dependents. In 1974, a reinvestigation ruled that she had killed herself "because she did not sufficiently understand the Cultural Revolution mass movement." This phrase meant an improvement in her family's political and economic status. The last document in Ding's file, dated September 17, 1979, completely overturned Ding's "bad element" label and called the decision to deport her a "mistaken judgment."[4]

Ding's story is tragic, but not unique. She was one of more than forty thousand people expelled from Tianjin under official deportation policies during the Cultural Revolution; 1.28 percent of the city's population.[5] Nationwide, hundreds of thousands of political outcasts from cities were relocated to villages.[6] Deportation to ancestral villages – not to be confused with administratively separate programs managing sent-down youth, May Seventh cadre schools, war preparedness relocation (*zhanbei shusan*), and labor reform (*laogai*) camps – affected work units and neighborhoods in many cities, and had a direct impact on housing and grain allocation in many villages. The few mentions of deportation in English-language memoirs and scholarly articles are vague and often imply that removal to villages was an ad hoc, spontaneous red guard punishment, arbitrarily applied during the chaos of late 1966.[7] On the contrary, the

[4] This decision followed a nationwide policy shift in June 1979. See "Zhonggong zhongyang, Guowuyuan guanyu chuli dangqian bufen renyuan yaoqiu fuzhi fugong huicheng jiuye deng wenti de tongzhi" [Party center and State Council circular on handling the employment and other problems of certain personnel who request to return to cities and return to work], June 4, 1979, http://www.law-lib.com/law/law_view.asp?id=43942.

[5] The official figure is 41,571 people, including 15,688 exiles and 25,833 accompanying family members. Zheng Zhiying, *Tianjin shi sishiwu nian dashiji*, 294.

[6] According to Wang Nianyi, 397,400 "monsters and freaks" were forced to leave China's cities before October 3, 1966; Wang Nianyi, *Da dongluan de niandai* [A decade of great upheaval] (Zhengzhou: Henan renmin chubanshe, 1988), 100. More were deported later in 1966 and again in 1968, pushing the actual number of deportees nationwide much higher than Wang's early figure, likely approaching one million. I base this estimate on numbers from Tianjin, where many outcasts were removed after October 1966, and where more than a third of deportees were expelled in 1968, not 1966.

[7] Yang Rae remembered taking a train with bad elements who had been "driven out of Beijing by the revolutionary masses"; Yang Rae, *Spider Eaters: A Memoir* (Berkeley: University of California Press, 1997), 133. Yue Daiyun's aunt was labeled a landlord and deported to rural Hubei from their home in Beijing; Yue Daiyun and Carolyn Wakeman, *To the Storm: The Odyssey of a Revolutionary Chinese Woman* (Berkeley: University of California Press, 1985), 176–77. Jiangsui He writes that Ma Zhongtai and his wife were "sent back" to the county seat and "brought to" their home village in Shaanxi in 1969; Jiangsui He, "The Death of a Landlord: Moral Predicament in Rural China, 1968–1969," in *The Chinese Cultural Revolution as History*, ed. Joseph W. Esherick, Paul G. Pickowicz, and Andrew G. Walder (Stanford: Stanford University Press, 2006), 140.

expulsion of political outcasts from Tianjin was a state-sanctioned policy, first handled by "Urban-Rural Liaison Stations" (Chengxiang lianluo zhan) in 1966, and later administrated by Deportation Offices (Qiansong bangongshi) in 1967 and Deportation Work Groups (Qiansong banshizu) under the authority of municipal and district revolutionary committees in 1968.

I have collected the files of seventy-eight deportees from Tianjin. Several, like the one about Ding Yun, are thick, detailed folders containing letters, official forms, reports, and testimonies. Most are briefer forms with a few pages of supporting documentation. All of the files but six are from the food supply systems in Tianjin's Hongqiao and Heping districts, which means that crimes involving grain and food loom especially large in my files. When I bought them at a used book market in Tianjin, the files from Heping were bound together in a single thick dossier. I found the other files separately on other visits to the market. The individual deportation files, together with policy documents and speeches, shed light on the broader patterns and implications of expelling urban residents to villages during the Cultural Revolution.

This chapter will first outline how the deportation program came to be institutionalized and bureaucratized between 1966 and 1968, apparently against Mao Zedong's wishes. I will then discuss who Tianjin's deportees were and how they responded to being sent to villages. Those targeted for deportation were not the prominent intellectuals, elites, and cadres who dominate victim-centered accounts of the Cultural Revolution.[8] Instead, the people who inhabit my files were lowly clerks and noodle-makers, among others. They were not party members. Not surprisingly, deportees fiercely resisted the prospect of losing their city jobs and residence permits for such transgressions as having an affair. Sometimes their resistance was effective, but it often backfired. Villagers also opposed what they viewed as an unwelcome influx of politically suspect people who were ill-equipped for farm work. In essence, forcing political outcasts to cross the rural-urban divide helped to define the boundary between city and countryside, for the practice cast cities as pure, privileged spaces and turned villages into dumping grounds for undesirables.

[8] Anne Thurston focuses on urban intellectuals, most of whom were not targeted for deportation, but who instead went to May Seventh Cadre Schools. These were isolated encampments that allowed little interaction with rural people; Anne F. Thurston, *Enemies of the People* (New York: Alfred A. Knopf, 1987). See also Wang Youqin, *Wenge shounanzhe* [Victims of the Cultural Revolution] (Hong Kong: Kaifang zazhi chubanshe, 2004).

Why Deport?

Mao Zedong launched the Cultural Revolution against "capitalist roaders in positions of power" in 1966. This phrase referred to leaders at all levels of the Communist bureaucracy who were insufficiently committed to socialism, and it represented an escalation of the war against revisionism that Mao had started with the Four Cleanups. People in Tianjin responded to Mao's call to "rebel against the headquarters" and to attack party leaders. After the city's top party secretary Wan Xiaotang came under criticism, he suddenly died on September 19, 1966 (his supporters said that he died of a heart attack, his detractors claimed that he had "killed himself to escape punishment," and some even speculated that he had been murdered). Zhang Huaisan, the Tianjin party secretary who had magnanimously forgiven a grain burglar in 1960, also came under attack. Rebels backed by radicals in Beijing, including Chen Boda, claimed that the two men were ringleaders of the "Wan-Zhang anti-party counterrevolutionary clique." Top party leaders, however, were not the only targets during the Cultural Revolution. An ever-expanding group of potential enemies of the revolution were also extremely vulnerable. Purported "counterrevolutionaries," "capitalists," and "bad elements" – in other words, the usual suspects in Mao-era political campaigns – made up the bulk of people subject to deportation from Tianjin.

Policy directives and speeches explained deportation during the Cultural Revolution in terms of security and punishment. "Bad elements" were considered threats to China's cities, which were more strategically important than villages because of the government offices and industrial development concentrated there. Class enemies were specifically targeted for punishment during the Cultural Revolution, and who better to supervise and reform them than the politically reliable poor and middle-lower peasants? There was precedent for expelling urban residents for security and disciplinary reasons. Tianjin's Communist government had removed various types of people from the city since taking over in January 1949, including political exiles, most notably landlords who had fled to Tianjin in the wake of land reform. After 1957, some rightists were expelled to villages, state farms, and labor camps, but most were not systematically deported to their native places. Other waves of urban-to-rural migration also predated the deportations of the Cultural Revolution, including sending cadres to labor in the countryside (*xiafang*), the "downsizing" (*jingjian*) of millions of workers addressed in Chapter 4, and the sent-down youth programs described in Chapter 5. These programs were more about easing urban employment pressures than about punishing bad elements, but they too buttressed the notion that urban space was privileged space.

During the Cultural Revolution, deportation originated in Beijing, apparently because of fears about the safety of Chairman Mao and other top leaders. Security was stepped up in the capital in response to an alleged coup attempt by General Luo Ruiqing, chief of staff of the People's Liberation Army. Rumors circulated that Lin Biao had surrounded Beijing with loyal troops in order to thwart a military takeover.[9] According to Zhou Enlai, Mao Zedong stayed away from Beijing for the first half of 1966 "because it was unsafe" (*jiu shi yinwei bu anquan*). People identified as landlords, rich peasants, counterrevolutionaries, and bad elements were then cleared out of the capital's public security and bodyguard organizations.[10] The Cultural Revolution unfolded in summer 1966 in this tense atmosphere of heightened security and fears of enemy plots. Mao's endorsement of the Destroy the Four Olds campaign at a rally at Tiananmen Square on August 18, 1966, sparked the removal of class enemies and bad types from the capital. According to MacFarquhar and Schoenhals, red guard organizations supported by the State Council General Secretariat and by city officials ransacked homes and forcibly deported people from Beijing. On August 30, 1966, Foreign Minister Chen Yi told red guards that he approved of removing the "five black categories" from Beijing, but he also urged moderation.[11]

Red guards in Tianjin, closely tracking events in the capital, followed suit. Beginning on August 23, 1966, red guards ransacked the homes of potential enemies. According to an official count, 107,720 households were raided during the Cultural Revolution in Tianjin.[12] As in Beijing, murders and suicides associated with the Destroy the Four Olds campaign spiked in late August 1966. During three terrible days at the end of August, 117 people attempted suicide and 79 died in Tianjin, mostly in Heping district, the site of Tianjin's most stately European-style homes.[13]

[9] On Luo Ruiqing in spring 1966, see MacFarquhar and Schoenhals, *Mao's Last Revolution*, 20–27. See also David Milton and Nancy Milton, *The Wind Will Not Subside: Years in Revolutionary China, 1964–1969* (New York: Pantheon Books, 1976), 157.

[10] *Zhou Enlai jiejian kexueyuan Jing qu ge danwei daibiao tanhua jiyao* [Abstract of Zhou Enlai's remarks upon receiving representatives from science academies in the capital region], January 21, 1967, in WDGW.

[11] MacFarquhar and Schoenhals, *Mao's Last Revolution*, 122.

[12] Zheng Zhiying, *Tianjin shi sishiwu nian dashiji*, 275.

[13] *Jin wan bao* [Tianjin evening news], November 24, 2004.

One Tianjin official responsible for compiling reports on the suicides estimated that more than one thousand people killed themselves during the Destroy the Four Olds campaign, many of them by throwing themselves in the Hai river.[14]

For some of Tianjin's "five bad types" (meaning people labeled as landlord, rich peasant, counterrevolutionary, rightist, and bad elements), fleeing to a village seemed like an attractive option compared to raids and beatings at the hands of urban red guards. An internal bulletin from Tianjin's Hexi district (rechristened "Red Flag district" in August 1966) reported that people were "requesting to return to villages." After a meeting for political enemies at a local police station on August 26, most of the bad types in the neighborhood voluntarily signed up to leave Tianjin, bringing their *hukou* booklets to the station to make the move official. In a process akin to the "self dekulakization" of fearful Soviet peasants during Stalin's collectivization of 1929 and 1930,[15] people in Tianjin preemptively brought personal property to police stations, shaved their heads, and displayed self-criticism posters outside of their homes.[16] Before the Cultural Revolution, Tianjin's class enemies were accustomed to regular study meetings and visits from neighborhood police. Faced with violence and humiliation at the hands of rampaging teenagers, many Tianjin residents saw familiar police officers as their protectors and viewed villages as temporary safe havens. Some preferred exile in the countryside because avoiding daily persecution became more important than the benefits attached to urban residence. Even though the goal of Ding Yun's protests and petitions was to maintain her city job and residency, she too sought refuge in the countryside when she felt threatened in Tianjin.

City officials must have been happy to oblige when people volunteered to leave Tianjin. From the very beginning, city leaders supported and managed deportation. On October 6, 1966, the Tianjin municipal government – under fire for having "suppressed the masses" during the first months of the Cultural Revolution – issued its first official order on deporting the five bad types to villages for "supervision and reform through labor." Over the next two months, city authorities refined deportation policy. One report about how to apply Beijing's experience to

[14] Interviewee 11.

[15] Lynne Viola, *Peasant Rebels under Stalin: Collectivization and the Culture of Peasant Resistance* (New York: Oxford University Press, 1996), 79–83.

[16] "Dangqian shehui shang de wulei fenzi he fandong zibenjia de jizhong dongtai" [Several current trends among five bad types and reactionary capitalists], *Tianjin shi Hongqi qu wenhua geming jianbao* 4 (September 12, 1966): 2, HDA, 1-6-33C.

TABLE 6.1. *People Deported from Tianjin during the Cultural Revolution*

	Deportees	Accompanying Family Members	Subtotal
Late 1966–Early 1967	10,292	15,621	25,913
After May 1968	5,396	10,262	15,658
TOTAL	15,680	25,883	41,571

Source: "Liu Zheng tongzhi zai shiwei luoshi qiansong zhengce he jiaqiang dui qingshaonian guanli jiaoyu gongzuo huiyi de jianghua" [Comrade Liu Zheng's speech at the work meeting on implementing deportation policy and strengthening management and education of youths], April 1, 1972, AC.

Tianjin targeted bad types who had come to the city from villages, towns, and county seats after 1945, and who could be "accommodated in their native places," as well as those "with rather big historical crimes and bad behavior." Furthermore, bad types with "reactionary thought" who lived in "strategic units and national security locations" and who had someone to support them in villages should be deported. If their children had no jobs in the city, the kids also had to leave. Bad types originally from big cities or who had lived in Beijing for "a long time (several tens of years)" were exempt from deportation.[17] The key was whether the target posed a potential threat to national security.

Tianjin officials invented new funding streams to pay for the removal of almost twenty-six thousand people in 1966–1967. An "extremely urgent" November directive from the Tianjin municipal government mandated that city work units were responsible for covering the travel expenses, living stipends, and settlement funds for deportees and accompanying dependents. If the deportation targets were jobless, the Tianjin Civil Affairs Bureau would pay. But this rule only applied when entire families were deported. If any family members remained on the job in Tianjin, they were ordered to cover deportation costs themselves, if necessary by drawing on funds and property that had been confiscated by red guards and handed over to state banks and security offices for safekeeping. If villages made additional financial demands to cover housing and food for deportees, these costs could also be supplemented by booty collected during house raids.[18] Tianjin officials not only explicitly legitimized deporting

[17] "Beijing dui guanyu chuli wulei fenzi banqian de yijian jianghua" [Talks on Beijing's opinion about handling the relocation of the five types], *Zhonggong Hongqi quwei wenge bangongshi cankao cailiao* 4 (October 27, 1966): 1, HDA, 1-6-33C.

[18] Tianjin shi renmin weiyuanhui, "Guanyu qiansong di fu fan huai you wulei fenzi huixiang jiandu laodong gaizao youguan wenti de buchong tongzhi" [Supplementary

political enemies by clarifying who to expel and how to expel them, they also endorsed red guards' home invasions by using confiscated money and property to fund the deportations.

Sociologist Yang Su has shown that events on the ground during the Cultural Revolution quickly outstripped central directives condemning violence and urging moderation.[19] This was also true of deportation work. In January 1967, Zhou Enlai told a group of representatives from science academies in Beijing that Chairman Mao disliked red guards' practice of forcing political enemies back to villages (*ganhui nongcun*). "I asked the chairman for instructions and he ordered that aside from certain *laogai* criminals, it is better to digest others oneself than to push the contradiction up or pass it down to the lower levels," Zhou explained. "What the chairman said about digesting them oneself is still correct."[20] Zhou's remarks, which were widely circulated, may have encouraged many deportees to return to cities on their own in early 1967, but they failed to halt the deportation program.

Even though deportation ran counter to Mao's instructions, Tianjin officials and zealous residents erred on the side of excess in trying to purify proletarian cities, much as they had in the Xiaozhan area two years earlier during the Four Cleanups. Their efforts were rewarded. In Tianjin, many families targeted by red guards for raids and deportation did not belong to the "five bad types" at all, but were still considered fair game because of a supposedly "bourgeois" background – or simply because someone had lodged an accusation against them. Central leaders in Beijing then legitimized red guards' actions after the fact by expanding the range of expulsion targets. In March 1967, party center circulated a new list of deportable individuals, called the "ten types of people" (*shi zhong ren*). This document was issued in response to the large number of deportees

order on issues related to deporting the five bad types to villages for supervision and reform through labor], (66) *Weimizi* 151 (November 14, 1966), HDA, 3-2-133C.

[19] Yang Su, "Mass Killing in the Cultural Revolution: A Study of Three Provinces," in Esherick, Pickowicz, and Walder, *The Chinese Cultural Revolution as History*, 119.

[20] *Zhou Enlai jiejian kexueyuan Jing qu ge danwei daibiao tanhua jiyao*, in WDGW. See also Michael Schoenhals, "Cultural Revolution on the Border: Yunnan's 'Political Frontier Defence' (1969–1971)," *Copenhagen Journal of Asian Studies*, no. 19 (2004): 38. By "digest others themselves," Mao and Zhou meant that work units should punish and supervise political enemies internally rather than sending them away. Schoenhals examines Mao's tendency to speak in digestive and scatological metaphors in his "Consuming Fragments of Mao Zedong: The Chairman's Final Two Decades at the Helm," in *A Critical Introduction to Mao*, ed. Timothy Cheek (New York: Cambridge University Press, 2010), 110–28.

who had "flowed back" into Beijing in early 1967 after power seizures took place in city offices and factories. Deportees, including Ding Yun, assumed that because the original deporting agency had been overthrown, their expulsion was invalid. Ding and many others returned to work and even had their urban *hukou* restored by whatever rebel organization had taken over the office.

The "ten types" document assailed the return to cities of people such as Ding Yun as "wantonly overturning the verdicts and unreasonably causing trouble." Party center had decided that even more individuals were disqualified from urban residency. The new list of deportable enemies cobbled together definitions of counterrevolutionaries and bad elements that dated from the mid-1950s.[21] The roster included:

1. Landlord, rich peasant, counterrevolutionary, rightist, and bad elements who maintain a reactionary standpoint (including those with bad behavior after being rehabilitated);
2. Landlord, rich peasant, counterrevolutionary, rightist, and bad elements discovered to have evaded detection, based on substantial evidence;
3. Puppet army (company commander and above), puppet government (baozhang and above), puppet police (chief and above), and spy elements with bad behavior;
4. Middle and small reactionary secret society leaders and professional sect employees with bad behavior;
5. Backbone elements from reactionary party organizations with bad behavior;
6. Capitalists and property owners who maintain a reactionary standpoint;
7. Elements with bad behavior after finishing prison, *laojiao* or detention sentences;
8. Embezzlers, thieves, and profiteers;
9. Family members of executed, jailed, detained, or escaped counterrevolutionaries who maintain a reactionary standpoint;

[21] For earlier definitions of enemies, see Zhongyang shi ren xiaozu, "Guanyu fangeming fenzi he qita huai fenzi de jieshi ji chuli de zhengce jiexian de zanxing guiding" [Provisional regulations on policy boundaries for explaining and handling counterrevolutionary and other bad elements], March 10, 1956, cited in Tianjin gongan ju, "Guanyu bianfa zhongyang youguan huading zhuanzheng duixiang zhengce jiexian de tongzhi" [Circular distributing party center's policy boundaries delineating targets for the exercise of dictatorship], November 23, 1963, AC.

10. Elements with criminally indecent or thieving behavior who have not reformed themselves after repeated education.[22]

This order – to be "forcibly" carried out by revolutionary mass organizations if individuals refused to leave voluntarily – meant that under categories six, eight, and ten, almost anyone could be expelled from cities. Why? Many city residents had broken rules in order to get food on the black market during the post-leap famine, which made them vulnerable to charges of theft or profiteering (category eight). Anyone accused of having an adulterous affair could be deported for "indecent behavior" (*liumang xingwei*, category ten). And anyone who had been part of a business or made a profit before nationalization in 1956 could be labeled a reactionary capitalist (category six).

Compared with life before the Cultural Revolution, 1967 was a turbulent year in Tianjin. But relative to events in many other parts of China, Tianjin was calm. Wan Xiaotang's rivals labeled his sudden death a suicide, factional battles took place, protesters temporarily halted rail service, a theater troupe performed the infamous *Madman of the New Age* play, rebels torched a prominent university administrative building, and the mother of a slain Tianjin rebel staged a sit-in outside of Zhongnanhai. But overall, a strong military presence in the city limited violence. MacFarquhar and Schoenhals call the establishment of Tianjin's Revolutionary Committee in December 1967 a "peaceful transition" that was "as orderly as could be expected."[23]

While Tianjin's political future was being hammered out in lengthy meetings in Beijing, additional directives from Tianjin's military leadership continued to endorse the deportation program. Authorities confirmed that even if the deported "ten types" had reacquired Tianjin *hukou* upon returning from villages in late 1966 or early 1967, they were still subject to redeportation. "Type six" capitalists indeed included people who had made profits between 1949 and 1956.[24]

[22] *Zhongfa* [1967] 101 (March 18, 1967), in WDGW.

[23] MacFarquhar and Schoenhals, *Mao's Last Revolution*, 242–43.

[24] Zhongguo renmin jiefang jun Tianjin shi gongan ju junshi guanzhi weiyuanhui qiansong bangongshi, "Guanyu guanche Zhongguo renmin jiefang jun Tianjin shi gongan ju junshi guanzhi weiyuanhui 'Guanyu wenhua da geming zhong bei qiansong hou fan Jin renyuan de chuli banfa' ruogan tiaowen de lijie yijian (caogao)" [Draft opinion on interpreting several clauses of the PLA Tianjin Public Security Bureau Military Control Committee's "On handling people who returned to Tianjin after being deported during the Cultural Revolution"], November 14, 1967, AC.

These rules were put on the books in 1967, but were not fully implemented until Tianjin's new Revolutionary Committee consolidated control in early 1968. Only then did most deportees who had made their way back to Tianjin face re-expulsion. Others who had never been deported also found themselves at risk. In March 1968, the Tianjin Revolutionary Committee established a Headquarters for Sorting Out Work (Qingli gongzuo zhihuibu) staffed by thousands of cadres and charged with getting people who had entered Tianjin during 1966 and 1967 – including rebels from other places, returned sent-down youth, and deportees – to leave the city.[25] The next month, the Revolutionary Committee issued a directive guiding deportation work for the year: Deporting the dregs of society in 1966 had "protected social order and strengthened the dictatorship of the proletariat," but unfortunately approximately half of the original deportees had returned to Tianjin "without permission." The Revolutionary Committee reorganized deportation "offices" into "work groups," affirmed previous directives about the ten types, and set financial guidelines for the renewed expulsion program. If political exiles were unable to pay for their own travel and living costs, the state could maintain them in villages at a level "lower than the standard of living of local poor and lower-middle peasants."[26]

It took several months of planning before the new wave of deportations began in summer and fall 1968. This coincided with the Cleansing of the Class Ranks campaign, and was often more brutal than the events of 1966. The leaders of Revolutionary Committees in factories and work units took revenge on deportees, many of whom had lost out in the factional disputes of 1967. Formal deportation papers issued by work units and district Revolutionary Committees in 1968 did not simply order "deport to native place," but stated, "after knocking him over with criticism and struggling against him rotten (*pi dao dou chou*), deport him to his native place for supervision and reform."[27] Tianjin's top leader Xie Xuegong, who had taken over the city's leadership in late 1966 after former party secretary Wan Xiaotang's death, placed his imprimatur on

[25] Tianjin shi geming weiyuanhui, Tianjin zhujun zhizuo lianluozhan, and Tianjin jingbei qu, "Guanyu jianli qingli gongzuo zhihuibu de jueding" [Decision on establishing a Headquarters for Sorting Out Work], March 20, 1968, AC.

[26] "Guanyu jixu zuo hao zai wenhua da geming zhong bei qiansong hou fan Jin renyuan chuli gongzuo de tongzhi" [Directive on continuing to do a good job in handling people who returned to Tianjin after being deported during the Cultural Revolution], *Jinge* [1968] 64 (April 1, 1968), AC.

[27] Deportation file 27, AC.

renewed deportations during a speech in May 1968. Xie's remarks are a smoking gun, leaving no doubt that Tianjin's municipal leadership supported forcible expulsions:

> A small handful of unreformed landlord, rich peasant, counterrevolutionary, bad, and rightist elements are seizing the opportunity to take action and retaliate. The red guard little generals kicked out these reactionary scoundrels, but last year when Tianjin was rather chaotic for a time, they ran back here, besieged neighborhood activists, and retaliated. Letting these people remain in Tianjin is tantamount to negating the contributions of the red guard little generals. Recently, our Headquarters for Sorting Out Work has attacked these landlord, rich peasant, counterrevolutionary, bad, and rightist elements, making them obediently return to their native places to accept reform.[28]

The deportations of 1968 were more about punishment and revenge than about urban security. They were a recipe for violence.

Approximately one third of all of Tianjin's deportees were expelled in 1968 (see Table 6.1). Only at the end of the year did deportations slow down, gradually coming to an end in 1969. This shift can be traced to Mao's December 1, 1968, order that the "scope of attack should be small, while the scope of education should be broad." Mao had made the statement after reading a report by the Revolutionary Committee of the New China Printing Plant in Beijing (run by PLA Unit 8341, the Politburo's bodyguard corps).[29] The report recommended that only landlords and rich peasants who had fled the countryside should be deported to their native places, so that the local masses could exercise dictatorship over them. All other people with political problems were to remain at the printing plant to be "digested" (*xiaohua*), supervised, and reformed through labor.[30] The ten types originally subject to deportation had just been reduced to two. Although no rationale was provided for singling

[28] "Yi Mao zhuxi zui xin zhishi wei gang, chengsheng qianjin, ba 'yi pi san cha' yundong jinxing daodi – Xie Xuegong tongzhi zai 'yi pi san cha' yundong jingyan jiaoliu dahui shang de jianghua" [Taking Chairman Mao's newest order as the guiding principle, advance on the crest of victory and carry out the "one criticize, three checks" movement to the end – Comrade Xie Xuegong's speech at the meeting to exchange experiences about the "one criticize, three checks" movement], May 5, 1968, AC.

[29] See MacFarquhar and Schoenhals, *Mao's Last Revolution*, 255.

[30] "Zhonggong zhongyang, zhongyang wenge pifa 'Beijing shi geming weiyuanhui zhuanfa Xinhua yinshuachang zai duidai douzheng zhong jianjue zhixing dang de "gei chulu" zhengce de jingyan de baogao'" [Party center and the Central Cultural Revolution Group circulate "Beijing Revolutionary Committee circulates the New China Printing Plant's report on its experience in resolutely carrying out the party's policy of 'giving a way out' in handling struggle"] *Zhongfa* [1968] 165 (December 3, 1968), in WDGW.

out landlords and rich peasants, the ruling was consistent with the party's land reform-era practice of sending rural exploiters to face the wrath of those they had oppressed.

Over the course of 1969, Tianjin work units gradually began reinvestigating and reclassifying deportees. It was a challenge to try to turn back the clock without admitting that the entire program had been wrong. The city's official line was that "deportation in the past was entirely correct. Not deporting anymore is carrying out Chairman Mao's newest order."[31] Partly motivated by reluctance to completely repudiate deportation policy, and also in keeping with escalating war fears that mandated dispersing China's urban coastal population to isolated areas, deportees and their families were ordered to stay in villages.[32] The reevaluations changed some deportees' political status from enemies to "return-to-village producers" (*huanxiang shengchanzhe*). This was the same label given to urban workers who had been downsized during the post-famine readjustment of the early 1960s, and it meant that rehabilitated deportees were now entitled to severance or retirement payments from their work units. But only in rare cases were people allowed to regain urban jobs and residency permits. Deportees hoping to return to Tianjin would have to wait for a fuller reinvestigation in 1972, and for most people relief did not come until after 1978.

Expelling urban political outcasts to villages was initiated in 1966 by red guards who were supported by central and municipal officials. Over the following two years, the deportation program was gradually institutionalized and governed by a bureaucracy with confusing rules and piles of paperwork covered with red stamps. By the time that party center began to back away from widespread deportations at the end of 1968, hundreds of thousands of people had been exiled to the countryside.

Fighting Deportation

Many of the deportees whose files I collected did not meekly accept their expulsions from Tianjin. They saw deportation as an unfair and illegal policy, and they used a variety of strategies – including writing letters,

[31] Tianjin shi di yi jixie gongye ju geming weiyuanhui, "Guanyu yi pizhun qiansong, bu zai qiansong chongbao pishi de tongzhi" [Directive on resubmitting orders to no longer deport already approved deportees], June 26, 1969, AC.

[32] Battles between Chinese and Soviet troops gave rise to the population dispersal policy. See Yang Kuisong, "The Sino-Soviet Border Clash of 1969," *Cold War History* 1, no. 1 (2000): 21–52.

visiting government offices, sit-ins, and threats of violence – to fight deportation orders. Writing of the disenfranchisement of millions of political outcasts in the Soviet Union during the 1920s and 1930s, historian Golfo Alexopoulous draws on individual appeals and petitions to show a "dual process" of exclusion and inclusion. When outcasts in the Soviet Union pleaded to regain their rights, they were actually asking to be included in – and thereby validating – a "class-based political community." Alexopoulous writes, "The deprivation and the reinstatement of rights form two aspects of a single campaign to construct a national community of the proletariat."[33] A parallel process took place in late 1960s China, but with an important distinction. Because the main point of deportation was to deprive outcasts of coveted urban residency, it actually split the national community in two: only politically pure individuals were allowed to enjoy the privileges of the city. Impurities were relegated to the countryside.

In Cultural Revolution-era China, the immediate goal of appeals was to clear one's name and remove political labels, but in most cases the ultimate motivation was to regain urban residency and employment. Even after deportees had been politically rehabilitated and reclassified as "return-to-village producers," they still fought to leave villages and return to Tianjin. Many exiles went back to the city without permission during the Cultural Revolution. In 1972, Tianjin's top public security official remarked that more than seventeen thousand deported people, more than 40 percent of the total, had "flowed back" to Tianjin.[34] Their disruptive presence in the city, where they slept at the train station or at the gates of their original work units, spending their days as full-time petitioners, played a major role in official efforts to reassess the deportation program and to rehabilitate deportees.[35]

[33] Golfo Alexopoulos, *Stalin's Outcasts: Aliens, Citizens, and the Soviet State, 1926–1936* (Ithaca, NY: Cornell University Press, 2003), 3.

[34] "Liu Zheng tongzhi zai shiwei luoshi qiansong zhengce he jiaqiang dui qingshaonian guanli jiaoyu gongzuo huiyi de jianghua" [Comrade Liu Zheng's speech at the work meeting on implementing deportation policy and strengthening management and education of youths], April 1, 1972, AC.

[35] "Some children of ten types and ten types [themselves] are vagrant in Tianjin, doing bad things or staying with relatives and friends and not returning to villages, avoiding being supervised and transformed by the poor and lower-middle peasants"; Nankai qu qingli gongzuo fen zhihui bu, "Guanyu jixu zhua hao qiansong gongzuo yijian de baogao" [Report on continuing to firmly grasp deportation work], March 20, 1969, circulated by the Nankai District Revolutionary Committee as *Nange* [1969] 18 (March 27, 1969), AC.

Fighting deportation was generally effective in making urban officials pay attention to exiles' demands. But for certain people, resistance could be terribly counterproductive, resulting in even worse punishment or violent reprisals. Whether resistance strategies were successful primarily depended on timing and the political atmosphere. Appeals backfired in summer 1968 but were viewed much more favorably in spring 1972, following a period of moderation in the wake of Vice-Chairman Lin Biao's death.[36] Other variables, including deportees' personal relationships, involvement in factionalism during the Cultural Revolution, health, "behavior" (*biaoxian*), and "attitude" (*taidu*), also affected how they were handled. The urban officials who had originally signed off on deportations were reluctant to admit mistakes and welcome back former rivals. They were also under tremendous pressure to limit migration to Tianjin. This meant that many deportees had to wait until the late 1970s to finally regain legal residency in the city.

Deportees from the Hongqiao district food supply system generally experienced the following pattern: deported in fall 1966; returned to Tianjin ("without permission") during winter 1966–1967; redeported in summer and fall 1968; reevaluated in 1969 or 1972. Reevaluations had several possible outcomes (see Table 6.2 for a tally from my files). First was no change in status, meaning that the deportee and his or her family had to stay in the village as enemies of the people. Second was reclassification of the original problem as a "contradiction among the people" (in other words, a non-antagonistic problem, as opposed to an enemy of the people), granting the deportee "return-to-village" status and earning her a severance or retirement payment but denying Tianjin residency. Third was complete rehabilitation and a return to Tianjin. How vigorously deportees appealed affected how their reinvestigations were handled. In 1972, people who had already returned to Tianjin in protest were reinvestigated before people who were still in villages; those who wrote letters and presented petitions were also given priority.[37]

[36] Lin and his family, accused of plotting against Mao, died in a plane crash on September 13, 1971 as they were fleeing China; Jin Qiu, *The Culture of Power: The Lin Biao Incident in the Cultural Revolution* (Stanford: Stanford University Press, 1999). Shocked by the apparent defection of Mao's trusted successor, many people questioned the Cultural Revolution and retreated from political involvement after Lin's death; Chan, Madsen, and Unger, *Chen Village*, 230–31.

[37] "Liu Zheng tongzhi zai shiwei luoshi qiansong zhengce he jiaqiang dui qingshaonian guanli jiaoyu gongzuo huiyi de jianghua."

TABLE 6.2. *Outcomes for 78 Deportees from Tianjin, through 1972*

Outcome	Number
Original verdict upheld, stayed in countryside	10
Political rehabilitation, stayed in countryside with "return-to-village" status	27
Political rehabilitation, regained Tianjin residency and job	24
Ordered to be deported but rehabilitated before leaving, allowed to stay in Tianjin	2
Died	7
Result unclear	8
TOTAL	78

Source: Deportation files, AC.

Guo Deren was an example of how forceful appeals sometimes backfired. In 1966, Guo was the thirty-seven-year-old manager of a neighborhood grocery store.[38] His family background (poor peasant) and class status (worker), offered no clue that he might suffer during the Cultural Revolution. But in October 1958, "because he was unhappy with the Great Leap Forward," he had refused to follow orders to sell large quantities of sweet potatoes (a common supplement when grain was short), resulting in a suspension from work. This was a mark against him, but the official reason for his deportation as a "bad element" was having had illicit sexual relationships with three of his female coworkers (his file was graphically, and, I suspect, pruriently specific: intercourse with two and mutual masturbation with the third). Guo was kicked out of Tianjin in September 1966, but the following January he returned to the city from his home village in Henan.

Back in Tianjin, Guo immediately appealed his deportation. He organized a group of "six or seven of the masses who were unclear about the truth" to advocate on his behalf, and "set up his own tribunal" (*si she gongtang*). Guo's organizing was effective in getting the political instructor at his shop to rehabilitate him and to burn materials related to his case. Guo also managed to convince officials from his home village to sign off on his rehabilitation. Happy at having reclaimed his urban salary and ration tickets, Guo celebrated by setting off firecrackers and by posting a notice of "glad tidings" (*tie xibao*). His happiness was premature. The Hongqiao District Revolutionary Committee deported Guo to Henan for a second time in September 1968. When he was finally reinvestigated in July 1972, the original verdict was upheld. Why? In 1967 Guo had

[38] Deportation file 25, AC.

"continued pursuing women and taking liberties with them, engaging in criminally indecent behavior," and he "sabotaged production" (by ruining a batch of cake batter). Moreover, after returning to his home village for a second time, Guo had not labored enthusiastically but instead had "incited the masses to struggle against one another."

The file does not include any letters from Guo himself, so we do not know his side of the story. But it is worth pointing out that he was deported for behavioral reasons, not political ones. His family background and class status were impeccable, but he was a nightmare of a coworker. His sexual misconduct may have ensured his redeportation in 1968, but was probably not enough to ruin his hopes for redemption in 1972. Instead, his energetic efforts to appeal and avenge his first expulsion sealed his fate. Because he went overboard in resisting deportation, he remained a political enemy in the countryside, presumably until the late 1970s.

This conclusion is supported by a similar case with a different outcome. Huang Yuanzhi, a man of middle-peasant background who was classified as a capitalist because he ran a noodle stand with his father between 1947 and 1956, continued making noodles in a collective after nationalization.[39] Like Guo Deren, Huang was deported from Tianjin as a "bad element" because he had sex with three women between 1958 and 1964. After being forced to move to his birthplace in Shandong in November 1966, Huang came back to Tianjin in February 1967. He approached the leaders of his work unit and complained. He asked, "On what basis did you send me out?" He argued, "Party center has regulations that allow everyone to return [to cities] now. Now that I'm back, arrange a job for me." These appeals were ineffective. Without employment, a salary, or ration tickets, Huang went to the grocery shop and demanded food, saying, "if the leaders won't give me grain, I'll eat the work unit's. They can't let me starve." Huang also threatened to "smash the dog heads who posted big character posters against me."

By mid-1968, these "dog heads" were likely calling the shots in the Huang's work unit. Unsurprisingly, Huang was redeported to Shandong in October 1968. When he was reinvestigated in 1972, his work unit recommended classifying him as a "return-to-village" laborer and giving him a severance payment, because "he is not consistently bad. His hooligan ways are not enough to make him a bad element." Huang Yuanzhi's original sexual misconduct was similar to Guo Deren's, but his appeals

[39] Deportation file 38, AC.

in 1967 were mild in comparison. While Guo had organized others, set up his own court of law, and adulterated cake batter, Huang had merely complained, argued, and taken enough food to stave off hunger. He had threatened to smash heads, but he never acted on the threat.

Huang's case was different enough from Guo's to convince his work unit to rehabilitate him. But when this decision was presented to the Hongqiao District Revolutionary Committee for approval, it was overruled in June 1972 with three terse sentences: "Huang's behavior in the village is bad, he should still be labeled as a bad element. Continue to supervise and reform. Treat as a deportee" (rather than as return-to-village). Remarkably, officials at Huang's workplace did not accept this judgment. They waited three months and resubmitted a duplicate reinvestigation report, hoping that district cadres would forget having already seen Huang's file (and that political loosening following the death of Lin Biao would filter through the system). It worked. In October 1972, the district signed off on the Food and Beverage Department's recommendation to remove Huang's "bad element" label and to treat him as a return-to-village producer. Huang was no longer an enemy of the people, but he was not completely satisfied. The final note on his file reads, "This person's opinion: requests to return to Tianjin" (*benren yijian yaoqiu hui Tianjin*). Regaining urban residence was often more important to deportees than political rehabilitation was.

Huang's political rehabilitation in 1972 meant material benefits, an end to social ostracism, and a restoration of citizenship rights. But Huang was still stuck in the countryside, unable to restore his Tianjin *hukou*. Regaining Tianjin residency was difficult but not impossible for deportees who achieved political rehabilitation. Sometimes the rationale for resettling exiles in the city was clear-cut. But it is often difficult to determine why some people remained shut out while others were allowed to return. One odd case involved a loose-tongued, liquor-loving man named Hao Baohua. Hao was of poor peasant background, but was approved for removal to Xinyang in Henan along with his wife and seven children as a "reactionary capitalist."[40] He was called a capitalist because he had run a tofu shop in Tianjin for twenty years, employing three laborers and accumulating capital worth almost three thousand yuan before nationalization. Ironically, Hao's eminently urban business was grounds for depriving him of city residency. Hao was labeled reactionary because he predicted the imminent return of Chiang Kai-shek in 1962, and during

[40] Deportation file 35, AC.

the Cultural Revolution he said he preferred pre-1949 theater to Jiang Qing's modern dramas, which sounded to him like "dogs fighting" (*gou dajia*). Also, Hao took advantage of the period's disorder to appropriate more than ten liters of liquor from a Tianjin warehouse.

Unlike the individuals in the previous examples, Hao was not forced to leave Tianjin in fall 1966. On June 30, 1968, during the second round of deportations from Tianjin, the Hongqi District Revolutionary Committee approved deporting Hao to Henan, but there is no evidence in his file that he ever left the city. It turned out that Hao did not have to leave, because a reexamination in 1969 allowed him to remain in Tianjin. On a form titled "no longer deporting people already approved for deportation," the neighborhood grocery store where Hao still made tofu recommended: "because Hao Baohua's ancestral home is Tianjin, there is no way to deport him." Instead he was to be supervised and educated in his original work unit. Four higher levels of bureaucracy endorsed this opinion, remarking that in the spirit of the "December 1 order" (Mao's late 1968 comment on uniting broadly and attacking narrowly, which put a halt to most new expulsions), Hao was no longer deportable, even though he was still considered a reactionary capitalist.

This is strange. Of course Hao could not be repatriated to the countryside if his "ancestral home" was Tianjin. It is unclear why his native place was listed as Xinyang on his deportation order, or why he was approved for deportation in the first place. According to the biography in his file, Hao had attended an elementary school in the Xiyuzhuang neighborhood of Tianjin, then worked as a cook for six years in the city before setting up his tofu shop. There is no indication that he actively protested his deportation order, or that he took any initiative during the Cultural Revolution aside from deriding Jiang Qing or drinking heavily. He simply never left the city, because there was nowhere else for him to go.

While Hao Baohua averted exile but kept his status as a political enemy, others who were expelled managed to find their way back to Tianjin. One seventy-three-year-old of rich peasant status – a category still marked for deportation even after Mao's moderating order of December 1968 – had his Tianjin *hukou* restored in late 1969 because he was elderly and ill.[41] This rationale was similar to the humanitarian exemptions granted to downsizing targets earlier in the decade. He returned

[41] Deportation file 59, AC.

to the city for good from his Hebei village. This ruling recognized that deportation could be a burden on villages, and also implicitly admitted that rural medical care was not up to urban standards.

While the rationale for the old Hebei man's return to Tianjin was clear, another returnee's case was less easily explained. A woman named Yao was deported twice to Hejian county in Hebei because she had illicit sexual relations with three men and stole 540 yuan in cash and grain tickets worth 480 kilograms during the famine.[42] Yao was given a capitalist label and her house was ransacked. When she was back in Tianjin in 1967, she reportedly said, "I'm not going to buy new furniture, I'll just confiscate some. I learned this from the working class." But in May 1969, her problem was reclassified because she had openly confessed to her misdoings and was willing to be reeducated. Yao was allowed to resettle in Tianjin, even though she was still considered a capitalist. We can only guess why someone with a capitalist label could return to Tianjin while others remained banished to the countryside after being exonerated. The results of deportees' petitions and appeals seem random because the process itself was arbitrary. The files do not reveal whether personal relationships, backdoor bribery, bureaucratic whims, or the employment needs of urban work units were decisive in determining outcomes. Deportees such as Yao must have been left scratching their heads about when and why their appeals were denied or accepted. What remained consistent, however, was that urban residence was a privilege worth fighting for.

Yao may have been disappointed that she was still considered an enemy of the people in 1969, but she did not complain about having her Tianjin residency restored. Less fortunate exiles completely lost hope. This is not surprising. The arbitrary handling of their cases devastated deportees who had no way of predicting when policies might change. Suicide was the most extreme type of resistance to the prospect of being expelled from Tianjin. Four of the deportees whose files I collected committed suicide (three killed themselves in Tianjin and one threw himself into a well after arriving in his home village).

Failed attempts to fight deportation likely contributed to the suicide of Liu Ende, who drank bittern (a liquid used to turn soy milk into tofu) the day before he was going to be forcibly removed from Tianjin. Liu was considered a capitalist during the early phase of the Cultural Revolution

[42] Deportation file 33, AC.

because he had run a wonton (*huntun*) stand before nationalization.[43] Red guards ransacked his home in fall 1966 but did not kick him out of the city at that point. Liu reacted angrily to the raid. The Hongqiao District Revolutionary Committee's August 1968 order to expel Liu, his wife, and three children to his home village in Shandong was based entirely on his vociferous opposition to mistreatment from red guards. According to his work unit, Liu needed to be deported because he acted hatefully toward the red guards who ransacked his home; he tried to overturn his verdict and directed his children to make demands at his office; and he maintained a reactionary standpoint. Liu's resistance annoyed and possibly threatened his superiors. They saw the second wave of deportations in 1968 as a convenient way to get rid of him.

When it became clear to Liu that his family's deportation was imminent, he argued against the action on legal grounds. He said that the Tianjin Military Affairs Committee's Notice Number Four of March 1967 (a document legitimizing Tianjin's deportation policy and clarifying the ten types) was "concocted by a few people. Because it has no mass base, Notice Number Four is invalid."[44] In retrospect, we can see that Liu had a good point. But in 1968, his questioning of a document issued by the military affairs committee was seen as a "venomous assault on the mighty PLA." His comment was added to his file as evidence against him.

When Liu poured poison down his throat on the eve of his deportation in September 1968, he had no idea that he would have been exonerated in 1972, if not earlier. A posthumous reassessment in July 1972 ruled that his wonton business was too small to make him a capitalist. His status should have been "petty proprietor" (*xiaoyezhu*). He had committed mistakes during his vigorous appeals to correct his class status, but this was a "contradiction among the people" and not grounds for deportation. Liu's suicide, much like Ding Yun's, was attributed to his "misunderstanding of policy" (*dui zhengce bu lijie*). Liu understood perfectly well that he had been wronged by the deportation program. In his despair, he may have failed to realize that if he had waited long enough, the policy would have changed.

By choosing death over exile in rural China, Liu Ende was in the minority. Most deportees lived in villages for years. Their hosts recognized

[43] Deportation file 43, AC. Even though Liu never left Tianjin, his deportation order from 1968 categorizes him as a "deported person" (*bei qiansong renyuan*).

[44] The full text of Notice Number Four is included in "Guanyu jixu zuo hao zai wenhua da geming zhong bei qiansong hou fan Jin renyuan chuli gongzuo de tongzhi."

the exiles' presence for what it was: the city dumping unwanted people on the countryside.

The Village Side

In an April 1, 1972, speech calling for full reinvestigations of deportation cases, Tianjin's top security official Liu Zheng ordered urban officials to travel to the countryside. City cadres were to cooperate with commune and village officials in researching the historical crimes and recent behavior of deportees. Likewise, if rural cadres arrived in Tianjin on deportation-related business, urban officials were to work enthusiastically with them. "Do not ignore them," Liu instructed. If reassessments of deportees were not handled well, Liu continued, "it will affect uniting the many, social order, the party's authority, urban-rural relations, and worker-peasant relations."[45] Liu was right, but his insights came rather late. Earlier policy documents and speeches about deportation never mentioned urban-rural relations, instead focusing on the disadvantages of letting political enemies remain in strategically important cities. Since fall 1966, the deportation program had indeed had immense implications for the relationship between city and countryside.

First, villages had to accommodate hundreds of thousands of city dwellers who had been away from their ancestral homes for decades. Some had never even set foot in the countryside. Unlike the millions of urban workers who also crossed the urban-rural divide when they were downsized during the early 1960s, the deportees of the Cultural Revolution often had little or no experience with agricultural work. Many villagers, including rural officials, saw the deportees as unwelcome competitors for limited housing and food.[46]

Second, the deportation program required regular communication and interaction between urban and rural officials. Village cadres haggled with city authorities about how to handle deportees. Some rural officials

[45] "Liu Zheng tongzhi zai shiwei luoshi qiansong zhengce he jiaqiang dui qingshaonian guanli jiaoyu gongzuo huiyi de jianghua."

[46] The other side of this coin was that deported outcasts freed up some of the most desirable real estate in Tianjin, leading the Tianjin Revolutionary Committee to prohibit "sudden moves" (*tuji banjia*) and squatting in deportees' vacant homes. Tianjin shi geming weiyuanhui, *Tongzhi* [Directive], *Jinge* [1969] 99 (June 9, 1969), AC. In 1972, Xinhua reporter Yang Jisheng discovered that the military had taken over some of Tianjin's best real estate. See his "*Neican* yinfa de jundui da banjia" [The great military move triggered by *Internal Reference*], *Yanhuang chunqiu* 3 (2011): 62–64.

demanded financial compensation or simply refused to accept exiles, forcing them back to Tianjin, homeless and jobless.[47] During the reinvestigations of 1972, rural and urban cadres met (usually in the countryside) to negotiate rehabilitations and changes in *hukou* status. City bureaucrats had orders to prevent deportees from returning to Tianjin, even if the exiles had been politically rehabilitated. The urban officials had an inherent advantage over their rural counterparts because they were higher in the administrative hierarchy – and were therefore in charge of "putting policy on firm footing" (*luoshi zhengce*, a euphemism that actually meant redressing injustices caused by the party). Village leaders felt pressure from above by commune officials demanding grain deliveries and from below by villagers who wanted their fair share of the crops. Gaming the system to maximize the amount of food that stayed in villages was a common practice for many rural residents during the 1960s and 1970s.[48]

The question of how to feed extra mouths without shortchanging other villagers vexed rural officials. In turn, aching hunger became a central concern for deportees, who rarely earned full allotments of work points and whose grain allocations were capped at the lowest possible rate. The family of one Tianjin man named Zhou was deported to his father's home village in Wuqing county.[49] Zhou's father had owned a small shoe workshop before nationalization. Predictably, this got his family deported in fall 1966. Zhou was twelve years old, and this was his first trip to the countryside. In 1967, a "mass organization" in the village kicked out Zhou's entire family and sent them back to Tianjin, calling the father's problem insufficient grounds to dump him in the countryside. In 1968, they were redeported to Wuqing, where they stayed until 1978.

Zhou remembered his time in the village in terms of hunger, not political discrimination. His father was periodically criticized at meetings, but Zhou recalled being treated like any other villager, especially after he abandoned his Tianjin dialect and began speaking like a local. Crossing the boundary between city and countryside made Zhou aware of one of

[47] As of May 1969, Heping district counted 135 deportees who had returned to Tianjin without permission. Of these, 51 came back to the city because villages refused to accept them, and 61 came back because they were too old or ill to support themselves in villages, or because their native places were in a strategic coastal or border region. Heping qu qingli gongzuo fen zhihuibu, "Guanyu xuexi guanche 'jiu da' jingshen luoshi zhengce, zuo hao qiansong gongzuo de anpai yijian" [Plan for studying and carrying out the spirit of the Ninth Party Congress on implementing policy and doing deportation work well], May 23, 1969, AC.

[48] Gao Wangling, *Renmin gongshe shiqi Zhongguo nongmin "fan xingwei" diaocha.*

[49] Interviewee 15.

the defining elements of cultural difference between the two realms, so he changed his speech and adapted. Annual summer flooding made grain scarce and expensive in the low-lying parts of Wuqing county. To help his family survive, Zhou strapped a small scale to a borrowed bicycle and rode on long overnight trips to areas unaffected by floods. Black market grain was cheaper, he said, in hilly Jixian and Zunhua counties. Zhou bought what he could and carted it back to Wuqing. He used his scale to resell the grain at higher rates after keeping enough for his family's own needs.

Zhou and his family survived in the village, raising few complaints, focusing on feeding themselves, and waiting until the Cultural Revolution ended to resettle to Tianjin. Other deportees were less cooperative and caused headaches for rural officials. Zhang Dajun, a clerk at a food shop in Tianjin's central Heping district, was expelled to Shandong in 1968.[50] His alleged crimes were almost all related to factional disputes during the Cultural Revolution, when he joined a rebel group and falsified his past, claiming to be a party member, martyr's son, and revolutionary soldier who had once worked for Chen Boda as a messenger. Lying about his identity made him a "bad element." After arriving in his Shandong hometown in 1968, Zhang attended two compulsory meetings for the village's political enemies. He then locked himself in a room and never came out again, refusing go to meetings or do farm work. Family members delivered his food. He did not even leave the room to urinate or defecate. In contrast, Zhang's wife (who also refused to work) went out often. She quickly blew the couple's settlement allowance of almost 600 yuan on food and liquor at a nearby rural market.

When Zhang was reinvestigated in 1973, village leaders, sensing a chance to get rid of Zhang and his wife, wrote a letter to his work unit in Tianjin:

> About the deportation of Zhang Dajun to us during the Cultural Revolution: At that time our village did not have a party branch and it was pretty chaotic. . . . After we established a party branch, in the process of putting all types of party policy on firm footing, we deemed that because Zhang's mistakes were committed in Tianjin, he should be reformed there and should not have been deported. Zhang's problem is still unresolved. Owing to poor production conditions here, every year Zhang often eats state-supplied grain and gets welfare relief. If he keeps living here it will be truly difficult. In accordance with the masses' complaints and multiple investigations, our party branch does not consent to settling Zhang in the village.

[50] Deportation file 75, AC.

After the reinvestigation was complete, Zhang's "bad element" label was removed. Because he did not work and the "village, commune, and county had gotten in touch many times and were determined to not accept him," Zhang and his family were allowed to return to Tianjin.[51] The village appeared to have won this battle. The real winner was Zhang himself, for his asocial behavior earned him the urban residency that he wanted so badly.

Village leaders successfully argued against Zhang's settlement in the countryside because he was a burden and his political problems had nothing to do with the village. This was a common line of argument from villagers who resented deportees. In spring 1967, a rural cadre in Shandong wrote a pleading letter to Tianjin officials about a fifty-seven-year-old man named Tao Ligong who had been deported as a "puppet army official":

> Tao left here when he was nineteen; he has been gone for thirty-eight years. During these thirty-eight years he cut off relations from his family. We only admit that according to his ancestral native place, he is from our village. In reality he is no longer from our village. When you sent him and his family here last October, we did not understand the situation and did not realize the difficulties they would bring to our village. Village life is mainly based on physical labor. But Tao Ligong is old and weak. His son is only six years old. Also we have many people here and land is scarce. It is difficult to survive. Under these circumstances, the villagers have big complaints about adding people who cannot labor. They also often gossip, saying, "Tao was away from home for thirty-eight years and had no contact with his family," "We do not admit that he is from our village," "We cannot labor for the sake of feeding him," "We cannot support him," "Let them go back to where they came from," and so on. This type of irresponsible talk has certainly brought difficulties, disunity, and a negative impact to our village. If this is not resolved quickly the villagers' complaints will surely be huge, affecting their production mood. The production team's opinion is that it firmly does not want him and his family. We ask that you accommodate him away from here.[52]

Tao's unwelcome presence in his ancestral home prompted rural people to define themselves in opposition to urbanites. Notably, the Shandong villagers expressed their idea of rural-urban difference in terms of community and labor, not the *hukou* system. Administrative structures such

[51] The family's return was approved by his work unit, the district vegetable company, and the district revolutionary committee, but the Tianjin Municipal Implementing Deportation Policy Office wrote, "does not meet all of the qualifications for returning to Tianjin." It is not clear if or for how long this ruling delayed Zhang's return, but a 1978 document in his file indicates that he and his family did return to Tianjin in 1973.

[52] Deportee file 52, AC.

as household registration and grain rationing shaped the rural-urban gap in socialist China, but difference came into clearest focus when people moved between the two realms and interacted with one another.

Even though Tao had been born in rural Shandong, villagers no longer considered him a native. He had been away for too long, had not bothered to write or visit, and did not contribute to the collective. The harsh response to Tao's arrival ("he is not from here," "go back to where they came from") reflects rural hostility to deportation. Rural people were not consulted about an official program that would cause them hardship. If villagers had a choice about which city residents to accept, they would have selected someone younger and stronger who fulfilled family and community obligations. They certainly would not have chosen Tao. Tao and his family did return to Tianjin in mid-1967, but they were redeported to Shandong the following year. When city officials reclassified his problem as a contradiction among the people in 1972, they ordered him to remain in Shandong as a return-to-village producer.

Villages were at a disadvantage in battles over how to handle unwanted exiles, but were not powerless. The Nankai district bureaucracy in charge of dealing with the fallout from deportations in 1969 reported that 243 people approved for expulsion had never left Tianjin. Village officials' steep demands for settlement funds from urban work units – as much as one thousand yuan per deportee – were partly to blame for this.[53] In addition, rural cadres sometimes appropriated entire severance payments that were intended to go to rehabilitated deportees. A document issued by the Tianjin Revolutionary Committee in August 1969 asked city officials to "persuade" villages to give the payments to individual deportees, but also acknowledged that the money was probably long gone. Tianjin's top leaders ruled: "If the payment went to the brigade, in principle seek the return of funds. If the village has genuine difficulties, this can be dealt with according to the situation."[54] This left a major loophole – what village in China could not claim difficulties in 1969? Villages were genuinely worse off than cities during the Mao period. Rural cadres played up this inequality in an attempt to get as much money as possible out of deportees and city offices.

[53] Nankai qu qingli gongzuo fen zhihui bu, "Guanyu jixu zhua hao qiansong gongzuo yijian de baogao."

[54] Tianjin shi geweihui hexin xiaozu, "Yanjiu guanyu chuli qiansong daoliu renyuan de yijian" [Opinion on researching how to handle deportees who flowed back], August 23, 1969, AC.

Rural officials made bald demands for cash when cadres from Tianjin showed up to sort out deportees' cases in 1972. The Tianjin Number Two Steel Rolling Mill's successful parrying of village demands was circulated citywide in a packet of "study and reference materials" about how to "put repatriation policy on firm footing." Factory bureaucrats went to Anxin county in Hebei to investigate a man named Chen who had been removed from Tianjin because of his "puppet army" history. They decided that Chen was not an enemy of the people and that he should remain in the village and receive a severance payment.

Factory bureaucrats then encountered opposition from village leaders, who reportedly said, "It was you who deported Chen here, now take him back." Village officials also pointed out that Chen's family had not earned enough work points to cover their grain needs, and that the family owed the production team more than three hundred yuan. That sum should be deducted from Chen's severance payment, the village leaders said. Factory cadres complained about this demand to commune headquarters, which sent officials to convince the brigade leadership to let Chen stay in the village and keep the money. "In order to express the policy's warmth, we secured the brigade's agreement that Chen's grain debt would not be deducted from his severance payment," factory officials reported. "First let Chen get his life in order, then let him gradually pay back the debt."[55] We do not know whether Chen ever repaid the village, but village leaders did not get the immediate windfall they had hoped for.

Urban officials tended to blame their rural counterparts for the problems that dogged deportation work. In 1969, Liu Zheng told Tianjin authorities to find out why villages had refused to accommodate deportees and to "do good political thought work on the village side."[56] Three years later, Liu said that almost twenty thousand exiles had flowed back to Tianjin because "they could not get appropriate accommodation in villages."[57] Liu criticized urban work units for expelling people without contacting villages first and for arbitrarily labeling undesirables (he was especially galled by such ridiculous grounds for deportation as "reactionary element who maintains the standpoint of a rich peasant's

[55] Tianjin shi geming weiyuanhui renmin baowei bu, *Tianjin shi luoshi qianfan zhengce jingyan xuexi cankao cailiao* [Materials for study and reference about experiences of putting repatriation policy on firm footing], July 26, 1972, AC.

[56] Heping qu qingli gongzuo fen zhihuibu, "Guanyu xuexi guanche 'jiu da' jingshen luoshi zhengce."

[57] "Liu Zheng tongzhi zai shiwei luoshi qiansong zhengce he jiaqiang dui qingshaonian guanli jiaoyu gongzuo huiyi de jianghua."

wife").[58] But Liu misplaced blame by criticizing villagers for rejecting or taking advantage of a policy they had no voice in making.

It was especially difficult for villagers to accept why they had to continue to house and feed deportees who had been exonerated and desperately wanted to return to Tianjin. The Tianjin Fabric Factory rehabilitated a deported worker named Li in 1970.[59] After changing his class status from "reactionary capitalist" to "staff member in the old society" (*jiu zhiyuan*), the factory paid Li more than sixty-five hundred yuan in severance funds (calculated on the basis of seniority and back wages). But in 1972, Li and nine of his family members showed up at his factory office in Tianjin, saying that because Li's name had been cleared, "we should return to Tianjin and get our *hukou* back for it to count as putting policy on firm footing." Li and his family had received a sizable windfall, but did not consider his case resolved until they regained Tianjin residency. Factory officials quickly rejected this argument, saying, "You cannot view the policy as being put on firm footing based on whether you return to Tianjin." Putting policy on firm footing (meaning fixing messes caused by deportation) was about addressing deportees' political and economic status, not about urban residency, the bureaucrats explained. "Neither we nor the village treat you as an enemy of the people, but rather as our own comrade. How can you say that the policy was not on firm footing?" they asked.

Li retorted that his family had been forced to return to Tianjin because the village did not want them. The family squatted at the factory and stayed for two months, interrupting policy lectures by shouting and threatening that "we won't leave even if it kills us. If anything happens, the factory is responsible." Finally the factory sent a work team to Li's home village in Weixian. The team first reported to the county party committee, where county leaders backhandedly commended the group for traveling such a long way and for not resting during the May 1 holiday. Next the factory cadres spoke with commune and village cadres. The village leaders said that in principle they supported keeping Li and

[58] "Gaoju 'jiu da' tuanjie, shengli de qizhi jin yi bu luoshi dang de ge xiang zhengce – Liu Zheng tongzhi liu yue ershiqi ri zai qu, ju fuzeren huiyi shang de jianghua jilu zhaiyao" [Hold aloft the Ninth Party Congress's banner of unity and victory, go a step further in putting all party policies on firm footing – Summary transcript of Comrade Liu Zheng's talk at a meeting of district and bureau leaders on June 27]. Reprinted by Yi jixie ju renmin baowei zu, July 10, 1969, AC.

[59] The following paragraphs are from Tianjin shi geming weiyuanhui renmin baowei bu, *Tianjin shi luoshi qianfan zhengce jingyan xuexi cankao cailiao*, 18–24.

his family. But because the village was poor, accommodating the large clan was difficult and villagers were complaining.

At this point the commune party secretary intervened, saying that more people in the village equaled more labor power. "Putting policy on firm footing is not about who has complaints, it is about who obeys Chairman Mao," the commune leader exhorted, adding, "Tianjin is so far away and these people have come to put policy on firm footing for Li." Overruled, the village cadre agreed to travel to Tianjin to persuade Li and his family to return. If he was forced to house the large and disgruntled family in the village, the least he could get in return was a junket to the city.

According to the fabric factory's report, Li's resistance crumbled when the village boss showed up in Tianjin and told him, "It is incorrect for you to say that the brigade does not want you . . . how could we not want you?" The next day, the factory party secretary authorized the use of the work unit's vehicle to return the family to the countryside. He told them to write a letter if they had any more troubles. Problem solved. The fabric factory's conduct was lauded as a model experience. Factory cadres had succeeded because they "relied on rural county, commune, and brigade party organizations to wipe clean ideological obstacles and unify understanding." What unified urban and rural officials was that none of them wanted to deal with Li and his family's complaints. This meant that whoever was lowest on the administrative totem pole was stuck with the family. If Li's village had managed to keep him out, his case would never have been circulated as a success story. Pushing off urban problems on the countryside, however, was considered model behavior.

Deportation and the Rural-Urban Divide

After cadres from the Tianjin Number Two Steel Rolling Mill convinced rural officials in Anxin county to keep deportee Chen and absorb his family's grain deficit, they wrote, "Putting deportation policy on firm footing gave us and the poor and lower-middle peasants an education in [class] line and policy, and established closer relations between city and countryside."[60] It is easy to dismiss this as the type of pablum that dominates official writings from the Cultural Revolution. But is it possible that the factory cadres were on to something? Did the deportation of political exiles actually end up bridging the rural-urban divide?

[60] Ibid., 15.

Inspired by the practice of sending landlords back to villages to face the wrath of the exploited masses, and justified by calls for heightened security in cities during the early days of the Cultural Revolution, deportation was never intended to shrink the gap between city and countryside. Expelling political exiles from cities was purely punitive. It punished deportees and the villages that hosted them. None of the lofty rhetoric that lauded the sent-down youth program – about tempering souls in the revolutionary countryside or bringing advanced culture to villages – accompanied deportation. The deportation program laid bare a system in which cities were politically and economically privileged, while villages became landfills for the "dregs of society." It bears remembering that the full name of the "meat grinder" that chopped up China during the 1960s and 1970s was the Great Proletarian Cultural Revolution.[61] Because most proletarians lived in urban areas, cities were special. In the era's heightened atmosphere of class struggle, urban zones had to be cleansed of impurities. There was only one way for impure elements to go: "down" to villages.

Why did Mao Zedong and Zhou Enlai's exhortations against passing contradictions down to the lower levels go unheeded for so long? Why, instead, was deportation effectively legalized? Why was it wholly abandoned and repudiated only after Mao's death? Deportation combined the revolutionary and modernizing elements of the Maoist project. In the eyes of the urban cadres in charge of deportation, protecting centers of modern industry from purported enemies of the revolution seemed like a safe course. It was a way to be revolutionary and to protect the fruits of socialist modernization. The cumulative effect of the policies that had disadvantaged rural China under Mao made it easy for the people who carried out deportations to assume that they were doing the right thing by sending political outcasts to villages.

Yet while the deportations of the Cultural Revolution were a massive injustice for deportees and villagers alike, in a sense the cadres from the steel rolling mill were correct that the entire experience had brought city and village closer together. Villagers learned about how the Cultural Revolution was unfolding in multiple ways, from red guards on the march to loudspeaker broadcasts. But the appearance of entire families of humiliated political outcasts in villages was a clear signal to rural residents

[61] The "Outline of Project 571" associated with Lin Biao's son Lin Liguo refers to China's state machinery during the Cultural Revolution as a "meat grinder" (*jiaorou ji*). Wang Nianyi, *Da dongluan de niandai*, 419.

that something important and unprecedented was taking place. For some villages, the methods and magnitude of the Cultural Revolution did not hit home until deportees arrived.

Later reassessments of deportees were another way that deportation bridged the rural-urban gap. How often during the Mao era did urban officials sit down with rural cadres to make deals? Probably more often than most scholars realize, but the reinvestigation of deportees in 1972 was a chance for city and village leaders to negotiate face-to-face about the sensitive issue of how to backtrack on deportation without negating the entire Cultural Revolution. To be sure, urban officials had the upper hand in these dealings. County and commune authorities, who did not have to deal with the headaches caused by deportees on a daily basis, usually sided with city reinvestigation teams against village cadres who complained about practical hardships. But local leaders sometimes stood their ground and pushed back.

The following chapter will trace how the complexities of everyday life during the 1960s and 1970s challenged state definitions of urban and rural space. In spite of administrative labels, all space in China during the Mao period remained relational and contested.

7

Neither Urban nor Rural

In-Between Spaces in the 1960s and 1970s

Picture a huge ironworks administered by the Tianjin Metallurgical Bureau, staffed by thousands of Tianjin workers. Next to the factory complex are dormitories, schools administered by Tianjin educational authorities, a Tianjin police station, and Tianjin banks and department stores. Steaming Tianjin stuffed buns are on sale, and vehicles displaying Tianjin license plates zoom by. What's strange about this scene? For one, it is 260 miles away from the actual city of Tianjin. The Tianjin Ironworks, these days known as the Tianjin Tiantie Metallurgical Group Corporation Ltd., is located in a steep mountain valley in the far southwest corner of Hebei Province. Since 1969, the ironworks has been an island of Tianjin land.

In 1956, another type of island was established much closer to Tianjin. The Worker-Peasant Alliance Farm is only a thirty-minute bicycle ride southwest of the city. Yet in a China divided into "urban" and "rural" spaces, the Tianjin-administered farm does not fit neatly into either category. Since its establishment, the farm has produced vegetables, milk, eggs, and grain, but the people doing the producing called themselves workers, not peasants. Even though they fed pigs and hoed fields all day long, people laboring at the Worker-Peasant Alliance Farm earned monthly wages and held non-agricultural *hukou*. Peasants in neighboring villages earned workpoints, not cash, for similar labor.

During the 1960s and 1970s, spaces like the Worker-Peasant Alliance Farm and the Tianjin Ironworks were located in geographically rural settings, but were enclaves where residents had urban identities. Enclaves' urban administrative status clashed with their rural physical space. They expose the inadequacy of analyzing China through fixed "urban" and "rural" labels. Household registration and grain rationing divided China into urban and rural spheres, but these administrative categories – even as they shaped life choices and opportunities – did not mesh with lived reality.

Enclave factories and state farms were far outnumbered by collective farms, county towns, and industrial cities. Nonetheless, they suggest that few spaces were exclusively urban or rural during the Mao Zedong era. Whether we define spaces by their population size or density, economic activity (farming or industry), residents' *hukou* status (agricultural or non-agricultural), or by what people called themselves and others (peasants, workers, villagers, city people), we discover that every officially "urban" space contained elements normally associated with the countryside, and vice versa. Many villages had industry; some city residents grew vegetables and raised chickens. Some people who lived in settlements of more than ten thousand residents held agricultural *hukou* and worked in the fields.

This is not to say that the *hukou* system was irrelevant during the Mao period, or that urban and rural labels were meaningless. *Hukou* status was crucial in people's everyday lives. How people who lived in in-between spaces negotiated the rural-urban divide shows just how central the benefits of a non-agricultural *hukou* were, especially when it came to decisions about work and marriage. When powerful administrative designations were clinically imposed on a complicated geographic and human landscape, individuals and families had to sort out the mess. Labels and categories pushed people into choices and situations that they might not have considered otherwise. But people pushed back.

This chapter focuses on the people in and around two unique spaces. I explain the rationale behind the founding of the Worker-Peasant Alliance Farm and the Tianjin Ironworks, and explore the mixing of different types of people at the farm and ironworks. I then discuss how intermediate space affected questions of marriage, family, and economic viability. People sent to the farm and ironworks from Tianjin fought hard to hold on to the benefits that came along with their official urban identities. Their interactions with local people made them acutely aware of how much they had to lose. In contrast, while the lives of villagers were disrupted, they discovered that they could take advantage of the enclaves next door.

Proletarian Peasants

In the latter half of 1955, as collectivization proceeded throughout much of rural China, Tianjin's municipal government ordered its labor bureau to establish a state farm on previously uncultivated swampland southwest of the city. The purpose of the farm was to provide paid jobs for unemployed city workers. The new unit was named "Worker-Peasant Alliance," an often-used theoretical construct in the mid-1950s. But at this point in the farm's history, there were no peasants, only workers.[1]

Cai Shiming, a city man who began working at the farm in 1962, heard that it had been named by Mao Zedong himself. Mao had visited the suburban village of Wangdingdi on January 12, 1956, to inspect the advanced unit's collectivization progress.[2] Standing on a hill outside of the village and gazing at the bog to the west, Mao reportedly said, "establish a farm there, worker-peasant alliance." Mao did visit Wangdingdi, but Cai's story is apocryphal, given that the labor bureau already had orders to found the farm before Mao's supposed utterance. Cai remains convinced of Mao's fateful hand in the farm's birth. "It's amazing how those few words changed my life and changed the lives of so many people," Cai said.[3]

Cai was right that the farm would eventually affect thousands of people, but it remained small in its early years. In March 1956 around two hundred unemployed workers from Tianjin moved to the farm. Their first tasks were to drain the bog and remove alkaline soil. Aside from swampland, this peripheral space on the outskirts of Tianjin included higher ground dotted with grave mounds. The workers labored to remove the tombs. By the end of 1956, workers had dug up more than thirty thousand "ownerless" graves.[4]

For the city workers, who lived in tents and earned monthly wages between twenty-eight and thiry-eight yuan, laboring at the farm was difficult. During the second half of 1957, more city factory jobs became available. The farm workers wanted out. They began taking long vacations, asking for sick leave, and skipping work. In 1957, the farm fell far

[1] NCS, 1.

[2] Zhonggong Tianjin shiwei dangshi ziliao zhengji weiyuanhui, ed., *Mao Zedong he Tianjin renmin zai yiqi* [Mao Zedong together with the people of Tianjin] (Tianjin: Tianjin renmin chubanshe, 1993), 27–29.

[3] Interviewee 16.

[4] NCS, 3.

short of its production targets, and had an operating deficit of more than three hundred thousand yuan. The labor bureau decided that relying on unemployed city workers as the only source of employees was "inappropriate," and anyone who wanted to leave the farm for a city job was allowed to go. Almost everyone left.[5] Tianjin agricultural officials transferred several hundred agricultural workers from other suburban state farms to Worker-Peasant Alliance, and the farm began hiring peasants as temporary workers.

Transforming "peasants" (*nongmin*) into proletarian "agricultural workers" (*nongye gongren*) was in tune with the national goals of state farms in the mid- to late-1950s. Model state farms were large, mechanized, and proletarianized. In other words, state farms were supposed to be more advanced and modern than village agriculture. As one pamphlet extolling the virtues of the model State Friendship Farm (Guoying youyi nongchang) in Heilongjiang explained, "a state farm is an agricultural factory on a large plot of state land that uses mechanized agriculture to carry out large-scale production. The producers are agricultural workers, they earn wages based on the quality and quantity of their labor, just like workers in a factory."[6] And unlike peasants in villages who used rudimentary tools to till small plots, it went without saying.

In the mid-1950s, China's state farms were modeled on the Soviet Union's *sovkhoz*, which employed "proletarians" who lived in huts, barracks, and dormitories. In 1952, a team of Chinese "peasant representatives" went to the Soviet Union to tour state farms. What the Chinese team learned about state farm organization and production was reprinted in pamphlet form at least three times, and Soviet advisers helped to establish the Friendship Farm in Heilongjiang.[7] In late 1957, there were 107 state farms in China. Twenty years later, there were more than two thousand.[8] State farms were intermediate spaces between rural and urban China. Their focus on cultivation and livestock seemed rural, but their administrative designation was more akin to urban factories. By the early 1960s, wages at Worker-Peasant Alliance were based on nationally-mandated salary standards for agricultural workers. Like city residents, they held non-agricultural *hukou* and received guaranteed grain rations.

[5] NCS, 5–6.
[6] Guo Wenyu, *Guoying nongchang* [State farms] (Beijing: Chaohua meishu chubanshe, 1957), inside cover.
[7] *Sulian de guoying nongchang* [Soviet state farms] (Beijing: Shidai chubanshe, 1956 [1953]).
[8] Guo Wenyu, inside cover; RMRB, November 20, 1977, 1.

Tianjin's Third Front

The Worker-Peasant Alliance Farm and other state farms established in the 1950s followed a Soviet model that aimed to mechanize the countryside and proletarianize peasants. In contrast, third front factories like the Tianjin Ironworks emerged during the anti-Soviet 1960s. Barry Naughton describes the third front of the 1960s and 1970s as a "purposive, large-scale, centrally-directed programme of development carried out in response to a perceived external threat with the broad support of China's national leaders."[9] The "big third front" refers to the dispersal of industrial projects in China's southwest, especially in Sichuan, Guizhou, and Yunnan, and in the northwest, including Ningxia, Gansu, and Qinghai. Mao Zedong, Zhou Enlai, Lin Biao, and other central leaders thought that building an industrial system in these remote areas would minimize damage from air attacks and allow China to fight a protracted war against the United States or Soviet Union. In addition to the big third front, each province and special municipality like Tianjin was to establish its own "small third front" of remote, dispersed industry.[10]

In 1969, Tianjin needed iron. The city had a steel mill but no local source of metals. Xie Xuegong, who had taken over as Tianjin's top leader after Wan Xiaotang died and who led the city through the late 1970s, traveled reluctantly to Shandong province to ask for iron. Xie procured eighty thousand tons of iron for the use of Tianjin's steel industry, but Tianjin officials wanted to be more self-reliant. Originally, Tianjin planned to build its ironworks near Tangshan, but the location did not meet "small third front" standards because it was too close to the coast and apparently more vulnerable to attack.[11]

Shi Zhirui was part of the investigation team sent by Tianjin's metallurgical bureau to the Taihang mountains in southwest Hebei to scout out mine and factory sites. Not only did there have to be sufficient iron and coal mines to fuel the ironworks, the site had to follow the "six-character principle" for third front construction: "mountainous, dispersed, and

[9] Barry Naughton, "The Third Front: Defence Industrialization in the Chinese Interior," *China Quarterly* 115 (1988): 351.

[10] Naughton, "The Third Front," 368. See also Lorenz Lüthi, "The Vietnam War and China's Third-Line Defense Planning before the Cultural Revolution, 1964–1966," *Journal of Cold War Studies* 10, no. 1 (2008): 26–51.

[11] Tianjin tiantie yejin jituan youxian gongsi, '*35 licheng* [35 year course] (n.p., 2004), 41.

concealed" (*kaoshan, fensan, yinbi*).[12] Shexian county, at the junction of Hebei, Shanxi, and Henan provinces, fit the bill. As one official put it, the site chosen for the ironworks was at the rear of Tianjin's small third front but was in the forward position of the national big third front.[13]

Because the area selected for Tianjin's ironworks was in Hebei province, the construction project was originally conceived as a collaborative effort between Tianjin and the province. But the alliance between the city and Hebei was short-lived. Although Tianjin had regained its status as a special provincial-level municipality in January 1967, the relationship between city and province remained tense. On August 5, 1969, national economic planner Xie Beiyi convened a meeting in Shijiazhuang, Hebei's provincial capital. The chair of the project team was from Hebei, the vice-chair from Tianjin. Meeting participants agreed that the ironworks would produce 1.5 million tons of pig iron annually for the exclusive use of Tianjin's steel industry, and would also produce 600,000 tons of steel and 500,000 tons of rolled steel per year. Hebei and Tianjin would cooperate in the plant's construction, which would be funded by the national government. The ironworks would be named "Project 6985," because that was the date of the meeting in Shijiazhuang.[14]

As planning continued during late summer and early fall 1969, Tianjin and Hebei officials clashed over resources, much as they had ten years earlier during the leap. The iron was for Tianjin, but the land was in Hebei. Each side wanted the final say on planning decisions. Fifty heavy trucks were assigned to the project. As soon as the vehicles arrived in Shexian, Hebei and Tianjin cadres demanded that their own drivers take control of the trucks.[15] Turf battles over scarce supplies had been part of the command economy since the 1950s, and this did not change during the Cultural Revolution. Authorities in Beijing caught wind of the dispute, and in November 1969 they awarded Tianjin full jurisdiction over the project. Tianjin was able to appropriate Hebei land for its own use.

Tianjin had once again won a battle against Hebei: the city would get its iron island in the mountains, but the specific site still had to be chosen.

[12] Shi Zhirui, "Tiantie jianchang zhichu de huiyi" [Memories of establishing the Tianjin Ironworks], *Tansuo yu yanjiu*, no. 3 (August 5, 1999): 302–3. Many, including Shi Zhirui, attribute this six-character phrase to Lin Biao, but recent research indicates that Zhou Enlai first came up with the principle in 1964. See Chen Donglin, *Sanxian jianshe*.

[13] Tianjin tiantie yejin jituan youxian gongsi, *'35 licheng*, 41.

[14] Shi Zhirui, "Tiantie jianchang zhichu de huiyi," 303; Tianjin tiantie yejin jituan youxian gongsi, *'35 licheng*, 43.

[15] Interviewee 17.

After Tianjin took over the ironworks project, city cadres and engineers made the long journey from Tianjin to Shexian. They sparred over where to build the plant. In this and all other decisions about the project, urban officials – and not local people – would dominate the conversation. But many local residents took advantage of the situation.

Encounters at the Ironworks Enclave

The top leaders of the ironworks project who arrived in Shexian county in late 1969 had all been forced out of office and detained in late 1966 and early 1967. They had been rehabilitated only a few months before being assigned to Project 6985. Most of them welcomed the opportunity to get away from Tianjin's highly politicized atmosphere. Yang Zhengmin was named director of project headquarters. Before the Cultural Revolution, he was Tianjin's vice mayor in charge of economic planning.[16] After arriving in Shexian, Yang met with other project officials, including former Tianjin Metallurgical Bureau director and Long March veteran Li Xianyuan, and Nie Bichu, who would become Tianjin's vice mayor in the late 1980s. Finding an appropriate site for the ironworks topped their agenda.[17]

Two locations made the final cut. Xigang was in a gorge close to the county seat. It had abundant water resources and some of the best farmland in the mountainous area. But in order to build there, about one hundred households would have to be moved. Xigang's water independence had not come easily. In 1958, girls from the village sold their braids and earrings to fund an irrigation project. The Gengle site was larger, but its topography was so steep, rugged, and rock-strewn that not as much arable land would be affected. Ironworks leaders presented these two options to Tianjin Revolutionary Committee Vice-Chair Chi Biqing. He chose Gengle.[18] The decision to build at Gengle was made in the city. But project leaders were aware that construction would disrupt village life, so they chose the site that they thought would have the least adverse impact. Gengle residents would soon have forty thousand new neighbors.

During planning and construction in 1969 and 1970, city officials interacted with villagers every day. Headquarters authorities moved into

[16] Yang was the son of Shaanxi warlord general Yang Hucheng, who, along with Zhang Xueliang, detained Chiang Kai-shek in 1936 in the Xi'an Incident.
[17] Shi Zhirui, "Tiantie jianchang zhichu de huiyi," 304.
[18] Ibid.

homes in Gengle, a large settlement of several connected villages with a population of 8,642 in 1970.[19] It is worth noting that the sheer size of Gengle stretches the definition of "rural." Most Gengle residents held agricultural *hukou* and farmed, but for a while, the size of their settlement dwarfed the ironworks' construction site. "Rural" and "urban" were more administrative categories than precise geographical descriptors. The ironworks was an intermediate space, but in its own way, so was Gengle. The non-agricultural *hukou* held by the newcomers from Tianjin were indeed an important marker of difference. Yet in everyday interactions, simple differences between insiders and outsiders, between locals and strangers, were more apparent than administrative designations.

Yang Zhengmin and Li Xianyuan lived with Gengle native Zou Shaorui. Yang sat down with his host and asked for local support. "If you peasants don't help us, we cannot build it," Yang told Zou. "Worker-peasant alliance, you know."[20] The official rationale for the ironworks was war preparation, not cooperation between city and countryside or rural development. But Yang Zhengmin knew that the project could ill afford local resistance, so he invoked the well-worn worker-peasant alliance bromide.

In practice, this meant monetary compensation for the terraced fields that would be destroyed and leveled for factory use. Ironworks employees also paid villagers for room and board until workers' dormitories were built. In exchange, Zou Shaorui and other local authorities were expected to convince villagers to accept the deal and to smooth over any conflicts that might arise. The ironworks had a home, but it immediately hit road blocks. In one dispute over land use, a village party secretary dug a deep ditch across the road heading to the ironworks site so that trucks loaded with construction supplies could not pass. County-level cadres finally arrived and persuaded the secretary to reopen the road.[21]

Much like the Four Cleanups work team members who had assaulted Xiaozhan in 1964, ironworks officials, even those originally from villages themselves, were shocked at the conditions they encountered in Gengle. Zhao Yingjie was an official in Tianjin's city government before he was sacked during the Cultural Revolution. He was sent to Shexian in

[19] *Gengle zhen zhi* bianzuan weiyuanhui, ed., *Gengle zhen zhi* [Gengle town gazetteer] (Beijing: Xinhua chubanshe, 2001), 231.
[20] Interviewee 18.
[21] Ibid.

late 1969. After arriving in Gengle, Zhao moved into a village home along with three other Tianjin people. Zhao paid 1 mao (.10 yuan) plus 150 grams worth of grain ration tickets for each meal. He gagged on the stir-fried rice chaff his hosts offered. "It was so poor there," said Zhao, who had grown up in a central Hebei village. "This place had been liberated for so many years, how could it still be this way?"[22] Zhao and his Tianjin colleagues always felt hungry. They regularly snuck off to a supply depot, bought eggs and potatoes, and hid them in the teapot in the center of their room. After their village hosts had gone to sleep for the night, the men quietly nibbled on their stash.

Long March veteran Li Xianyuan also remarked on the poverty of the area. "You can really call it a 'poor and out of the way place,'" he wrote, "it had a bit of the flavor of the war of resistance." Hardy Li could handle everything except Gengle's water. The nearest river was about thirteen miles away, too far for daily trips. Instead, Gengle villagers dug holes in their yards and drank the rain and snowmelt that accumulated there. Almost all Tianjin people who stayed in Gengle reacted with horror to the murky "pit water" (*yao shui*). "There were lots of bacteria in the water," Li Xianyuan wrote, "We could even see insects, roots, and dirt. It was enough to make city people terrified." Li remembered that Yang Zhengmin made a point of gulping the yellow water, bugs and all, in front of his village hosts.[23] He did not want to disrespect them, and there was nothing else to drink anyway. Other Tianjin people, less concerned about offending the locals, filtered the water through handkerchiefs before drinking it.

The first few dozen officials stationed in Gengle in late 1969 got along well with their hosts. Yang Zhengmin and Li Xianyuan exchanged Spring Festival gifts with their village "landlord" (they used the neutral term "*fangdong*," not "*dizhu*," which referred to class enemies) and helped him years after the two Tianjin cadres were transferred away from Project 6985. But when tens of thousands of outsiders arrived in the valley in 1970, tensions were impossible to avoid.

Distinct groups came together to build the ironworks: hundreds of technical experts from the Baotou and Beijing steel mills; around five thousand demobilized soldiers from the Beijing Military Region's Tianjin garrison; about ten thousand Tianjin middle school graduates from the

[22] Interviewee 17.
[23] TJRB, November 13, 2001, 11.

classes of 1969 and 1970; and at least ten thousand *mingong* (peasant contract laborers on temporary leave from their Hebei communes).[24] The *mingong* returned to their communes after the initial construction ended, while the ex-soldiers and Tianjin youth stayed on as salaried employees and officials at the project's factories and mines. Other Tianjin units were also transferred to Shexian to serve the ironworks. Doctors and nurses from the well-regarded Tianjin Number 3 Hospital moved their entire operation, including all staff and equipment, to the plant site. Several thousand Tianjin construction workers charged with building dormitories and office space also arrived in the valley.

We know very little about the thousands of *mingong* who cycled through the construction site. The historical record privileges the memories of the Tianjin middle school graduates. Commemorative literature and television programs focus on city youth who cried when they disembarked at the empty train station near Gengle in 1970 and who sob when they retell the story today. Working in isolated Shexian was undeniably arduous; perhaps terrible untold stories cause the tears to flow. According to Wu Yifu, who was the project vice-director in charge of personnel, "there were lots of accidents and many workers were killed and injured, they sacrificed for the project."[25] Urban youths' memories reflect genuine difficulties, but also reveal a sense of entitlement and an assumption of natural difference between life inside and outside the ironworks island.

According to one teen who was sent to ironworks-affiliated mines, an assignment to 6985 was actually coveted by Tianjin youth. Most students from previous graduating classes had been assigned to rural communes and ordered to become peasants. In contrast, the ironworks offered worker status, decent salaries, guaranteed grain, and the chance to retain an urban *hukou*.[26] The enclave was geographically distant, but it was still officially Tianjin. The ironworks' administrative status meant that it might be possible for the youths to return to Tianjin in the future, an option denied to teens who were sent to villages.

[24] Sources differ on the size of each group. The range for demobilized soldiers is three thousand to seven thousand; for Tianjin youth, three thousand to twelve thousand; and *mingong* from a low of ten thousand to a high estimate of fifty thousand. Tianjin tiantie yejin jituan youxian gongsi, *'35 licheng*, 43–44, 46; TJRB, November 13, 2001, 11.

[25] Tianjin tiantie yejin jituan youxian gongsi, *'35 licheng*, 45. Judith Shapiro writes that the death rate for workers at the Panzhihua Steel Mill, a massive third front construction site in Sichuan, averaged a shockingly high 5.42 percent; Judith Shapiro, *Mao's War against Nature: Politics and the Environment in Revolutionary China* (New York: Cambridge University Press, 2001), 152.

[26] Interviewee 19.

Because of the strategic nature of the third front, the ironworks was technically secret. Students had to have favored class labels and meet high political and performance standards before being approved to work there.[27] Even though the ironworks was more desirable than becoming a sent-down youth in a village, for most graduates it still seemed worse than staying in Tianjin proper. Urban authorities raised the expectations of the teens, which led to disappointment after they arrived in Shexian.

One of the first trainloads of youths arrived in March 1970. The train stopped at Piandian station, which had no platform, only a hut. The students thought that the conductor must have made a mistake. They expected an expanse of tall buildings and smokestacks, with wide roads extending in all directions. But they saw no roads at all, only a few one-story buildings. In the distance, a group hiked toward the train, pounding drums, beating gongs, and waving red flags. It dawned on the new arrivals that this was a welcoming party of Tianjin youths who had arrived a few days earlier. "Oh my God, this is 6985?!" they exclaimed. "That's right, get off the train!" the conductor ordered.

The youths had also been misinformed that Project 6985 was near the south, "where all seasons are like spring." They were told to leave their long underwear behind. Shexian was indeed south of Tianjin, but the mountain air was frigid, and the winter was long. It snowed as late as April that first year.[28] They were the best of the class of 1970. They came from the most revolutionary of class backgrounds. This was their reward? Many of the students felt tricked. They had not gone to school for years in order to make bricks or build roads in this forsaken place.

Some of the students began to act up and demand better conditions, making life difficult for their supervisors, many of whom were demobilized soldiers. "It was tough to manage them," acknowledged one ex-soldier originally from a Hebei village. "They could not adapt" to the difficult conditions. They often stirred up trouble, forming gangs and brawling over trivial matters, the veteran said.[29] During the early 1970s, in administrative terms these workers lived on an urban island, in that their wages and Tianjin *hukou* differentiated them from unpaid rural people in nearby villages. But before the first blast furnace and dormitories

[27] Interviewee 20; interviewee 21.

[28] Tianjin tiantie yejin jituan youxian gongsi, *Tiantie jingshen tiantie ren* [Tiantie spirit, Tiantie people] (n.p., 2004), 117.

[29] Interviewee 21.

were complete, there was no physical barrier that kept the youths apart from local peasants. What happened when they met?

At first, the students and villagers looked at one another with mutual suspicion. Often, this distrust was warranted. Liu Hongwu, a Tianjin student who arrived in Shexian in 1970, said that "the city people looked down on the peasants. They wore dirty cotton clothes and just sat in their doorways, they even ate their meals sitting on the stoop." Liu noticed that locals interpreted the Tianjin youths' new, clean clothes as a sign that the city youths "did not work" (*bu gan huor*). "Because we came to their hometown, they thought we should obey them," Liu complained.[30] The teenager sensed that the villagers could not stand the students. He was right.

"We couldn't stand the students," said Zou Shaorui, the Gengle native who had been a friendly host to top ironworks leaders. Villagers' main complaint was not that the students did not work, but that they stole fruit, corn, and nuts from village fields and orchards. Persimmons and walnuts normally ripened in August, but the students picked and ate them in July.[31] Liu Hongwu admitted that he was part of a group of Tianjin youths who stole walnuts from a vendor in the Shexian county town. This was a fun diversion for the city teenagers, who probably did not pause to consider that they were robbing villagers of a crucial source of income.

Students flaunted their sense of entitlement. The youths requested that their hard physical labor be rewarded with dumplings every Sunday. Peasants could afford the luxury perhaps once a year. The demand was granted, but only for young women.[32] In 1970, around one-third of the Tianjin youths were female, and they were organized into a separate work unit. Male workers at the ironworks were allowed an annual *jiaozi* meal, but women could eat them weekly. Pulling off the weekly dumpling feast presented logistical difficulties for the young Tianjin women. The nearest meat shop was three miles away from their worksite. On one occasion, five female workers pushed a cart to the shop. By the time they arrived, the day's meat had already sold out. They argued with the local butcher and begged him to make an exception. When that did not work, they all started crying. The exasperated man fetched a hog

[30] Interviewee 19.
[31] Interviewee 18.
[32] Interviewee 22.

and slaughtered it right in front of the sniveling teens. Before handing over the meat, he said, "Don't you cry, my pig's life was only one day shorter."[33]

The Tianjin youths flouted rules and ignored the costs of their stealing and wheedling. It was, therefore, no surprise when locals took what they could from the factory. According to a history of public security at the ironworks, "owing to the complicated make-up of the personnel and the effects of the Cultural Revolution," construction materials and funds were stolen at an alarming rate in 1970.[34] The report does not specify who was robbing the site, but the formation of a new *hukou* inspection team in September 1970 aimed to keep villagers out. One of the stated goals of the *hukou* team was to keep "population from nearby villages from flowing into the construction site."[35] The island's boundaries were taking shape, but they were never impermeable.

Ten years after the factory produced its first iron in 1972, peasants had literally torn holes in the wall around the ironworks. In the early reform period's atmosphere of uncovering corruption and inefficiency, the *Economic Daily* splashed an exposé of fiscal disarray and looting at the ironworks on its front page. Although the report is from the early 1980s, its contents, along with public security histories, suggest that looting occurred throughout the 1970s. Two photos accompanied the article. The first showed "a few peasants from around the factory" sneaking metal through a hole in the wall surrounding the ironworks' perimeter. The next photo was a close-up of a Shexian man selling stolen iron at an open-air market. He told *Economic Daily* reporters, "I go [to the ironworks] once a day and take 50 kilograms. The commune buys it for 6 fen (.06 yuan) per kilogram, so that's 3 *kuai* (yuan). It's better than doing farm work."[36]

According to the article accompanying the photos, peasants from Gengle and Jingdian communes carried off fifty tons of iron, one hundred tons of coke, and one hundred tons of coal in 1982. The problem continued in 1983: materials continued to disappear, and in the dry season, peasants "from all over the factory district" used factory water to irrigate

[33] Tianjin tiantie yejin jituan youxian gongsi, *Tiantie jingshen*, 118.

[34] Lu Jinjun, Yu Xianbiao, and Zhao Jie, "Pijing zhanji dandang tiecheng weishi" [Hacking our way through difficulties, bodyguards of the iron city], *Tansuo yu yanjiu*, no. 3 (August 5, 1999): 204.

[35] Ibid., 205.

[36] *Jingji ribao* [Economic Daily], December 18, 1983, 1.

their fields, costing the ironworks several hundred thousand yuan. For the people who made off with free iron and water, the benefits of having an ironworks next door was making up for the fruit and nuts stolen by the spoiled Tianjin youths.

Not all of the advantages reaped by villagers were illicit, nor were all interactions between locals and outsiders antagonistic. Throughout the 1970s, peasants and ironworks employees met at twice-weekly markets. They also traded and bartered in other settings. A boy who grew up in a nearby village carried persimmons, corn, walnuts, and eggs on a shoulder pole to the ironworks. He followed the plant's work calendar, going straight to the ironworks perimeter on Sundays, not on customary market days. Peddling to Tianjin workers supplemented his family's income.[37]

Some Tianjin youths pilfered extra corn buns from their own cafeteria. After dark, they snuck down to Gengle to trade the buns for walnuts and persimmons. They also took their extra ration tickets down the hill and traded them for eggs.[38] Workers and peasants even exchanged gifts. One Tianjin teen who worked in the ironworks' mines brought sacks of high-quality paddy rice back from his vacations in Tianjin. He gave them to the families who had hosted him during his first two years at the mines. When he returned to Tianjin for good in 1974, his village friends sent him off with bags of local products.[39]

After the blast furnace opened in 1972, a clearer line demarcated the urban enclave from the village. Roads were better and buildings taller inside the island; higher-quality schools and hospitals catered exclusively to ironworks staff and dependents. Perimeter walls went up. Yet people could still cross the line. Sometimes villagers entered the ironworks compound to enjoy performances; ironworks employees also watched movies, opera, and political meetings in Gengle.[40] These were perhaps the most pleasant interactions of all. In the early 1970s, Tianjin youths formed a performance troupe, putting on shows like "I Vow to Give My Youth to the Third Front" and "Taihang Battle Song." One former member of the troupe recalled that huge crowds of peasants always turned out for their shows in Shexian.[41] The annual performance in Gengle by a Henan-style drama group was a treasured ritual for villagers and an inscrutable

[37] Interviewee 23.
[38] Interviewee 19.
[39] Interviewee 20.
[40] Interviewee 24.
[41] Yang Dianqi, "Gongdi shang de wenyi xuanchuan dui" [Culture and propaganda team at the construction site], *Tansuo yu yanjiu*, no. 3 (August 5, 1999): 307–8.

spectacle for Tianjin youths, who loitered around the edges of the village square, unable to comprehend the local dialect.[42]

Even though the two groups intermingled at markets and shows, they were easily distinguishable. Those with regular jobs inside the ironworks considered themselves urban workers. They had Tianjin *hukou* to prove it. Locals' lives were hugely affected by the presence of the industrial compound, especially by the pollution poisoning their air and water. But they could not become a part of that world, at least not until the mid-1980s. Some did not want to become ironworks workers. Zou Shaorui thought that he could have asked his former tenants for a factory position. "I needed to plant my fields," he said. "I don't understand the blast furnace, I don't have that ability. I could have asked and they would have given me a job, but I did not want to bother the leaders."[43]

Finding Middle Ground at the State Farm

Both the ironworks and the Worker-Peasant Alliance Farm were privileged spaces compared to the surrounding countryside. The ironworks had a clear, consistent goal throughout the 1970s: to produce metal for Tianjin. In contrast, the farm's name, mission, and administrative status changed repeatedly. In the 1950s the farm was controlled in succession by the Tianjin Labor Bureau; the municipal Agriculture, Forestry, and Irrigation Bureau; the city's Nankai District; and by the Tianjin Livestock and Poultry Bureau. In the 1960s the city's Agricultural Cultivation Bureau was in charge, but for a year during the Cultural Revolution, the farm was caught in a tug-of-war between the agricultural bureau and the city's education system. With each administrative change, production tasks swung wildly. The farm's main products were usually paddy rice, vegetables, eggs, and milk, but in September 1958, as part of the leap's hygiene drive, all cows within the Tianjin city limits were shipped to Worker-Peasant Alliance over the course of three days. Many of the animals fell ill, froze, or starved to death because of a feed shortage.

A year later, the farm pioneered a model "pig cafeteria" that garnered national recognition. The cafeteria was meant to "transform the backward way of feeding pigs separately in individual stalls," by cycling the hogs in shifts through a two-story collective dining hall (farm employees lived on the top floor). Over the course of eight months in 1959,

[42] Interviewee 19.
[43] Interviewee 18.

the farm's pig herd grew from 335 to 1,842, and numbers continued to skyrocket after the Agricultural Publishing House in Beijing published a short book praising the experiment.[44] As forward thinking as the cafeteria was, it failed in winter 1960, when there was not enough food to sustain humans, let alone hogs. Even after grain was transferred from the farm's liquor distillery to save the animals, most of them starved: 4,255 pigs and 82,825 chickens died at the farm in 1960.[45]

At least 250 farm employees suffered from edema at the height of the famine, but the farm recovered and received infusions of new workers in the 1960s and 1970s. While personnel at the Tianjin Ironworks remained relatively static during the 1970s, Worker-Peasant Alliance was home to many different types of people over the years. People from villages in the Tianjin region got jobs at the farm in the late 1950s and early 1960s. Urban people labeled as "rightists" (375 of them in 1959) and, during the Cultural Revolution, as "freaks and monsters," were sent there for punishment and reeducation. Two waves of Tianjin "educated youth" (*zhiqing*) were assigned to work at the farm: almost one thousand in 1962 and 1963, and twenty-two hundred between 1973 and 1979.[46]

Less easily categorized groups moved in, including 643 "personnel without *hukou* who flowed back to Tianjin" (*daoliu fan Jin wu hukou renyuan*) in 1961. These were mostly people who had been removed from Tianjin by state fiat (thousands were sent to Qinghai province in the 1950s; more than half of them returned to the city without official authorization).[47] They wanted back into the city, but their *hukou* remained outside of Tianjin. As a compromise, the "backflow households" were allowed to settle at the state farm, an intermediate zone between villages and the city.[48]

Barber Xing Bo did not care whether his customers were city people or ex-peasants like him. As long as they lived at the farm, he cut their hair. Xing Bo came from a long tradition of Baodi barbers. He learned to cut hair in his Baodi village, and continued to ply the trade after

[44] Tianjin shi xumu ju, ed., *Tianjin shi gongnong lianmeng xumuchang chuangban "zhu shitang" de jingyan* [The Tianjin Worker-Peasant Alliance Stock Farm's experience in setting up a "pig cafeteria"] (Beijing: Nongye chubanshe, 1960), 1, 3.

[45] NCS, 13, 18.

[46] Ibid., 29–30, 130.

[47] On the migrants to Qinghai, see Guo Fengqi, ed., *Tianjin tong zhi: minzheng zhi* [Tianjin gazetteer: Civil affairs gazetteer] (Tianjin: Tianjin shehui kexueyuan, 2001), 176–77.

[48] NCS, 28–29.

migrating to Tianjin in 1958 at the age of seventeen. Freelance haircutting was unsteady. When Xing heard that forty other men from his village, including his uncle, were getting temporary jobs at the Worker-Peasant Alliance Farm, he jumped at the opportunity. The sojourning men had permission from their home village, which docked their wages. During the leap famine, many of Xing's fellow villagers returned home when daily food rations at the farm were slashed. Along with four other men from his village, Xing Bo stayed on until he retired in the 1990s. By 1961, he was allowed to keep his own wages, and in 1964, he obtained non-agricultural *hukou* status. Garrulous and self-deprecating, Barber Xing was quick to befriend co-workers. His buddies were mostly men from villages next to the farm who had been hired on during the late 1950s and early 1960s, men like Wu Mengyong, from the nearby village of Yangwuzhuang. Xing and Wu became mentors to the city youth sent to work on the farm's vegetable team.

The farm's first group of urban youth came from Tianjin technical schools that had shut down during the post-leap retrenchment. Hundreds of teenagers who had been trained as technicians suddenly learned that they would become "agricultural workers." Fixed wages and rations, plus the farm's proximity to the city, tempered the youths' disappointment. Cai Shiming had hoped to become a factory worker. When he was assigned to Worker-Peasant Alliance, he thought that state farms were all prison camps.[49]

After he made the short bus trip to the state farm, Cai learned that even though some rightists were detained there, he was not a prisoner. Farm work was tough, but he earned a decent salary and could go home frequently. During the 1960s, urban youths bicycled to Tianjin for family visits every weekend. Barber Xing remembered that by the 1970s, recently hired Tianjin youth essentially lived at home in the city and commuted to the farm by bicycle every day. Xing and friends like Wu Mengyong rode their bicycles to Tianjin as often as they could. At the parks, movie theaters, and restaurants where the men spent their wages, they tried to fit in with other city workers. When Xing chatted with the rightists or educated youth whose hair he cut, he discovered that he had visited more Tianjin attractions than they had.

One farm worker, a driver, entered Tianjin quite often. He delivered fresh milk to a city milk station every night at 11 P.M. In late 1958, the

[49] Interviewee 16.

farm's single truck was too small for the volume of milk produced by an influx of new cows, so the driver towed a massive vat of sloshing milk behind a tractor. The tractor's engine blasted like an artillery explosion every half-second, shaking city residents awake each night.

After several weeks of interrupted sleep, people who lived near the milk depot revolted. They set up a road block and emptied buckets of water on the road, which froze in the frigid winter air. Protesters stood their ground and the driver was unable to deliver his milk. This was a problem for the farm and for city authorities in charge of the urban food supply system. Urban officials quickly approved the farm's request for a large new truck.[50] The outcome of the confrontation between city people and the tractor driver was positive for both sides. Tianjin residents caught up on their sleep, while the farm got a brand new vehicle.

Barber Xing Bo's friend, dairy worker Wu Mengyong, was overjoyed when he had saved enough money to purchase new wheels. His bicycle allowed him to take occasional weekend trips to Tianjin with Barber Xing. More often, he cycled to see his family in Yangwuzhuang. With his stable farm job, Wu felt luckier than other villagers, who had only enjoyed salaried life for four years before their wages were cut off. Yangwuzhuang was one of two villages right next to Worker-Peasant Alliance Farm. In 1960, the farm expanded its boundaries and absorbed the villages. Yangwuzhuang and Huazhuang, with a combined population of about twelve hundred residents, attained the strange administrative status of "transitional villages" (*guodu cun*).[51]

The villages maintained their original collective work teams and still handed over grain to the state, but the farm invested in electricity, irrigation, drainage, and machinery. It also paid villagers regular wages for tasks like providing hay for the farm's dairy cows. Villagers made 20 percent less than regular state farm salaries, but 30 percent more than they had ever earned as commune members. Infrastructure improvement and guaranteed incomes made Yangwuzhuang and Huazhuang beacons for outside families with marriageable daughters. Bachelors became hot commodities, and forty-three women married into the two hamlets over the course of two years. Not surprisingly, peasants in neighboring villages clamored to "transition" into the farm.

Problems soon arose. Farm authorities waited in vain for policy guidance about how to formally turn villagers into state farm workers, and

[50] NCS, 21–22.
[51] Data on transitional villages are from NCS, 23–25, and interviewee 25.

the "transitional" villagers wondered if they would ever become full-time agricultural employees. They received salaries for collecting hay, but had little incentive to do regular collective work. Salaries kept coming in as weeds sprouted and tools disappeared. Wandering sheep gobbled up seventeen acres of Yangwuzhuang's spinach crop.

The experiment fell apart in 1964. The villages' transitional status was cancelled, and most residents no longer received wages. Thirty-six fortunate villagers, including Wu Mengyong, were hired on as full-time farm employees. Wu moved to the dairy team and milked cows every day next to a Tianjin woman who had been sent to the farm after her technical school shut down in 1962. A few years later, the pair got married in Yangwuzhuang. By then, his fellow villagers envied Wu's salaried job. They had been fired by the farm, but the two villages were technically still part of Worker-Peasant Alliance territory – rural enclaves stuck within the state farm island.

The failed transitional village experiment and the diverse backgrounds of people at the farm highlight its position in the middle of an urban-rural hierarchy. Yangwuzhuang and Huazhuang were administratively subordinate to the state farm, whether or not villagers earned state wages. Since the farm's inception, rural people eagerly sought job security there. With their salaries, new bicycles, and leisure time, agricultural employees from village backgrounds considered themselves on par with city factory workers. A job at the farm meant upward mobility for rural people. But for city youth sent there in the 1960s, it seemed mediocre, and not what they had hoped for. For political outcasts exiled from the city during the Cultural Revolution, the farm was punishment.

The Cultural Revolution In Between

Neither the Worker-Peasant Alliance Farm nor the Tianjin Ironworks were spared from the Cultural Revolution's upheavals. The ironworks, founded in 1969, was itself a product of the period's international tension and urban turmoil. The course of the Cultural Revolution in the two spaces highlights their intermediate status.

Worker-Peasant Alliance was similar to much of rural China in that its Cultural Revolution effectively began in 1964 with the Four Cleanups movement. In September 1964, a two hundred-member work team from the Tianjin Agricultural Cultivation Bureau arrived at the farm. City cadres viewed the state farm as a rural space full of corruption. Much like the work teams who went to Xiaozhan, the Tianjin agricultural officials attacked malfeasance among state farm cadres and re-investigated the class status of employees. By 1965, well before most city residents could have predicted the turmoil of the coming year, the state farm hosted intense struggle meetings. At one study session, a jittery cadre blurted out that China had two guiding principles. The first was the "United Nations," the second was "class struggle." He was right about the latter concept, but horribly confused about the former (in 1965, *People's Daily* was full of articles denouncing the international body as a handmaiden to American imperialism). The man suffered through multiple struggle sessions after his misstatement.[52]

In July 1965, the work team announced the end of the Four Cleanups. Seven people had attempted suicide (two of them died), and two people with "historical problems" had simply disappeared. Li Zhi, the official who had led the farm since 1957, was demoted because of his "unclear class line," "excessively patriarchal work style," and "capitalist management." Members of the work team stayed on to take charge of farm operations: the new farm party secretary and one party vice-secretary, plus a vice-director, were from the work team. The Four Cleanups movement was primarily rural, and through early 1966, the farm was following a rural pattern.

In June 1966, Tianjin's agricultural bureau sent another work team to the farm. This "Four Cleanups Reinvestigation Work Team" was quickly rendered obsolete by the developing Cultural Revolution. Now, the farm followed what was happening in Tianjin. Like people in city schools and offices, farm employees pasted big-character posters and formed revolutionary mass organizations.[53] Wu Mengyong and other workers rode bicycles to Tianjin to join mass marches and read big-character posters. Educated youth at Worker-Peasant Alliance united with workers at other state farms to establish the short-lived "Tianjin State Farm Rebel Corps."[54]

Rebels overthrew the farm leadership, which was still dominated by former members of the Four Cleanups work team. Two main rebel factions emerged in January 1967. After three months of struggle, the January 31 faction claimed victory when security officials in Tianjin declared the January 23 faction an illegal counterrevolutionary organization and arrested its top leader. In April, victorious rebel chief

[52] NCS, 38–39.
[53] Ibid., 45.
[54] Interviewee 26.

Feng Jinsheng took over as chair and old party secretary Li Zhi became vice chair of the farm's temporary leadership group. When the farm's Revolutionary Committee was officially established in December 1967, the two had switched positions.

Supporters of the vanquished January 23 faction fled to Tianjin, linked up with other disaffected rebels there, and made occasional forays into Worker-Peasant Alliance territory. They threatened to "wash the farm in blood" and warned that a convoy of thirty trucks loaded with five hundred warriors would soon attack. In response, the new Revolutionary Committee organized armed patrols on horseback and set up road blocks. The threatened attack never came.[55]

Because Worker-Peasant Alliance was part of Tianjin's agricultural bureaucracy, it was hit relatively hard by the Four Cleanups movement, like parts of rural China. But its proximity to Tianjin enmeshed the farm in urban turmoil in 1966 and 1967, as employees marched down Tianjin streets and representatives of city rebel groups came and went. More than any other factor, however, state-mandated migration marked the farm as an intermediate space during the Cultural Revolution. On the one hand, the settlement of twenty-two hundred urban educated youth at the farm during the 1970s colored the space rural, even though unlike youth sent down to villages, those at the farm held non-agricultural *hukou*. On the other hand, beginning in 1968 the farm carried out the national policy of deporting political outcasts to villages. As we saw in Chapter 6, the official rationale for removing the "ten types of people" from cities was ostensibly based on national defense: China's cities were more strategically important than villages. But the message received by citizens was that political outcasts were not qualified to enjoy the privileges of urban life.

During the Cultural Revolution, Worker-Peasant Alliance deported ninety-nine people to villages.[56] The more deportations farm leaders made, the more revolutionary they appeared. The official national list of the ten types of deportable people left plenty of room for interpretation at the local level. It was up to each sending unit to determine whether suspects' "reactionary standpoint" and "bad behavior" warranted deportation. A fifty-two-year-old farm employee was deported to his home village on the basis of his landlord-capitalist label, but the village refused to take him, pointing out that he had been reclassified as an

[55] NCS, 46–47.
[56] Ibid., 48.

agricultural laborer during the Four Cleanups. One educated youth sent to the farm in 1963 had a clean family background, but had grumbled about the new Revolutionary Committee. This offense was enough to deport him, along with his wife and two children, to his father's home village.[57]

That the farm was a receiving point for educated urban youth but a sending unit for political outcasts underlines its in-between spatial status. Worker-Peasant Alliance during the late 1960s and early 1970s combined aspects of rural and urban life. In the case of the Tianjin Ironworks, it is more accurate to refer to a third front Cultural Revolution. Work started on the ironworks after the initial phase of the Cultural Revolution had ended, but the entire rationale for the enclave was based on one of the period's defining slogans: "prepare for war, prepare for famine, for the sake of the people" (*bei zhan, bei huang, wei renmin*).[58]

Debate about where to put the ironworks – in water-rich Xigang or in rugged, dry Gengle – became so heated that beleaguered Tianjin officials who were relieved to flee the city felt that Cultural Revolution politics had followed them to the mountains. According to Shi Zhirui, the conflict turned acrimonious and led to criticism meetings. Author Ran Huaizhou fictionalized this dispute in his 1974 novel, *Jianshezhe* (Builders). In the 534-page novel, a nerdy engineering expert named Zhang tries to persuade his colleagues that the flat, well-irrigated site is the only realistic place to put a functioning ironworks. But other officials, along with local peasants, want the site to be concealed deep in the mountains in accordance with war preparation principles. Fortunately, peasants know about a plentiful mountain spring near the steep Gengle site (called Wohupo in the book). Meanwhile, a local landlord and a "landlord-capitalist" from Tianjin hatch a plot to sabotage construction. They plan to take advantage of nerdy Zhang's reasoning to get construction started at Xigang (fictionalized in the novel as Caomawa). Once the building site had eliminated the best agricultural land in the county, the class enemies would derail the project by accusing it of "destroying the worker-peasant alliance."[59] Ironically, the bad guys had formed their own rural-urban alliance – a fictional example of class identity trumping spatial difference.

Naturally, in the novel heroic poor peasants and wise leaders thwart the plotters and build the ironworks in the precipitous valley. Tianjin

[57] Ibid., 47–48.

[58] Judith Shapiro's translation; Shapiro, *Mao's War Against Nature*, 145.

[59] Ran Huaizhou, *Jianshezhe* [Builders] (Tianjin: Tianjin renmin chubanshe, 1974), 128.

TABLE 7.1. *Production and Profit at the Tianjin Ironworks, 1970–1991*

Year	Pig Iron (tons)	Profit/Loss (RMB)	Year	Pig Iron (tons)	Profit/Loss (RMB)
1970			1981	391,348	−19,910,000
1971			1982	425,386	−13,090,000
1972	41,018	−12,450,000	1983	505,576	−10,750,000
1973	59,161	−18,796,000	1984	702,659	1,362,000
1974	56,618	−17,678,000	1985	816,529	20,799,000
1975	129,753	−27,890,000	1986	911,280	17,634,000
1976	154,561	−31,290,000	1987	1,015,449	20,676,000
1977	320,074	−22,485,000	1988	979,371	14,005,000
1978	430,687	−22,995,000	1989	1,081,444	24,199,000
1979	403,178	−30,880,000	1990	979,371	25,541,000
1980	451,307	−16,418,000	1991	1,081,444	30,266,000

Source: Tianjin tiantie yejin jituan youxian gongsi, '*35 licheng*, 14–15.

leaders indeed chose the less practical site for the ironworks. This required extensive earth moving and road building, and contributed to injury-causing accidents and major delays. Ran Huaizhou may have invented the landlord plot, but the decision to build at Gengle was real. This choice, made in the Cultural Revolution atmosphere of war fears and anxiety about not seeming revolutionary enough, triggered a series of problems that would take years to resolve.

Problems and Resolutions

Naughton writes that third front construction "was immensely costly, having a negative impact on China's economic development that was certainly more far-reaching than the disruption of the Cultural Revolution."[60] The Tianjin Ironworks was certainly costly. For twelve years, the project was deep in the red (see Table 7.1). Of all the industrial units under Tianjin's control in the 1970s and early 1980s, the ironworks was the city's biggest money loser; its massive deficits ranked second in the metal industry nationwide.[61] Far from being separate from the Cultural Revolution's tumult, however, the third front was very much a part of the period. Like the ransacking of homes by red guards and the deportation of political outcasts from cities, which observers have

[60] Naughton, "The Third Front," 351.
[61] *Jingji ribao*, December 19, 1983, 1.

mistakenly called chaotic "disruption," the third front was sanctioned by the state and managed by a massive bureaucracy.

The ironworks did not bleed money simply because it was built at an isolated, topographically challenging site. Construction was rushed and sloppy. Leadership constantly changed, and employees complained, protested, and tried to leave. The plant was functioning, but only barely. In February 1972, employees fired up the site's coke furnace. Two months later, when the blast furnace began producing pig iron, Tianjin's number two party secretary General Wu Dai was there for a ribbon-cutting ceremony. On May 15, 1972, top leader Xie Xuegong welcomed the arrival of the plant's first delivery of iron to the Tianjin train station; three days later, the event was celebrated in *Tianjin Daily*.[62]

Behind his smiles in public, Xie was fuming. The original plan had the ironworks producing 1.5 million tons of pig iron each year, plus steel, but even after the plant's second coke and blast furnaces opened in July 1975, the flow of pig iron that actually passed quality control standards was a mere trickle. Steel was completely out of the question. That year, Xie traveled to the ironworks. At a huge meeting of officials and employees, Xie railed that the plant's low output defied the principles of mathematics. He said that at the ironworks, "one plus one equals one," because the two blast furnaces were not even producing what a single one should. "Produce more iron, produce good iron," he exhorted workers.[63]

Production did increase somewhat after Xie's criticism, but as long as leaders and workers were unstable and unhappy, the ironworks would continue to underperform. Between 1969 and 1983, there had been thirteen different directors at the ironworks; the shortest term was less than half a year. One account published after the Cultural Revolution charged that plant leaders were clueless: "most did not understand production technology and management, and they did not work hard to become experts. Some even bragged that they were 'clods' (*da laocu*)."[64]

To be fair, ironworks leaders were bedeviled by shifting national policies. After Lin Biao's death in September 1971 and China's rapprochement with the United States, the third front had become less politically relevant. In 1972, investments decreased and plans were cut back. National planners classified the Tianjin Ironworks as a unit on which to "delay

[62] Tianjin tiantie yejin jituan youxian gongsi, '*35 licheng*, 37, 42; Tianjin tiantie yejin jituan youxian gongsi, *Tiantie jingshen*, 120.

[63] Tianjin tiantie yejin jituan youxian gongsi, *Tiantie jingshen*, 120.

[64] *Jingji ribao*, December 19, 1983, 1.

building" (*huan jian*), and central government investment in the project dried up.[65] As Tianjin struggled to fund the plant on its own, the scale of the project shrunk. More than four thousand of the Tianjin construction workers at the site and more than three thousand Tianjin youths were reassigned back to the city. Many of those left behind in Shexian requested transfers, but as former factory leaders remembered, "the city government was afraid that the hearts and minds of people at the site were chaotic, so it adopted a lockdown policy of not allowing even one [more] worker to return to the city."[66]

When little changed after Mao's death and the end of the Cultural Revolution, ironworks employees' passive slowdowns turned into open resistance. Workers demanded transfers back to Tianjin. At the very least, they wanted better lives at the ironworks. This second demand centered on marriage and family issues. The demobilized soldiers assigned to the site in 1970 were mostly from villages in north China. By 1978, they had been living apart from their wives for more than ten years, and were only allowed home leave every year or two. The men held Tianjin *hukou*, but their wives and children had agricultural *hukou* and were not allowed to move to the ironworks.

While ex-soldiers asked to be reunited with their wives, the Tianjin youths demanded wives, period. By 1978, most of the Tianjin middle-school graduates left in Shexian were men. They were in their mid-twenties, with no good marriage prospects. The young men ruled out marrying local women because of cultural differences, the tense history between the ironworks and nearby villages, and, most important, the women's rural *hukou*. This last issue was particularly relevant because future children would assume their mother's *hukou* status (unlike official class labels, which were inherited from the father).[67] Workers at the ironworks remembered that the frustrated Tianjin men organized marches and sit-ins at factory headquarters. More than three hundred of them even traveled back to Tianjin for sustained protests in 1979. There, the

[65] Wang Jinming, "Jiannan quzhe de fazhan licheng – Tianjin tiechang sanshi nian jingji fazhan huigu" [Difficulties and setbacks on the course of development – Looking back on thirty years of economic development at the Tianjin Ironworks], *Tansuo yu yanjiu*, no. 3 (August 5, 1999): 41.

[66] Tianjin tiantie yejin jituan youxian gongsi, *'35 licheng*, 47.

[67] Potter and Potter speculate that this "departure from customary assumptions about the inheritance of status" may have come from the state's desire to "restrict mobility as effectively as possible. Since men are much more likely to shift status than women, having the child take the mother's status means that far fewer children will shift status." Potter and Potter, *China's Peasants*, 304.

men occupied offices, lay down in front of the municipal government gate, and held a "teach-in" (*xuanjiang*) that attracted a crowd of onlookers. On three occasions the protesting ironworks employees marched through city streets and blocked traffic, yelling "we want jobs, we want democracy, we want freedom, we want wives" (*yao gongzuo, yao minzhu, yao ziyou, yao laopo*).[68] This last demand was the most pressing of all. Finally, ironworks leaders agreed to listen to the men's demands at a large meeting in the main auditorium back in Gengle.

As Nie Bichu recalled, ironworks and Tianjin officials worked together to address the "youths' conjugal fate."[69] Hao Cheng, the ironworks' party secretary between 1978 and 1980, arranged a novel solution called the "recruit fiancées" (*zhao weihunqi*) policy. The men were given two options. They could quit the ironworks and return to Tianjin, but they would receive no assistance in finding jobs and wives. With thousands of returned sent-down youth already crowding the city and looking for work, this was a risky choice, but many took it. Or, the Tianjin men could agree to stay at the ironworks and the factory would help resolve their conjugal fate.

The demobilized soldiers put out word to their home villages in Hebei and Shanxi that ironworks employees required wives. Eligible village women who were chosen by ironworkers would get non-agricultural *hukou* and paying jobs on-site. Young women, eager to receive these benefits, made their way to Shexian (by the hundreds, according to one source). What followed was a remarkable state-sanctioned singles meetup. The Tianjin men who had chosen to stay at the plant met with rural prospects (collectively dubbed Qiu Xiang, after the folk tale "Tang Baihu Chooses Qiu Xiang") in a series of interviews that ended when both parties assented to a match. Not all women who came were chosen. Generally, women with some education who were from villages near Tianjin were the hottest picks, because their customs and cooking were familiar to the Tianjin men. We can only imagine what rural bachelors were thinking as the most attractive women in their region packed their bags and left to marry urban strangers.

Gengle villagers did not have a problem with the arrangement. They knew about "choosing Qiu Xiang" (*dian Qiu Xiang*), but it affected few

[68] Tianjin shi geming weiyuanhui, *Tongzhi* [Directive], *Jingefa* [1979] 33 (April 10, 1979), AC.

[69] Tianjin tiantie yejin jituan youxian gongsi, '*35 licheng*, 41. The following narrative is based on conversations with interviewees 18, 19, 24, and 27.

of them directly. Gengle militia leader Zou Shaorui was still friendly with ironworks leadership. Hao Cheng tried to arrange for Zou's daughter to become a Qiu Xiang. This would have meant a salary and a non-agricultural *hukou* for the young woman, but she refused. There were very few marriages between ironworks workers and locals, Zou said, because Gengle people did not like to marry outsiders. "We're pretty conservative," Zou explained.

The Tianjin men had either quit and returned to the city, or, buoyed by martial bliss, stayed behind to continue working at the ironworks. But demobilized soldiers, who had played a major role in arranging the Qiu Xiang matches, still endured separation from their own families. By 1980, the veterans had the option of retiring and being "replaced" (*dingti*) at the factory by one of their children. Most of them were too young to retire. If the Tianjin youths' Qiu Xiang could move to the factory, why were the soldiers' families still shut out?

The ex-soldiers' consternation may have contributed to a protest in 1982 called the "February 19 incident," when people "surrounded and besieged" factory leaders.[70] Again, loud resistance got leaders' attention. Tianjin Vice-Mayor Hao Tianyi visited the ironworks in 1983 and surveyed employees. Family problems and a shortage of meat and eggs topped the list of complaints. In February 1984, Nie Bichu, Tianjin's vice mayor in charge of economic planning, called a meeting of top city officials to discuss problems at the ironworks. Tianjin officials decided that ironworks employees would be guaranteed a quarter kilogram of meat and eggs per month. Workers were also allowed to quit the ironworks and reunite with families in their home villages. If they chose to stay in Shexian, two of each worker's children could be hired as ironworks employees under a deal remembered as the "recruit old workers' children" policy. Once the army men's children entered the ironworks, their wives began to arrive, too. The women were finally granted non-agricultural *hukou* status in 1985.[71]

The family problems of some workers had been resolved, but so many people had left the ironworks in the late 1970s and early 1980s that the site was experiencing a labor shortage. Ironworks leaders admitted that because of the "reality that the ironworks is in a mountain village . . . it would not work to transfer new employees and cadres in from Tianjin any more." In 1970, faced with a choice between a job at the ironworks

[70] Lu, Yu, and Zhao, "Pijing zhanji dandang tiecheng weishi," 205.
[71] Tianjin tiantie yejin jituan youxian gongsi, '35 *licheng*, 48; interviewee 27.

and becoming an unpaid sent-down youth in a village (which meant being locked out of the city indefinitely), the Tianjin youths had gone to Project 6985. After the sent-down youth program was cancelled, nobody from Tianjin wanted to go to Shexian. The ironworks needed a new source of labor.

The plant began hiring people from Shexian to fill its empty production positions.[72] Locals were hired on as long-term contract workers. They kept their agricultural *hukou* and did not get guaranteed grain rations. A March 1984 *People's Daily* article lauded the ironworks' recruitment of 550 "peasants who work at the factory during the day, eat and live at home after work, and can plant their fields in their spare time and on holidays." The article baldly celebrated the advantages of employing peasant contract workers: "if they do a good job, they can extend their contracts; if they do a bad job, the factory has the right to fire them."[73]

The influx of local contract workers accompanied other big changes at the ironworks in the 1980s. The December 1983 *Economic Daily* exposé about the factory was a signal that problems at the ironworks had attracted the attention of central authorities. Indeed, Vice Premier Wan Li visited officials in Handan, Shijiazhuang, and Tianjin to discuss the possibility of Hebei province assuming control of the plant. Hebei leaders were interested, and some Tianjin officials welcomed the chance to jettison the costly enterprise. The patch of Tianjin land was on the verge of being recovered by Hebei.

Tianjin vice mayor Hao Tianyi, who had been the top party secretary at the Baotou Steel Mill in the late 1970s, wanted the ironworks to remain Tianjin territory. In the reform period, the city still needed metal. Hao convinced his reluctant Tianjin colleagues that the city should keep the enclave. He traveled to Beijing and persuaded national economic planners that the ironworks simply needed good management. Central authorities decided that the enclave would still be part of Tianjin, but under a new arrangement. The city would no longer cover the plant's economic losses, but in the event that the ironworks actually made money, Tianjin would not receive profits either. In order to survive, the ironworks had to become financially sustainable. It could reinvest its profits in future improvements, but its iron still had to go to Tianjin.

In 1984, the ironworks turned its first profit. It began producing steel in 1994. By 2005, the Tianjin Tiantie Metallurgical Group Corporation's

[72] Tianjin tiantie yejin jituan youxian gongsi, '35 *licheng*, 48.
[73] RMRB, March 29, 1984, 2.

fuel, lime, iron, and steel factories lined the highway for miles east of Gengle. Chief Executive Officer and party secretary Liu Zhijia, a former electrician who moved to Project 6985 from Tianjin in the early 1970s, had become a national labor model. When workers with Tianjin *hukou* retire, the company gives them comfortable apartments, but not in Shexian. The dwellings are in a gated community on the outskirts of Tianjin. It is taken for granted that the workers want to retire to the city.

On the other side of Tianjin, huge new buildings have appeared at the Worker-Peasant Alliance farm in recent years, but for different reasons. Tianjin's expanding urban boundaries have reached the farm. The road from Wangdingdi (where Mao visited in 1956) to the farm's vegetable team passes by several new schools, research institutes, and businesses. These stand on what was once Worker-Peasant Alliance farm land. The road then passes a set of decrepit four-story apartment buildings, known as the Worker-Peasant Mansions, built for farm workers in 1979. In 2005, the farm's vegetable team remained as it was in the 1960s and 1970s: single-story brick houses and dirt alleys.

The farm and ironworks experienced similar difficulties in the 1970s and 1980s, including leadership change, worker flight, and economic losses, but saw different outcomes. Many of the twenty-two hundred educated youth sent to the farm in the 1970s were unenthusiastic about their assignment. Picking vegetables and milking cows next to political exiles felt like punishment. They spent as much time in the city as possible, and left the farm as soon as they had the chance. Five hundred were assigned to city jobs in 1976 and 1977. By 1980, all of the educated youth sent to the farm during the 1970s had returned to Tianjin.[74]

All spaces are constructed and shaped by social, economic, and political forces. But the ironworks and state farm were more artificial than Tianjin neighborhoods or north Chinese villages. These intermediate zones were established by state mandate. Without state intervention, the spaces would wither and die. That is what happened at the Worker-Peasant Alliance Farm, which has slowly disappeared. The ironworks was such an artificial state-constructed space that without the policy of recruiting wives for Tianjin workers, it was impossible for residents to reproduce and sustain the island.

The state farm, the ironworks, and other spaces like them challenge the stock image of a sharp dichotomy between rural and urban China during the 1960s and 1970s. The islands of Tianjin land in the suburbs and

[74] NCS, 74.

in the Taihang mountains carried urban administrative designations, and the people who worked inside the enclaves called themselves urban workers. But the spaces' geographic settings – and the villagers who knocked holes in their walls – clashed with official designations. During the Mao period, the state had the power to bestow labels on people and spaces, and it had the carrots (material benefits for urban residents) and sticks (restrictions on movement and forced requisition of grain) to make its categories meaningful. Black-and-white administrative categories, however, did not automatically simplify a complex society, nor did they guarantee obedience. At the Worker-Peasant Alliance and the Tianjin Ironworks, city people seeking happy family lives and villagers in need of extra income not only contested the urban-rural divide, they won significant victories against it.

The experiences of people affected by the state farm and ironworks illustrate the variety of factors that defined "urban" and "rural" in Mao's China. Administrative categories, notions of work and labor, and cultural differences including food, clothing, and language all came into play. Early visitors to Gengle had trouble adjusting to the local diet, choked on the dirty water, and gaped at villagers' dirty clothing. Villagers eyeballed the outsiders' clean suits and assumed that the ironworks employees did not do real work. The two groups sometimes came together for cultural functions and to trade steamed buns for fruit and nuts, but these interactions were not entirely friendly. Villagers mistrusted young ironworks employees who pilfered fruit, while factory officials struggled to keep locals from stealing industrial products. Mutually unintelligible dialects increased the likelihood of misunderstandings.

All of these factors converged in the handling of the marriage problem at the ironworks. *Hukou* and jobs shaped the conflict and determined its resolution. Tianjin women who already held urban *hukou* would have been the most desirable match for the young men, but few were willing to relocate to a remote mountain compound. In contrast, the promise of non-agricultural *hukou* and paid work offered a rare opportunity for rural women to leave their home counties and improve their economic standing. Women from areas of Hebei province closer to Tianjin seemed more attractive to ironworks men than Gengle women, who ate strange food and spoke a different language. The feeling was mutual. Gengle women were uninterested in marrying into the factory, even though they could have received jobs and Tianjin *hukou*. Rural-urban difference in the 1970s combined cultural signifiers with administrative distinctions. Face-to-face interactions and state-imposed categories reinforced each other in a mutual feedback loop.

The final chapter turns to another unique place: a village called Xiaojinzhuang north of Tianjin where residents sang revolutionary opera, wrote poetry, and, beginning in 1974, guided tours for thousands of urban visitors. Like residents of Gengle, the people of Xiaojinzhuang had to contend with an invasion of disruptive outsiders from Tianjin. They also took advantage of this turn of events, and some even became famous. Their fame was fleeting, however, and did not translate into power.

8

Staging Xiaojinzhuang

The Urban Occupation of a Model Village, 1974–1978

As I stepped out of a minivan and greeted Wang Zuoshan, the sixty-nine-year-old former village party secretary of Xiaojinzhuang, my taxi driver suddenly realized that he recognized the old man. Driver Li had last seen Wang in the late 1970s, when Li was an elementary school student in the Baodi county seat, a town about forty-five miles north of Tianjin and fifty-three miles southeast of Beijing. Li was part of a crowd of ten thousand watching transfixed as Wang, kneeling on an elevated stage in the town's main square, bowed his head and accepted the slaps and insults of his accusers.[1] This was a time of political upheaval in China. Mao Zedong had died, and his wife and the rest of the "Gang of Four" were arrested as the curtain fell on the Cultural Revolution. But after Mao's death, Wang Zuoshan was the target of a classic Cultural Revolution ritual, the mass criticism and struggle meeting.

Wang Zuoshan had the misfortune of being the leader of Xiaojinzhuang, a village of 101 households on the Jian'gan river. His village, about a thirty minute drive east of the Baodi county seat, became a national model for arts and culture after Jiang Qing visited in June 1974 and called it her "spot." Wang and other villagers emerged as the poetry-writing and opera-singing stars of a political drama sponsored by Jiang and staged by her allies in the Tianjin municipal leadership. Xiaojinzhuang's fortune was tied to Jiang Qing and other "radicals" who sought power by affirming the anti-capitalist, collectivist Cultural Revolution policies of constant class struggle and strict artistic standards. The model village became a weapon in the radicals' 1974–1976 political

[1] Interviewee 28, Interviewee 29.

battle against "moderate" targets of the Cultural Revolution like Deng Xiaoping, who advocated economic pragmatism, a limited return to private plots in agriculture, and more relaxed arts policies.[2]

Yet Xiaojinzhuang and its residents were more than just bit players in the mid-1970s drama over whether to embrace or repudiate the radical politics of the Cultural Revolution. As a rural model, Xiaojinzhuang was presented to all of China as a cultural utopia worthy of emulation. The fantasy image of Xiaojinzhuang, which included a vibrant night school, prolific poets, skilled singers, and policies encouraging gender equality, was only loosely based on village reality. It was instead the invention of urban politicians who disdained and distrusted rural residents. While the most prominent aspects of Xiaojinzhuang's model utopia changed according to the shifting needs of city authorities – from agricultural advances in the early 1970s to education, culture, and women's equality in 1974, and finally to anti-Deng Xiaoping insults in 1976 – villagers' lack of political influence remained constant. Xiaojinzhuang's inferior position allowed city officials to colonize the village and transform it into their cultural theme park. This development sparked discontent from people who lived in and around Xiaojinzhuang. In spite of their political subjugation, villagers asserted themselves in a variety of ways. Some embraced the experience of living in a model village and garnered national fame, while others complained about the urban-imposed changes.

When Wang Zuoshan knelt in front of thousands and winced from stinging slaps in the late 1970s, he and his village were double losers. Not only was their political line deemed incorrect after Jiang Qing's arrest, but they were victims of a system that put villages on the lowest rung of a political hierarchy dominated by city officials.

This hierarchy helps to explain how the countryside became a dumping ground for urban political exiles during the Cultural Revolution, and it is also what allowed urban officials to colonize model villages while denying villagers a voice in political and economic decisions. Yet while urban politicians had the upper hand in establishing and manipulating models, some residents of model villages enjoyed newfound privileges and benefits, however short-lived. Because city officials felt the need to cultivate prominent rural models during the 1970s, villagers like Wang Zuoshan who collaborated in the model-making process were able to

[2] Edward Friedman, "The Politics of Local Models, Social Transformation and State Power Struggles in the People's Republic of China: Tachai and Teng Hsiao-p'ing," *China Quarterly* 76 (1978): 874.

gain more power, fame, and leisure time than they had ever imagined. Wang and his village's rise and fall can be explained by a political culture that publicly celebrated rural China while privately scorning villages and the people who lived in them.

With fewer than six hundred residents, Xiaojinzhuang is a small village by north China standards. The village was known for growing garlic but boasted no remarkable achievements during the 1950s and early 1960s, when it suffered from constant flooding and low-yielding saline-alkaline soil. During the Great Leap Forward in 1959, villagers labored for a month removing water from low-lying land near the river. They threw seeds onto the exposed mud and reported their success to commune headquarters, but a few days later a rainstorm washed away their hard work. Xiaojinzhuang residents went hungry and gnawed on raw garlic for sustenance.[3]

Rural Baodi had long enjoyed a rich cultural life. Many villages had their own opera troupes, and most villagers could sing a few lines of *pingju*, the local opera of north China.[4] During the Cultural Revolution, old opera ensembles were dismantled, but some people in Baodi continued to sing the didactic revolutionary model operas promoted by Jiang Qing. Xiaojinzhuang itself escaped major turbulence during the early stage of the Cultural Revolution. There was no temple to smash, so people burned books and struggled against a poor soul who was designated a "capitalist roader."[5] During the power seizures that swept across China in 1967, some Xiaojinzhuang brigade leaders were forced to "step aside."[6] Wang Tinghe, a longstanding leader who had served as village party secretary, was punished for his "capitalist roader mistakes," but he returned as a vice-secretary shortly after Xiaojinzhuang's government was reconstituted as a revolutionary committee.[7] This was a typical pattern in rural north China, and there appeared to be little about the village's experience in 1966–1969 to foreshadow Xiaojinzhuang's meteoric rise.

Setting the Stage: The City in the Countryside

Without question, it was Jiang Qing's visit in June 1974 that catapulted Xiaojinzhuang to national prominence. In the immediate wake of Jiang's

[3] Liu Bingrong, "Wo suo zhidao de Xiaojinzhuang" [What I know about Xiaojinzhuang], *Dangshi bolan* 6 (2002): 40.
[4] Ibid.
[5] GJG:1, 5.
[6] Interviewee 30.
[7] GJG:2, 12.

tour, the city headed for the countryside, an event which intimated drastic changes for the village. In effect Xiaojinzhuang was set apart from the surrounding countryside, even though its physical location in rural China was never in question. Tianjin-based authorities and work team members occupied the village and packaged it into their utopian vision of rural China. This image was the product of urban officials' imaginations and the political dicta of the time, which required rhetorically supporting the virtues of rural socialist construction. Urban and military models were fine, and Jiang Qing had those too. As an ambitious politician and cultural revolutionary, however, she needed the jewel in the crown of the "worker-peasant-soldier" triumvirate. She needed a rural model, and Tianjin leaders placed it in her lap. For Jiang, it was immaterial that the city's role in staging the Xiaojinzhuang show would shape the village into a repository of urban imaginings of the countryside.

If Jiang Qing was seeking a model village, why did she settle on Xiaojinzhuang? A confluence of village achievements, county-level model-making efforts, city involvement, and national elite politics set the stage for the 1974 occupation. Xiaojinzhuang's rise was neither random nor predetermined. Instead, it was the product of a political environment that pressed local officials into grooming potential rural models so that provincial, municipal, or national officials could use them for symbolic or publicity purposes. Ubiquitous propaganda trumpeted rural advances, but only partially concealed the contemptuous view many urban elites held of Chinese villagers. The model-making process – coupled with anti-rural attitudes – denied local autonomy and sparked intra-village friction, even as it led to fame and new opportunities for some residents.

Xiaojinzhuang first appeared as a blip on the radar screens of Baodi county and Tianjin municipal leaders during the early 1970s. Local authorities had learned not to expect much from the small village. With its poor soil and vulnerability to flooding, Xiaojinzhuang was known as a place with long-standing problems. Things began to change after 1969, when villagers worked during the winter transporting frozen earth to fill in salty swampland near the river.[8] They also dredged the riverbed, built a dyke, and covered the saline-alkaline soil with river mud.[9] These efforts began to pay off with several seasons of increased agricultural yields that attracted the attention of commune and county officials. By 1973, the year that Baodi county became a part of the newly established Tianjin

[8] GJG:1, 5.

[9] Interviewee 31; Pien Tsai, "Peasant Poets of Hsiaochinchuang," *Chinese Literature* 10 (1974): 96–97.

municipality, Xiaojinzhuang produced 551 catties per *mu* and was recognized for its successes by Tianjin authorities.[10] Breaking out of mediocre economic performance was a precondition that had to be met before any village could garner model status.

Crucial to Xiaojinzhuang's local notoriety was the long-term residency of a Baodi county cadre named Hu Penghua. In April 1972, the county propaganda department dispatched Hu to Xiaojinzhuang with orders to develop the village into a model unit. Hu, a Baodi native who graduated from a local high school in 1964, visited a number of other villages before finally settling on Xiaojinzhuang as a promising site. Xiaojinzhuang caught Hu's eye because of its united leadership, comparatively educated populace, and recent agricultural gains.[11]

One of Hu's main tasks in Xiaojinzhuang was to work with the brigade party branch to establish a political night school (*zhengzhi yexiao*) as part of the national movement to study Dazhai, China's most famous model village. The school met three nights a week and provided basic literacy training for illiterate and semi-illiterate residents, along with courses for young people in current events, politics, and agricultural technology.[12] If energetic youth had time they sang model opera excerpts and invented lively political jingles.

Hu's work directing the night school would have attracted little attention had he not produced a steady stream of glowing reports for county officials about Xiaojinzhuang's educational and agricultural progress. Two journalists from a local newspaper in Hebei province caught wind of Hu's reports and decided to visit Xiaojinzhuang. Hu recalled that the propaganda articles he co-authored with the two journalists resulted in several full page spreads on Xiaojinzhuang. This publicity led to inspection visits by Hebei provincial propaganda officials and Zheng Sansheng, second party secretary in Hebei and commander of the Tianjin garrison. But in August 1973, administrative reshuffling placed Baodi county under the control of Tianjin municipality. Hebei authorities could not foster the

[10] On local honors see TJRB, December 19, 1973; on grain yields see Ren Xizeng, "Jiang Qing shu Xiaojinzhuang de qianqian houhou" [The whole story of Jiang Qing establishing Xiaojinzhuang], *Guoshi yanjiu cankao ziliao* 1 (1996): 18. See also Wang Yan, "Xiaojinzhuang yishi" [Xiaojinzhuang anecdote], *Lingdao kexue* (October 2002): 14; and GJG:1, 5. Before August 1973, when Tianjin became the administrative equivalent of a province (*zhixia shi*), Baodi county was part of Hebei province's Tianjin prefecture.

[11] Interviewee 31.

[12] Ren Xizeng, "Jiang Qing shu Xiaojinzhuang de qianqian houhou," 18; Interviewee 31. See also *Xiaojinzhuang zhengzhi yexiao ban de hao* [Xiaojinzhuang's political night school is good] (Beijing: Renmin chubanshe, 1974), 4.

promising village as a potential model anymore, because Xiaojinzhuang was no longer under their jurisdiction. As we have seen in previous chapters, Tianjin and Hebei had been competing for resources since the 1950s. Once again, the city won out over the province. Tianjin could now draw on advanced rural units in Baodi in upcoming campaigns.

Xiaojinzhuang would have remained a simple local success story, had Major General Wu Dai not taken an interest in the village. Wu, along with his fellow Tianjin party secretaries, particularly cultural leader Wang Mantian and first secretary Xie Xuegong, were perfectly situated to become the producers and stage managers of the Xiaojinzhuang show. Much as municipal authorities had facilitated Chen Boda's intervention in Xiaozhan during the Four Cleanups, they worked with Jiang Qing to elevate Xiaojinzhuang to national stardom. They publicized the model in the Tianjin press, invited village representatives to city meetings, and funneled resources to prettify the village. Just as important, Tianjin leaders' reputations as cultural revolutionaries allowed them to bring the village to Jiang Qing's attention. While Wu Dai was a survivor, a military man who rose in prominence after Lin Biao's death, Xie Xuegong and Mao Zedong's cousin Wang Mantian were politicians whose careers took off during the Cultural Revolution. All three promoted their city as a base from which Mao's wife could bolster herself and her politics.

Agriculture in Tianjin fell under the purview of General Wu, who was serving concurrently as vice political commissar of the Beijing military region and Tianjin's second party secretary. Wu's military background made him averse to sitting behind a desk in his city offices. He much preferred driving around the countryside on impromptu inspection visits.[13] Wu enjoyed touring villages, chatting with cadres, and checking up on agricultural production. He visited Xiaojinzhuang and other nearby brigades several times and built up amiable working relations with local officials.[14]

In spite of the good impression Wu Dai had of Xiaojinzhuang, by early 1974 he had not yet settled on the village as a favored spot. In January 1974, Wu Dai sent a ten-person "Spread Dazhai Counties Work Team" (Puji Dazhai xian gongzuo zu) to Baodi county. The work team bypassed Xiaojinzhuang and set up shop instead in Dazhongzhuang, a

[13] Interviewee 11.

[14] Journalist Gao Jianguo reports on the first visit of a general in a jeep from Beijing, GJG:1, 4; Wang Zuoshan told a reporter in March 2002 that Wu Dai inspected the village on several occasions, Wang Yan, "Xiaojinzhuang yishi," 14.

larger village and commune headquarters that had come to Wu Dai's attention on one of his rural tours.[15] But only a few weeks after the work team's arrival, a new nationwide political movement blew on the scene, confounding the outside cadres in Dazhongzhuang and paving the way for Xiaojinzhuang's rise.

Perhaps Wu Dai viewed Dazhongzhuang as the most appropriate spot for a work team to preach the Dazhai message of self-reliance and innovation in agriculture. Yet the new campaign to criticize Lin Biao and Confucius, initiated by Jiang Qing and her allies with the approval of Mao at the end of 1973, was better suited to Xiaojinzhuang. At the national level, this campaign pitted political beneficiaries of the Cultural Revolution like Jiang Qing against veteran officials linked to Premier Zhou Enlai. Both sides used esoteric historical arguments to battle over the significance of the past eight years and who would lead China after Mao.[16] Not surprisingly, in Chinese villages the campaign bore scant resemblance to the epic struggle between Confucianism and Legalism depicted in the national press.

According to the former head of the 1974 work team, farmers in Dazhongzhuang, like their counterparts throughout rural China, were unenthusiastic about the anti-Confucius campaign.[17] The work team struggled to connect with residents who had never read any of Confucius's works. Under pressure from superiors in Tianjin to produce positive reports about the campaign, harried urban cadres called meetings and urged farmers to rail against feudal sayings. Although *Tianjin Daily* featured several vague front-page articles praising Dazhongzhuang's achievements, the unwieldy anti-Confucius movement was threatening to sink the village's utility as a model.[18]

Meanwhile, Tianjin municipal leaders including Wu Dai learned that Jiang Qing wanted to visit their city after she read an internal report about vigorous "Criticize Lin Biao, Criticize Confucius" activities at the Tianjin railway station. She would be coming to promote the campaign by identifying and publicizing additional models, including an army unit and a village.[19] Wu Dai was well aware of his work team's troubles in Dazhongzhuang. He realized that smaller Xiaojinzhuang, with its night

[15] Interviewee 11.

[16] Maurice Meisner, *Mao's China and After: A History of the People's Republic*, 3rd ed. (New York: Free Press, 1999), 392–93.

[17] Interviewee 11.

[18] TJRB, February 12, 1974, 1; TJRB, March 1, 1974, 1.

[19] Interviewee 11.

school and more lively cultural activities, might be just what Jiang Qing was looking for.

On June 19, 1974, Jiang Qing spoke in Tianjin at a large meeting about the historical struggle between Confucianism and Legalism.[20] After her speech, Tianjin leaders puffed up the package they were offering to Jiang Qing. At a Tianjin hotel, municipal officials reported to Jiang on a number of advanced villages in the region. None especially interested Jiang until Wu Dai mentioned an exciting village that boasted a successful night school and lively cultural activities.[21] Tianjin authorities carefully stressed that Xiaojinzhuang's night school not only excelled at political study, but also featured revolutionary model opera singing and poetry readings.[22] The mention of singing got Jiang Qing's attention. As the promoter of officially sanctioned model dramas during the Cultural Revolution, it was pleasing to hear that villagers in rural China were singing "her" songs.[23] "I want to go to Xiaojinzhuang," Jiang said, and after perfunctory protestations that the road to the village was too rough, her Tianjin allies assented to the visit.[24]

Propaganda about Xiaojinzhuang ramped up. On the morning of June 21, 1974, a report about the village's night school appeared on the front page of *Tianjin Daily*.[25] Wu Dai also summoned Baodi county leaders and Xiaojinzhuang's party secretary Wang Zuoshan to a meeting in Tianjin.[26] Wang called back to the village and told his colleagues in the party branch to expect an inspection visit from a central leader. Municipal authorities informed villagers of their scripts, instructing them to prepare a meeting to criticize reactionary sayings and to be ready to sing excerpts from

[20] Copies of her speech were first circulated as important study materials, but after 1976 were distributed again as examples of her ambitious "bid to be empress." Ross Terrill, *Madame Mao: The White-Boned Demon*, rev. ed. (Stanford: Stanford University Press, 1999), 265. *Jiang Qing tongzhi zai "Tianjin shi ru fa douzheng shi baogao hui" shang de zhongyao jianghua* [Comrade Jiang Qing's important talk at the Tianjin meeting on the history of the struggle between Confucianism and Legalism], June 19, 1974, 1, 9, 11, AC.

[21] Interviewee 11; Ren Xizeng, "Jiang Qing shu Xiaojinzhuang de qianqian houhou," 18.

[22] GJG:1, 5.

[23] Xiaomei Chen debunks the notion that Jiang Qing created the eight model works all by herself, but it is clear that Jiang was proud of her role in shaping and producing the operas, dramas, and ballet. Xiaomei Chen, *Acting the Right Part: Political Theater and Popular Drama in Contemporary China* (Honolulu: University of Hawai'i Press, 2002), 86, 105–7.

[24] GJG:1, 6.

[25] TJRB, June 21, 1974, 1.

[26] Interviewee 32.

revolutionary model operas. Baodi cadre Hu Penghua scrambled to coach seventeen hand-picked villagers on their lines.[27]

To many villagers, a visit from Mao's wife was an honor and an exciting diversion. Just as Chen Boda's perceived proximity to the chairman allowed him to convince people in the Tianjin region to do his bidding, Jiang Qing's apparent closeness to Mao was the main source of her authority. Power emanated from the center, but not much of it trickled down to the village level. Xiaojinzhuang was enmeshed in a model-making process that kept political control out of villagers' hands. They had become tools of urban politicians eager to earn points in an environment that required rhetorical celebration of rural models.

By encouraging Mao's wife to visit Xiaojinzhuang, Tianjin leaders had placed the village on a national stage. The urban invasion of Xiaojinzhuang began in earnest when Jiang Qing stepped out of a sedan in the center of the village on the morning of June 22, 1974. She was wearing a skirt and white sandals, and she was not alone. Her entourage totaled around forty people, including opera singers, cultural officials, Tianjin leaders, and members of the Liang Xiao writing group (a team of professors from Tsinghua University and Peking University who were the rhetorical brain trust behind a series of historical articles linking Lin Biao's "revisionism" to Confucius).[28] Also on hand were Hou Jun and Xing Yanzi, Baodi county's two famous "iron girls" (*tie guniang*) who had been celebrated as models since the early 1960s for volunteering to return to their villages instead of pursuing city jobs or university educations.[29] Thanks to Jiang's visit to Xiaojinzhuang, several village residents would soon join Hou and Xing as national celebrities.

Jiang Qing toured the village and nearby fields, and then the preselected Xiaojinzhuang villagers joined Jiang and her entourage for a meeting.[30] Young women sang excerpts from revolutionary operas, which pleased Jiang. In an anti-Confucian mood, Jiang also took it upon herself to suggest name changes for villagers whose names she deemed "too feudal." Thus Wang Xiaoxian, an instructor in Xiaojinzhuang's

[27] Interviewee 31; GJG:1, 6.

[28] "Liang Xiao" was the pen name under which articles by the writing group were published. This was a homonym for "two schools," meaning Tsinghua and Peking Universities.

[29] Hou Jun, *Jiang Qing san ci qu Xiaojinzhuang de bufen jianghua he huodong* [Parts of Jiang Qing's talks and activities during her three visits to Xiaojinzhuang], October 14, 1976, AC.

[30] Wang Yan, "Xiaojinzhuang yishi," 14.

political night school, became Wang Miekong (Wang "Exterminate Confucius").[31] After over an hour of reports, singing, poetry reading, and name changing, the meeting broke up.

Xiaojinzhuang would do, Jiang Qing decided. As she was preparing to leave, she turned to the Tianjin leaders at her side. "Comrade Xie Xuegong, you must come here often," she told the municipal first secretary. "This is my spot (*wo de dian*), and if you don't run it well you'll be prodded." She asked to be given status reports on Xiaojinzhuang in the future, "because I don't know how often I'll come around to my spot."[32] Jiang would only make it back to the village twice, once with Imelda Marcos in September 1974 and again in August 1976, when she was embroiled in a struggle over who would succeed the ailing Mao as China's leader. But Jiang's loud claim during her first visit that she was representing party center and Chairman Mao, plus her instructions to Xie Xuegong, were enough to change everything for the village. A few days after Jiang Qing's visit, a joint Tianjin-Baodi work team, along with Beijing-based writers, teachers, and coaches, moved into Xiaojinzhuang and the commune guesthouse down the road.[33] This outside work team – and not the village's party branch – became the center of political power in the village. It plunged into producing and staging the model village.

Two leading journalists from the national Xinhua news agency traveled to Xiaojinzhuang and wrote a confidential article that was distributed to party center and provincial leaders throughout China. The piece alerted officials to prepare propaganda materials. A separate article by the Liang Xiao writing group about Xiaojinzhuang's night school garnered Jiang Qing's approval for nationwide dissemination and appeared in *People's Daily* and *Tianjin Daily* on September 8. By fall 1974, extensive publicity had enshrined Xiaojinzhuang as a national model, and visitors began to flow into the village to view opera performances and poetry readings.

If the new work team, Xinhua journalists, and Liang Xiao writers produced these performances, then what was the script that villagers were expected to follow? In 1970s China, urban politicians did not share a uniform vision of the countryside. The image of Xiaojinzhuang presented to the nation reflected one specific use of rural China by such leaders as Jiang Qing and her Tianjin allies whose political careers depended on celebrating, defending, and continuing the Cultural Revolution. In the face of

[31] Liu Bingrong, "Wo suo zhidao de Xiaojinzhuang," 42.
[32] Hou Jun, *Jiang Qing san ci qu Xiaojinzhuang*, 2.
[33] Interviewee 31.

challenges from moderates like Deng Xiaoping who emphasized production, Xiaojinzhuang had to confirm the benefits the Cultural Revolution had brought to villages. This vision mandated that cultural advances and attention to political movements could not be sacrificed to the details of agricultural work.

A pro–Cultural Revolution script emphasizing transformation in culture and consciousness guided Xiaojinzhuang as it ballooned from a modest local advanced unit to a national model during the summer and fall of 1974. On August 4, a front page *People's Daily* article about "Xiaojinzhuang's ten new things" conveyed the essence of radical urban elites' utopian vision of the countryside.[34] The "ten new things" script, penned by Xinhua and *Tianjin Daily* journalists, along with Baodi propaganda cadre Hu Penghua, wildly exaggerated the village's achievements.[35] Xiaojinzhuang's ten innovations included starting a political night school, building up a team of poor and lower-middle peasants versed in Marxist theory and anti-Confucian history, singing revolutionary model operas, establishing an art propaganda team, writing poems, opening a library, telling revolutionary stories, developing sports activities, and "transforming social traditions, destroying the old and establishing the new" (*yifeng yisu, pojiu lixin*). This item, number ten on the list, focused mostly on gender equality, including encouraging newly engaged women to return betrothal gifts and delay their wedding dates. The article applauded married women for drawing up birth control plans and convincing their husbands to share in household chores.

Missing from the roster of ten new things was agriculture, one of the advances that attracted county officials to Xiaojinzhuang in the first place. The script instead emphasized the village's "revolution in the superstructural sphere" (*shangceng jianzhu lingyu geming*), a key message for culture-first politicians during the mid-1970s.[36] The cultural bent of the ten new things comprised the main theme of the Xiaojinzhuang show, and subsequent publicity, as well as the physical appearance of the village

[34] RMRB, August 4, 1974, 1. This article was reprinted in at least seven books about Xiaojinzhuang and also appeared in provincial newspapers all across China.

[35] Interviewee 31. Before Jiang Qing's visit Hu was involved in writing an article on Xiaojinzhuang's "Eight New Things," which was revised and augmented later in 1974.

[36] Jiang Qing was following Mao's reversal of the Marxist idea that social being determines consciousness. Mao believed that instead of material advances leading to cultural change, only a remolding of people's consciousness through revolutionary cultural offerings could transform the other realms of Chinese society, including economic life. Meisner, *Mao's China and After*, 315. See also Roxane Witke, *Comrade Chiang Ch'ing* (Boston: Little, Brown and Company, 1977), 3.

itself, had to reflect this script. Resources, advisers, coaches, journalists, and tourists poured into the village, in effect creating a cultural theme park. In addition to funds spent on fixing the road into Xiaojinzhuang, the village received 100,781 yuan in grants, 51,800 yuan in loans, 370,000 bricks and tiles, 135.99 cubic meters of wood, 155 tons of fertilizer, and 92 kilograms of steel products. Around 9,000 yuan were spent to improve toilet facilities.[37]

How did Xiaojinzhuang residents handle their roles in the political drama that had overtaken the village since June 1974? Although urban politicians had taken control of the village for their own purposes, villagers still had room to maneuver. Some enjoyed the privilege of living in a model village newly rich from state resources, while others rejected the city-imposed script. A few, like village leader Wang Zuoshan, rose to become stars of the show. But life in the spotlight was not easy.

Stars and Show Stealers: Model Villagers Scripted and Unscripted

Wang Zuoshan, village party secretary since 1969, received the most national exposure of anyone from Xiaojinzhuang. For the producers pushing the Xiaojinzhuang message, this hard-working young cadre was an ideal leading man. According to their script, Wang Zuoshan was undeniable proof of the success of the Cultural Revolution in rural China. Yet Wang would later self-effacingly describe himself to visitors as an "ignorant peasant," a "donkey in a stable awaiting orders," and a "dung beetle on an airplane, stinking to high heaven."[38] There is no question that Wang Zuoshan soared like an airplane from 1974 to 1976. He threw himself wholeheartedly into his prominent role as a rural promoter of the Cultural Revolution, traveling extensively, giving speeches to cheering crowds, and bantering with such prominent figures as table tennis star Zhuang Zedong. Model villages required model village leaders, and Wang played the role with brio.

Wang Zuoshan was a young man of "poor peasant" background whose family, fleeing famine conditions elsewhere, settled in Xiaojinzhuang earlier in the twentieth century.[39] His status as a relative outsider may have helped him rise in the village's leadership ranks during

[37] Journalist Gao Jianguo gathered these figures from documents he viewed in the Baodi county archives during the 1980s; GJG:1, 11.

[38] Interviewee 32; Liu Bingrong, "Wo suo zhidao de Xiaojinzhuang," 42; GJG:2, 9.

[39] Interviewee 31; Interviewee 33.

the Cultural Revolution (later, this lack of local ties would hasten his downfall). He became Xiaojinzhuang's party secretary in 1969, when the village's party branch was reconstituted after the Ninth Party Congress. Wang was twenty-six years old at the time. After taking charge, he promoted the agricultural improvements that led to three straight bumper harvests and local recognition for the village. Young Wang Zuoshan's considerable successes centered on increased agricultural production. Until Jiang Qing visited the village on June 22, 1974, he had managed to successfully balance the competing demands of rural residents and his superiors.

Jiang Qing's first visit was going smoothly for Wang Zuoshan until he unwittingly offended Mao's thin-skinned wife. After deferentially reporting to Jiang, the young secretary accompanied her and Tianjin city leaders to a wheat field, where Jiang wanted to stage photos harvesting with a sickle.[40] Jiang took a few awkward whacks at the wheat stalks, and a concerned Wang urged her to stop, fearing that she would get tired. She exploded at the well-intentioned cadre. "Leave me alone! What the hell are you doing?" (*Ni bu yong guan wo, ni shi gan shenme de?*) she yelled.[41] After this incident, Tianjin officials decided to keep Wang away from Jiang Qing. He was not allowed to leave his home when Jiang accompanied Imelda Marcos to Xiaojinzhuang in September 1974. He had a cold, he said, and city leaders were afraid he might be contagious.

Wang Zuoshan's run-in with Jiang Qing may have diminished Tianjin leaders' confidence in him, but he continued to host visitors to Xiaojinzhuang, including the writer Hao Ran, who wrote glowingly of the party branch secretary as a "heroic grassroots cadre."[42] Wang still carried symbolic power as a new kind of villager, a creative achiever who could combine agricultural success with cultural advances. He remained the public face of Xiaojinzhuang and was honored as a representative and standing committee member of the Fourth National People's Congress in January 1975. Wang Zuoshan attempted to patch up his relationship with Jiang Qing by sending her positive reports. For Wang, as for so many other people in China during the Cultural Revolution, Jiang's proximity to her deified husband made her a representative, if not an incarnation, of

[40] GJG:2, 7–8. A member of Jiang Qing's entourage described Wang Zuoshan as "fawning upon" (*bajie*), "pandering to" (*yinghe*), and "flattering" (*fengcheng*) Mao's wife, which must have been common responses to her commanding presence. Interviewee 34.

[41] Interviewee 32; GJG:2, 8.

[42] *Xiaojinzhuang de shenke biange* [Xiaojinzhuang's profound change] (Changsha: Hunan renmin chubanshe, 1975), 62, excerpted from RMRB, October 1, 1974, 5.

Mao himself. Wang had journalists stationed in the village write to Jiang to affirm his loyalty to her and Mao – and to their Cultural Revolution, which had transformed him into one of China's most famous villagers.

Jiang Qing appreciated Wang's enthusiasm and reportedly scribbled a note that said, "Wang Zuoshan is a good cadre."[43] After this, Tianjin leaders could not touch him, even if some of them still thought he was "uneducated and clueless" (*mei wenhua, ye mei tounao*).[44] Under Jiang Qing's sponsorship, Wang attended the Central Party Academy in Beijing for six months in 1975, was promoted to Baodi county secretary in 1976, and reportedly received internal approval for a promotion to head a state-level ministry.[45] Wang appeared to relish his prominence and threw himself into the project of defending the Cultural Revolution and his sponsor in speeches and essays. But Wang was too deeply intertwined with Jiang Qing to survive her arrest in October 1976. His promotion to county leader had been based on her support, and for Tianjin leaders, he represented a perfect symbol in the new campaign against the Gang of Four. Many city officials used Wang in order to gain favor with Jiang Qing, but then were the first to blame him when things turned sour. Xiaojinzhuang and Wang Zuoshan were political resources for Jiang Qing and other city leaders, more symbols than real people.

Wang Zuoshan stuck to his script, perhaps too closely, while trying to make the most out of his village's model status. He was the only villager who was incarcerated and publicly pilloried after his patron fell, but other prominent village stars also felt let down by the end of their show's run. For Zhou Kezhou, Yu Fang, and Wang Xian, the energetic young women whose very identities were shaped by Jiang Qing, the village's rise was an empowering rush.

Memoirs and scholarly works have highlighted the pride and excitement many young, unmarried women felt during the Cultural Revolution as they emulated the stars of revolutionary model operas and assumed local leadership roles.[46] In Xiaojinzhuang, Zhou Fulan, Yu Ruifang, and

[43] Interviewee 30; GJG:2, 8.

[44] GJG:2, 8.

[45] Probably the Ministry of Agriculture. Interviewee 30; Zhonggong Tianjin shiwei zuzhibu, Zhonggong Tianjin shiwei dangshi ziliao zhengji weiyuanhui, Tianjin shi dang'anguan, eds., *Zhongguo gongchandang Tianjin shi zuzhi shi ziliao, 1920–1987* [Materials on the history of the Tianjin CCP organization, 1920–1987] (Beijing: Zhongguo chengshi chubanshe, 1991), 392; GJG:2, 7.

[46] Xiaomei Chen, *Acting the Right Part*, 33–46; and Xueping Zhong, Wang Zheng, and Bai Di, eds., *Some of Us: Chinese Women Growing Up in the Mao Era* (New Brunswick, NJ: Rutgers University Press, 2001).

Wang Shuxian belonged to this group. When Jiang Qing first visited the village, she bestowed new revolutionary names on the three women. Jiang's magic touch made the women's identities even more entwined with promoting revolutionary culture. Zhou Fulan, the head of the brigade's women's association, became Zhou Kezhou (Zhou "Overcome Zhou").[47] Yu Ruifang, the women's leader of a village production team, became Yu Fang after Jiang eliminated the offending character "*rui*," which means "auspicious." Wang Shuxian (*shuxian* means "gentle and virtuous"), a militia and youth league member, was now Wang Xian (Wang "First").[48] The young women activists were some of Xiaojinzhuang's busiest stars, performing opera excerpts, giving poetry readings daily for the thousands of visitors to the village, and traveling across China and even to Japan for promotional speaking engagements. These were unique, confidence-building opportunities that would have remained out of Zhou, Yu, and Wang's reach had Jiang Qing chosen another village for her model.

Zhou Kezhou, Wang Xian, and Yu Fang eagerly embraced their leading roles as revolutionary young women, and promoted policies including equal pay for equal work, returning or refusing betrothal gifts, and matrilocal marriage.[49] But while Xiaojinzhuang was a model for equal compensation for women's labor and fighting what Zhou Kezhou called "the buying and selling of women" in marriage, entrenched views about proper gender roles limited the scope of change, particularly in villages that were not prominent models.[50] Even within Xiaojinzhuang, published images reveal the limits of efforts for gender equality in rural China. Wang Xian, the captain of the village's celebrated women's volleyball team, said that the team was formed at the behest of local leaders. They feared that Jiang Qing would lodge accusations of male chauvinism if the only sport

47 This apparent attack on Premier Zhou Enlai was cited after Jiang Qing's arrest as one of her most heinous acts in Xiaojinzhuang. See RMRB, January 12, 1978, 2, and Hou Jun, *Jiang Qing san ci qu Xiaojinzhuang*, 1. During the "Criticize Lin Biao, Criticize Confucius" movement, Jiang directed her writing groups to attack the Duke of Zhou and the Confucian rites (*zhouli*), both of which were alleged to be attacks on Zhou Enlai after the arrest of the Gang of Four.

48 Interviewee 30; Hou Jun, *Jiang Qing san ci qu Xiaojinzhuang*, 1; GJG:1, 6–7.

49 Interviewee 31; Interviewee 33.

50 Women were elevated to local leadership positions throughout China during the "Criticize Lin Biao, Criticize Confucius" campaign, but according to Friedman, Pickowicz, and Selden most men throughout north China were unenthusiastic about policies offering women equal pay. Outside of model villages male leaders ridiculed and blocked measures promoting gender equality. Friedman, Pickowicz, and Selden, *Revolution, Resistance, and Reform in Village China*, 198–202.

played in the village was men's basketball.[51] Interestingly, no one thought to form a women's basketball team or a co-ed team. Basketball was for men, volleyball for women. And in publicity photos of the village's party branch, Zhou Kezhou sits quietly as Wang Zuoshan and four other men lead the discussion.[52] The proper place for the young woman heroes of Xiaojinzhuang was in the propaganda team and women's groups. The party branch belonged to men.

Of the men in the village's party branch, Wang Du was the most politically savvy. A Xiaojinzhuang native, he graduated from the commune high school in 1972 at the age of twenty-one and then became a teacher in the night school, head of the village militia, and vice-secretary of the party branch by 1973.[53] County cadre Hu Penghua lived in Wang Du's home for the full three years he was stationed in Xiaojinzhuang. Hu took Wang Du under his wing and the two collaborated closely, planning the night school's curriculum and writing propaganda together. Wang Du quickly gained the trust of Tianjin leaders and Jiang Qing. Wang Du was more aware than most villagers that Xiaojinzhuang's model experience was highly scripted and he participated actively in creating and modifying the script. He was able to let his writing talents shine, but ended up frustrated by the limits of his rural status. For Wang Du, being a star within the confines of the model village was not enough.

Wang Du was the best poet in Xiaojinzhuang, a village full of farmer bards. While residents of rural Baodi county were renowned for their singing, humorous banter, jingles, and doggerel, Wang Du took these rhymes to a new level and reshaped his neighbors' poems into publishable form. Seven of his poems were included in the 1974 *Xiaojinzhuang Poetry Anthology*, and he considers reciting his "My first visit to Beijing" at a study meeting in the capital to be one of the proudest moments of his life.[54] Wang Du was a product of the forgotten educational successes in China's countryside during the 1970s, when more rural youth attended elementary and middle school than at any other time in China's history.[55] His training allowed him to return home to teach farmers basic Marxism and to become a prolific writer and editor.

[51] GJG:2, 13.

[52] "Xiaojinzhuang de xinshi" [Xiaojinzhuang's new things], *Renmin huabao* (March 1975): 28.

[53] Interviewee 30; GJG:2, 11.

[54] Tianjin renmin chubanshe, ed., *Xiaojinzhuang shige xuan* [Xiaojinzhuang poetry anthology] (Tianjin: Tianjin renmin chubanshe, 1974), 20–21.

[55] Meisner, *Mao's China and After*, 362.

The problem was that Wang Du did not especially want to return to Xiaojinzhuang. He hoped to go to university. During the Cultural Revolution, however, rural primary and middle schools expanded while universities languished. University entrance examinations were abolished and the only route to college was for students classified as "workers, peasants, and soldiers" to rely on personal relations. Wang Du knew full well how this worked. At a meeting in Beijing, he established a good relationship with Liu Zehua, director of the history department at Tianjin's Nankai University. Liu recognized Wang Du's academic potential and sent university representatives to Xiaojinzhuang with an official admission letter. The next step was securing approval from county and Tianjin authorities, which should not have been a problem, considering Wang Du's regular interaction with Tianjin leaders and Jiang Qing. The architects of the Xiaojinzhuang model, however, had different plans. They needed Wang Du right where he was, pumping out poetry.

When Tianjin cultural leader Wang Mantian heard of Wang Du's wishes, she approached him in the village and shook her head. "So, you want to go to university?" she asked. "Isn't Xiaojinzhuang one of the best universities in the country?" His hopes were dashed. "She was a city party secretary, a real big shot," he said. "She had spoken, what could I do?"[56] City elites had their own uses for the countryside and its inhabitants. The Cultural Revolution had expanded educational opportunities in rural areas, but increased schooling bred resentment and frustration when young villagers were not allowed to use their education to advance their careers.

Unable to attend college, Wang Du continued contributing to the Xiaojinzhuang script. When the village was at the forefront of the 1976 campaign to criticize Deng Xiaoping, he was quoted in *People's Daily* excoriating Deng's "nonsense and lies," and wrote poetry blasting the anti-Gang of Four April Fifth Tiananmen protests as "noxious winds and evil waves."[57] Wang Du, like village leader Wang Zuoshan, was deeply implicated in the criticism of Deng, but much better attuned to the changing political winds. He egged Jiang Qing on when she lashed out at Deng during her August 1976 visit to Xiaojinzhuang, yet after her arrest he was quickly in print criticizing her as a "scheming double-dealing counter-revolutionary."[58] Always a master at adhering to and

[56] Interviewee 30; GJG:2, 11.
[57] RMRB, August 29, 1976, 1.
[58] RMRB, November 26, 1976, 3. For a text that depicts Wang Du encouraging Jiang Qing to criticize Deng Xiaoping, see Hou Jun, *Jiang Qing san ci qu Xiaojinzhuang*, 5.

elaborating upon the scripts of the Cultural Revolution's political drama, Wang Du knew that his old lines were passé and adopted new ones.

The celebrities of Xiaojinzhuang collaborated enthusiastically in the village's rise and participated in shaping its political script. They enjoyed their newfound fame and relished the excitement of traveling to the capital and other cities for meetings and speeches. But less prominent villagers scorned the model experience, especially when Xiaojinzhuang's stardom led to tension between opera-singing stars and laboring farmers. In late 1974, politically correct outsiders reportedly criticized discontented villagers for circulating subversive doggerel (*shunkouliu*). One sarcastic rhyme about the "ten ranks of people" recounted how Xiaojinzhuang's rise to national fame had privileged cultural performers and tour guides over laboring farmers.[59] As Perry Link and Kate Zhou have shown, *shunkouliu* provide a vivid glimpse of otherwise hidden popular sentiment.[60]

The "ten ranks" jingle began with the "first rank," people out making deals, living in hotels, eating bread, lavishing gifts and getting reimbursed. It ended with those in the lowly tenth rank, the "old black class" of political enemies who had to engage in compulsory labor without earning work points. Also near the top were the broadcasters who read reports over the loudspeakers (second), the party secretary and militia leader (third), who were almost impossible to find, and propaganda team members (fifth), who could receive a full day's worth of work points just by "singing a few lines of opera." Those in the bottom half of the status ratings included cart drivers (sixth), livestock raisers (eighth), and lowly tillers and farmers (ninth), who "wield a hoe and gasp for air."

Perhaps unaccustomed to the biting doggerel of rural north China, outsiders chastised villagers for reciting lines so at odds with the public image of Xiaojinzhuang as an idyllic farmer's utopia. But for the circulators of the jingle, developments in Xiaojinzhuang since Jiang Qing's visit seemed upside-down and patently unfair. Divisions within villages had always existed, and the miserable lot of those unlucky enough to be classified as landlords and counterrevolutionaries (the "old blacks") had

[59] GJG:1, 10. This *shunkouliu* was not invented in Xiaojinzhuang, but at the time rhymes on the "ten ranks of people" were circulating throughout north China. Interviewee 31. The phrase "ten ranks of people" (*shi deng ren*) is quite different from the "ten types" of deportable people (*shi zhong ren*) described in Chapter 6.

[60] Perry Link and Kate Zhou, "*Shunkouliu*: Popular Satirical Sayings and Popular Thought," in *Popular China: Unofficial Culture in a Globalizing Society*, ed. Perry Link, Richard P. Madsen, and Paul G. Pickowicz (Lanham, MD: Rowman & Littlefield, 2002), 89, 91.

been a constant since the 1950s.[61] Yet the village's rise to national fame heralded a disturbing new development. Not only had life been disrupted by an endless stream of urban cadres and tourists; villagers whose main talent was farming, not opera singing or poetry recitation, felt denigrated and excluded.

While thousands of tourists visited Xiaojinzhuang daily during the model's high point, some outsiders stayed on for longer periods. At one point, sixty or seventy outside cadres, over one hundred journalists, and more than one hundred volleyball coaches, poetry tutors, and opera teachers lived in the village.[62] Some stayed for as long as six months, earning wages and food rations and eating in a newly established cafeteria.[63] The tillers of the land who called themselves "ninth rank" villagers certainly benefited from the material improvements brought about by the colonization and occupation of their home, but they had to deal with constant disruptions. Tianjin authorities installed experimental drip irrigation systems on 170 acres of surrounding land and lavished fertilizer on the village, but when it came time to harvest, many young villagers were too busy receiving guests and could not work the fields.[64] The brigade decreed that members of the propaganda team were exempt from agricultural labor, and an army unit was sent in to help collect the harvest.[65]

If the farmers who circulated the "ten ranks" jingle heard about the front page *People's Daily* article celebrating how Xiaojinzhuang's campaign to criticize Lin Biao and Confucius had spurred agricultural production and led to a bumper harvest, they must have found fodder for more subversive verses. The October 1974 piece trumpeted the notion that cultural advances supposedly lead to improvement in material life, but everyone in the village knew that the harvest required outside assistance in order to take place at all.[66] Songs and poetry were supreme, but the details of agricultural production were an afterthought, not a result of Xiaojinzhuang's "advanced superstructure." As a model village, Xiaojinzhuang was required to have yearly bumper harvests and the appearance of agricultural abundance. But a model village featuring only sweating farmers toiling around the clock would have been boring and at

[61] On the long-term scapegoating of rural "class enemies," see Friedman, Pickowicz, and Selden, *Chinese Village, Socialist State*, xx, 270.

[62] GJG:1, 10; GJG:2, 12.

[63] GJG:2, 12.

[64] GJG:1, 11.

[65] Interviewee 29; Interviewee 30; GJG:1, 10–11.

[66] RMRB, October 28, 1974, 1.

odds with the point Jiang Qing and her Tianjin allies wanted to make. In their vision, villagers had to be portrayed as the source of creativity and positive knowledge. No matter that farm work required real investments of time and energy. Why not just call in the troops to take care of it?

Some residents of the village felt that stars like women's leaders Zhou Kezhou and Wang Xian had let their suddenly acquired fame go to their heads. A sent-down youth from Tianjin who moved into the village with seven of her high-school classmates in October 1974 remembered that Wang Xian's imperious and tough manner of speaking scared other villagers.[67] Baodi cadre Hu Penghua was horrified at how arrogant certain village cadres had become, ordering others around and seeking personal benefits. "I was behind the scenes," Hu said. "I wrote the articles but who got the credit? They did! They weren't mentally prepared to be big stars. It was like they'd drunk half a *jin* of liquor."[68] At one meeting Hu criticized Zhou Kezhou for circumventing proper channels to obtain rationed wood for a new house. Shortly thereafter he requested to be transferred out of the village. The friction that arose after his carefully groomed test point became a national model had become too painful for Hu to bear.

It may not have been the intent of the Tianjin-based managers of the Xiaojinzhuang model to sow discord among rural residents and to devalue farm work, but that was the end result of their show. Disgruntled villagers accustomed to being looked down on by urbanites made light of their plight by circulating wry jingles, but the irony of being nationally celebrated as an advanced model village while suffering new humiliations must have stung. The officially sanctioned cultural achievements seemed ridiculous and exclusive to those who witnessed the occupation of their village, so they made up their own lines and made the best of the situation. Those dissatisfied with the state of affairs must have known that it could not last forever. Indeed, payback time came after Jiang Qing's arrest, when humbled former members of the propaganda team returned to the fields. Even into the early 1980s, farmers who had classified themselves into the "ninth rank" made a gleeful show of carefully supervising the ex-stars' every swing of the hoe.[69]

Neighboring villagers also relished Xiaojinzhuang's downfall. The only thing worse than being in a model village was living right next to one.

[67] Interviewee 33.
[68] Interviewee 31.
[69] GJG:1, 14.

A man who lived near Xiaojinzhuang remembered that his village had to start a political night school after Jiang Qing's visit. Farmers there memorized and recited Mao's quotations at night after toiling in the fields, not as fortunate as Xiaojinzhuang's agriculture-exempt propagandists.[70] More than thirty-four hundred political night schools were established in the Tianjin suburbs after Xiaojinzhuang became famous.[71] These night schools served as safety valves for local officials required to follow their neighbor's example. If superiors asked, village cadres could report on the glorious advances of their own political night school, but after Xiaojinzhuang fell the schools quickly disappeared. In 1977, when Xiaojinzhuang residents like former vice-party secretary Wang Tinghe ventured outside the village, they faced snide comments from put-upon neighbors: "Oh, you're from Xiaojinzhuang? Why don't you sing or read some poetry?"[72]

When Xiaojinzhuang was riding high, other rural Baodi residents felt a mixture of envy and fear about their neighbors' soaring stature. Some attempted to capitalize on the Xiaojinzhuang brand name. Before Xiaojinzhuang became a model, the main access to the village was by boat across the Jian'gan river. To handle the huge influx of tourists in 1974, the state allocated funds for a new bridge. Laborers from around the Tianjin region came to build the bridge and after completing the job each worker received a commemorative shirt. The top half of the shirt displayed "Xiaojinzhuang" in three large characters, while the bottom half read "bridge-building souvenir" (*xiuqiao liunian*) in smaller script. These flashy shirts were a coveted prize for some workers. The bridge builders tucked their new shirts deeply into their pants, concealing the part identifying the shirt as a souvenir. They then went to Tianjin, where they swaggered and blustered behind the Xiaojinzhuang brand name, acting so intimidating that others dared not question them.[73]

For the workers who built the bridge to Xiaojinzhuang, the three Chinese characters making up the village's name connoted power and status. By wearing new costumes and acting tough back in the city, the workers enacted roles quite at odds with the official script lauding Xiaojinzhuang as a happy pantheon of advanced culture and gender equality. Yet at

[70] Interviewee 29.
[71] GJG:1, 13.
[72] Ibid.
[73] GJG:2, 12. According to journalist Gao Jianguo, Wang Tinghe's point in telling this story was to show that Xiaojinzhuang indeed made mistakes but that much of its bad reputation came from people outside the village.

the same time, the tucked-in wannabes were unintentionally engaged in a wholly accurate form of model emulation. In fact, the bridge builders had leapt beyond the showy froth of model propaganda and grasped its essence – Xiaojinzhuang meant power in the city. Far from emulating Wang Zuoshan or other model villagers, the workers proudly strutting their association with Xiaojinzhuang back in the city were excellent copies of Jiang Qing, Wu Dai, Wang Mantian, and Xie Xuegong. Urban political elites had constructed a rural paradise; Tianjin workers had built a bridge. But both groups used their ties to an idealized, concocted rural China in order to strengthen their own agendas – and egos – in Tianjin.

Xiaojinzhuang's Audience: Consumers, Tourists, and Copycats

The Tianjin bridge builders actively utilized Xiaojinzhuang's reputation for their own purposes, but most people who read or heard about the village were more passive cultural consumers. Their concern was figuring out the message behind the model. What, then, did Xiaojinzhuang mean to its audience throughout China? How aware was the public of the model's concocted nature? The reactions of cultural consumers, revolutionary tourists, and potential emulators varied according to their vantage points and the prevailing political winds. While the producers of the drama were primarily based in large cities and the model's stars hailed from the countryside, the show's intended audience was both rural and urban. Media coverage urged rural cadres to learn from Xiaojinzhuang's opera and poetry. Propaganda also provided clues to city dwellers about the relative influence of Jiang Qing and her allies. Most of Xiaojinzhuang's audience never set foot in the village, but read about it from afar or viewed it on television. People familiar with the political use of model units knew not to accept articles at face value.

Daily newspapers were the best source for decoding shifting messages about Xiaojinzhuang and its links to national politics. After Jiang Qing's first visit, a trickle of reports on the village gave way to a cascade of references. Thirty articles mentioning Xiaojinzhuang appeared in *People's Daily* in late 1974, including eight front page pieces exclusively dedicated to political education, poetry, women's equality, and opera singing. In 1975, Xiaojinzhuang's media prominence first soared but then dropped off entirely. Newspaper readers could have correctly concluded that the model and its sponsors had fallen into political disfavor. Sixty-two *People's Daily* pieces referring to Xiaojinzhuang appeared before June, but as the year progressed, Deng Xiaoping took control of government tasks, Mao criticized his wife for her political activities, and Xiaojinzhuang's national exposure dwindled to zero. During the four-month period between August 26 and December 26, 1975, the village vanished completely from the pages of China's main newspaper. Xiaojinzhuang residents wondered what had happened to so thoroughly stifle their village's year-old fame. At first they had no idea that Deng Xiaoping's distaste for Jiang Qing's rural model was behind the silence. Had the curtain fallen for good on the Xiaojinzhuang show, or was the media silence simply a long intermission?

The answer partly depended on the outcome of the political battle between radicals like Jiang Qing and moderates represented by Deng Xiaoping. The ailing Mao Zedong, however, played a decisive role in creating the political atmosphere necessary for Xiaojinzhuang's return to national prominence. Mao's comments about art and literature, along with the general trend of moderation in mid-1975, helped banish Xiaojinzhuang to temporary obscurity. In July, Mao complained to Deng Xiaoping about the paucity of artistic offerings. "There are too few model dramas, and if people make even small mistakes they are struggled against," he said. "There are no novels or poetry."[74] We do not know whether Mao ever read the large-type anthology of Xiaojinzhuang's poems that Jiang Qing arranged to have printed for his ailing eyes – if he did, he must not have considered it genuine poetry.[75] Xiaojinzhuang stayed invisible until Mao decided that Deng's policies, including his proposals on reforming industry, developing science and technology through borrowing from abroad, and reviving higher education, had gone too far in rolling back the Cultural Revolution.[76] Mao approved a new campaign attacking Deng in late 1975, and the curtain rose on Xiaojinzhuang's strident second act. Thanks to shifting elite politics, the rural cultural utopia morphed into an anti-Deng Xiaoping model.

People's Daily readers who had forgotten Xiaojinzhuang received a blunt reminder on December 27, 1975. A front page article declared, "Everyone's familiar with Xiaojinzhuang, an advanced model. Many concerned people are asking, 'What new changes have occurred in Xiaojinzhuang?'"[77] The model was back with a vengeance and recovered

[74] Mao also complained to Jiang Qing, "we are lacking in poetry, novels, prose, and literary criticism." MWG, vol. 13 (1998), 443, 446.

[75] Baodi qu dang'anguan, *Xiaojinzhuang "dianxing" shimo* [Xiaojinzhuang as a model from start to finish] (Unpublished draft manuscript, 2004), 39.

[76] Meisner, *Mao's China and After*, 401.

[77] RMRB, December 27, 1975, 1.

its position as a mainstay in the pages of *People's Daily* during 1976, the final period of primacy for Jiang Qing and her allies. Three of the year's total of eighty-two articles that referred to the village were front page screeds dedicated to Xiaojinzhuang residents' criticism of Deng Xiaoping. Twenty-four other references to Xiaojinzhuang in 1976 mentioned the village in the context of larger articles attacking Deng and proclaiming the triumph of the Cultural Revolution over its purported enemies. Readers who may have been somewhat confused about how to react to the initial 1974 coverage of Xiaojinzhuang (Should we just write poetry? Sing more often?) could make no mistake about the model's message in 1976: criticize Deng, squash any kind of market activity or agricultural sideline, and defend the glorious fruits of the Cultural Revolution from all doubters. By this time, it was clearer than ever that Xiaojinzhuang was a political tool.

The publicity blitz elicited both positive and negative reactions. Some consumers were moved to write to the village. People from at least five provinces wrote letters to Xiaojinzhuang accusing local cadres in their provinces of various infractions.[78] What kind of criticism would writers include in their correspondence to Xiaojinzhuang? They probably wrote to lament the inadequate emulation efforts of local officials back at home. This was likely a tactic to gain leverage in local power struggles by supporting what seemed to be a "Maoist" project. How better to challenge local cadres than to appeal to the mecca of rural cultural transformation itself?

Letter writing was one of the only methods for people in China to raise complaints or accuse cadres of wrongdoing during the 1970s. Likewise, an inspection tour of a model unit was one of the few chances Chinese people had to travel during the final years of the Cultural Revolution. Around one hundred thousand sightseers toured Xiaojinzhuang during 1975, and for many visitors the opportunity to leave home and view a rural theme park was refreshing.[79] Xiaojinzhuang residents working in the village's new reception office ascertained the rank and origin of each visiting group, and arranged tours accordingly.[80] Leading cadres at the county level or higher enjoyed special treatment, including meetings with the Xiaojinzhuang party branch and opera and poetry performances. Average tourists were treated to a simpler program: look around,

[78] RMRB, January 12, 1978, 3.
[79] Baodi xian zhi bianxiu weiyuanhui, *Baodi xian zhi*, 68.
[80] Ren Xizeng, "Jiang Qing shu Xiaojinzhuang de qianqian houhou," 19.

watch a film, and hear a report about the model.[81] Even this abbreviated itinerary excited city visitors, including one young Tianjin student who toured Xiaojinzhuang on an elementary school field trip. After inspecting a farmer's home and attempting to plant wheat in a nearby field, the student left the village impressed by its "advanced" design and exhilarated by the opportunity to see real farm fields.[82] For him, the rural utopia invented by Tianjin politicians was magnificent.

Other tourists approved of Xiaojinzhuang's physical appearance. The village had become a cleaner, brighter place since Jiang Qing's visit, when one writer accompanying her remembered it as "average" and "nothing special."[83] Since then, material improvements had transformed the village. A city writer who visited Xiaojinzhuang after it became a model recalled that the village lacked the "messy" qualities he expected to see in the countryside (*meiyou luan de*), and he found the poetry performance "very simple and sincere" (*hen pushi*).[84] The Xiaojinzhuang theme park's combination of rural simplicity and cleanliness catered to the tastes of city visitors. They could maintain a sense of superiority over the village's "simple farmers," without dealing with the odors or messiness that were part of agricultural life.

Rural visitors to Xiaojinzhuang who knew what life was really like back on the farm had a different experience. They knew that the whitewashed buildings, inevitable bumper crops, and hours of free time for cultural activities were impossible to attain without massive infusions of state resources. Going on a trip was still an adventure, but figuring out how to copy the model was vexing. One young woman from Wugong village in Hebei province visited Xiaojinzhuang as part of a cultural delegation in September 1974. Wang Zuoshan was "too busy" to receive her group, but as she listened to Wang Du's report on Xiaojinzhuang's poetry and singing, she fretted about how to explain its significance to her village party branch. Wugong, like other villages near Tianjin, ended up copying what it could. Political night school classes commenced, villagers wrote verses, and farmers took breaks from agricultural work to sing and listen to arias.[85]

Local models began to earn praise for studying Xiaojinzhuang during fall 1974. Villages relatively close to Xiaojinzhuang and Tianjin were the

[81] GJG:1, 10.
[82] Interviewee 35.
[83] Interviewee 34.
[84] Interviewee 36.
[85] Friedman, Pickowicz, and Selden, *Revolution, Resistance, and Reform*, 203–4.

first to receive national recognition for opening night schools, forming political theory teams, and singing opera tunes.[86] Later, units far from Tianjin became advanced "study Xiaojinzhuang" models.[87] Often the villages singled out for successfully studying Xiaojinzhuang had already been honored for copying China's most famous rural model, Dazhai. Xiaojinzhuang itself started down the road of national fame by becoming a local advanced "study Dazhai" unit. In 1964, Mao called on the nation to emulate Dazhai's collective agriculture and self-reliance.[88] Mao's elevation of Dazhai, a brigade in Shanxi's Xiyang county, gave the model a magic aura and it remained prominent throughout the Cultural Revolution, only to be briefly eclipsed by Xiaojinzhuang in late 1974 and again in early 1976.

Tension between Dazhai and Xiaojinzhuang was unavoidable. Dazhai and Xiaojinzhuang were not natural antagonists, but national politics placed them in opposition. As Edward Friedman notes, both rural models were political tools.[89] The bigger a national model got, the less control villagers had over their own destiny. Many of Xiaojinzhuang's poems lavishly praised its model predecessor, but Xiaojinzhuang's rapid rise caused friction. It was irrevocably linked to Jiang Qing, while Dazhai's message had gone through so many contortions that everyone tried to claim it as a badge of legitimacy. In 1975, Deng Xiaoping contributed to the perception that the two model villages were combatants. When Deng criticized Xiaojinzhuang for getting rich from state funds, a charge that would have been equally valid against Dazhai, he also complained, "now it's study 'small' (*Xiao*), not 'big' (*Da*)... Xiaojinzhuang does not study Dazhai."[90] Deng, in favor of private plots and agricultural modernization, appealed to his own pro-mechanization version of Dazhai to attack Jiang

[86] See RMRB, October 13, 1974, 1, for an article on Hebei's Xiong county, and RMRB, December 8, 1974, 1, for a mention of how Hebei's Zhengding county managed to study both Dazhai and Xiaojinzhuang at the same time.

[87] Propagandists awarded this label to such places as Shendaokou brigade in coastal Shandong or an army unit in Lanzhou in an informal manner, much like Xiaojinzhuang itself rose without the benefit of official directives. RMRB, July 31, 1975, 5; RMRB, May 15, 1975.

[88] Tang Tsou, Marc Blecher, and Mitch Meisner, "National Agricultural Policy: The Dazhai Model and Local Change in the Post-Mao Era," in *The Transition to Socialism in China*, ed. Mark Selden and Victor Lippit (Armonk, NY: M. E. Sharpe, 1982), 266–99.

[89] Friedman, "The Politics of Local Models," 885.

[90] Xiaojinzhuang literally means "Little Jin Village"; Dazhai means "Big Stockaded Village," RMRB, February 26, 1976, 1. Deng was blasted in 1976 for "putting the experiences of Dazhai and Xiaojinzhuang in opposition," RMRB, August 16, 1976, 3.

Qing and belittle her "spot." All of China's leaders paid lip service to Dazhai, regardless of where they fell on the political spectrum.[91]

In the end, there was room for both Dazhai and Xiaojinzhuang only while the latter's patron was politically strong enough to bolster her utopia. Dazhai lingered on as a catch-all rural model until 1980, but soon after Jiang Qing was arrested Xiaojinzhuang became an anti-model. Even after Xiaojinzhuang's final fall from grace, urban politicians and propagandists refused to let go of the village and its potent symbolism. Xiaojinzhuang's night school, once lauded as a creative fountainhead, was condemned as an institution that stifled technological innovation.[92] Rural opera singing and poetry writing no longer shone as cultural beacons, but were presented as obstacles to agriculture and scientific education.[93] Even after the tourists, journalists, and poetry coaches departed, Xiaojinzhuang remained on stage as a negative example until gradually fading from public view. This was a welcome development for many residents who resented the consequences of the village's stardom. For them, the only thing worse than being denigrated during the model's high point may have been the humiliation of living in an anti-model.

The blessed media silence after 1978 did not signal a return to normalcy for Xiaojinzhuang's ex-stars. Former leading man Wang Zuoshan struggled to adapt to a changed script. After Jiang Qing's arrest, Wang languished in detention in Baodi for almost a full year, only leaving his cell to make appearances at criticism meetings. Festering conflict in Xiaojinzhuang contributed to Wang's woes. Because his family was relatively new in the village, he lacked the longstanding lineage ties that could have softened his fall. Leaders from the dominant lineage group reportedly heaped blame on him and protected themselves.[94] Wang's party membership was suspended until 1984, when a Tianjin committee restored his status. One factor the committee cited in its decision was that "he is a farmer, after all, and is uneducated" (*ta bijing shi ge nongmin, you meiyou wenhua*).[95] Even as the relieved Wang Zuoshan celebrated this long-awaited good news, the insults continued. Wang's humbling experience with confession and self-criticism made him an adept spinner of the

[91] David Zweig, *Agrarian Radicalism in China, 1968–1981* (Cambridge, MA: Harvard University Press, 1989), 65–69.

[92] RMRB, August 12, 1978, 3.

[93] RMRB, May 21, 1978, 1; RMRB, December 11, 1978, 3.

[94] Interviewee 33.

[95] GJG:2, 6.

last official word on Jiang Qing and Xiaojinzhuang.[96] "Jiang Qing was plucking peaches," he often said, meaning that Jiang stole rural innovations and used them for her own political purposes.[97]

There is truth to this version of the story, but the Xiaojinzhuang model's rise and fall is too complicated to fit into a simple "plucking peaches" trope. The village was doomed by its subordinate position in a political system dominated by urban politicians. Yet villagers' adoption or rejection of the model script confirms that local agency endured. In 1999, Wang Zuoshan defended himself to a local visitor, saying that he had simply followed orders. "What they made me do, I did," he claimed; "What they made me say, I said."[98] Granted, Wang's position as a rural cadre pressured by Tianjin officials, coupled with his understanding of Jiang Qing as a representative of the divine Mao, put him in a difficult bind. But Wang enjoyed some tasty "peaches" too. He followed his orders with flair and was honored by appointments to the National People's Conference and Central Party Academy. Similarly, Wang Du, who would go on to run a chemical fertilizer factory in Baodi, retained fond memories of his stardom, and Wang Xian's 1975 trip to Japan as a representative of Xiaojinzhuang was a rare chance for a rural woman to travel outside of China.[99]

Tianjin leaders criticized and abandoned Xiaojinzhuang soon after Jiang Qing fell, but the decollectivization and money making of the reform era also left the village behind. In October 1991, Wang Zuoshan took a bus to Daqiuzhuang, a village near Tianjin that gained notoriety in the late 1980s and early 1990s as a model of reform. The new model's enterprises had transformed it into China's richest village, and Wang took his pilgrimage in order to ask Daqiuzhuang's leader Yu Zuomin for financial support. One wonders what Wang, who was more aware than anyone of the shaky stilts on which China's model villages were built, could have been thinking as he made his appeal. Xiaojinzhuang's one small metal processing factory had failed, Wang Zuoshan explained as Yu Zuomin listened sympathetically. Yu cut Wang a check for sixty thousand

[96] In late December 1976, *People's Daily* published an article by *Tianjin Daily* editors accusing Jiang Qing of "plucking peaches," RMRB, December 24, 1976. This article, along with "Jiang Qing yu Xiaojinzhuang" [Jiang Qing and Xiaojinzhuang], RMRB, January 12, 1978, 2, remain the official verdict about the village's model experience.

[97] Interviewee 32; Wang Yan, "Xiaojinzhuang yishi," 14.

[98] Liu Bingrong, "Wo suo zhidao de Xiaojinzhuang," 42.

[99] Baodi xian zhi bianxiu weiyuanhui, *Baodi xian zhi*, 68.

yuan, treated him to a banquet, and sent him home in a limousine.[100] Yet when Wang Zuoshan reported this development to the Baodi county party secretary, the county official, fearful of the implications of horizontal ties between individual villages, ordered that Wang return the money. Wang continued to negotiate with Daqiuzhuang and eventually succeeded in garnering financial support.

Daqiuzhuang was totally discredited in 1993, when a court sentenced Yu Zuomin to twenty years in prison for stealing state secrets, hiding criminals, and obstructing justice.[101] Xiaojinzhuang was tainted again because of its connection to its disgraced neighbor. When I visited, Xiaojinzhuang seemed lackluster, with no industry and many young people away in the cities laboring as second-class citizens. In the reform period, city officials have largely ignored Xiaojinzhuang and surrounding villages. Tourists and work teams have disappeared from the village, much to the relief of many people, but guaranteed education and health care have also vanished. It is difficult to imagine someone like Wang Zuoshan becoming a county party secretary in the reform period. A villager becoming vice premier of China – as Dazhai's leader Chen Yonggui did in 1975 – now seems out of the question. Cultural Revolution-era paeans to the gloriousness of rural China were rarely more than lip service, but for some people, lip service may have been preferable to no service.

[100] Bruce Gilley, *Model Rebels: The Rise and Fall of China's Richest Village* (Berkeley: University of California Press, 2001), 106–7.

[101] Yu Zuomin died in 1999; Gilley, *Model Rebels*, 177–78.

Epilogue

On a recent visit to Beijing, I was walking across a pedestrian overpass when an elderly woman from the countryside approached me and asked for money. A well-dressed middle-aged man quickly intervened. He pushed the woman aside violently, told her she was making China look bad, and apologized to me on her behalf. My first thought was that it was not the rural woman whose behavior looked bad. Whenever we see such signs of rural-urban discrimination and inequality in today's China, we are seeing a product of the Mao period. The imprint of Mao's revolutionary modernization project becomes visible when city people like the man on the overpass feel embarrassed by rural people, when city governments bulldoze schools for the children of migrant workers, and when urban management officials (*chengguan*) bully and confiscate property from street peddlers.[1] It can also be seen in a university admission process skewed in favor of urban children, in the struggles of peasants to obtain decent medical care, and, until recently, in the unequal representation for rural deputies in China's National People's Congress.[2]

[1] On *chengguan*, see Austin Ramzy, "Above the Law? China's Bully Law-Enforcement Officers," *Time*, May 21, 2009, http://www.time.com/time/world/article/0,8599,1899773,00.html.

[2] Municipalities and provinces set quotas for local students, giving urban applicants a leg up in testing into universities, almost all of which are in cities. See "China Begins to Reform Its Controversial College-Entrance Exam," *Chronicle of Higher Education*, June 7, 2010, http://chronicle.com/article/China-Begins-to-Reform-Its/65804/. For a poignant story of a rural family's attempt to get treatment for a sick child, see Peter Hessler, "Kindergarten," *New Yorker* 80, no. 7 (April 5, 2004): 58–67. Before the National People's Congress amended the electoral law in March 2010 to mandate equally weighted representation for rural and urban deputies, rural deputies represented a population four times that of

In December 2008, China celebrated the "thirtieth anniversary of reform and opening up," meaning that the reform period had lasted longer than the Mao era. In many ways, China's history since 1978 has been as dynamic, diverse, and tumultuous as the history of the Mao years. Some social scientists tend to assume that recent developments in China are wholly new and have little to do with the Mao era. But as Timothy Cheek, Sebastian Heillman, and Elizabeth J. Perry argue, the habits, practices, and structures of the Mao period have shaped almost every aspect of contemporary China, including discourse, interpersonal relations, governance, and the gap between city and countryside.[3] The continuing salience of the rural-urban divide in the twenty-first century is a testament to the enduring legacy of Mao's revolutionary modernization project. But the Maoist period was so complex and fraught with tensions that when it comes to the gap between city and countryside, it is more accurate to speak of multiple legacies rather than a single inheritance. These legacies include the overlapping themes of inequality, interaction, and development.

The unequal incomes, rights, and benefits enjoyed by urban and rural residents today are the most striking and painful consequence of the policies and practices of the Mao years. During the Mao period, revolutionary modernization's institutional underpinnings (household registration and food rationing) and political hierarchy (cities at the top) disadvantaged rural China. This was not Mao's intention. It resulted instead from a spiraling series of contingent decisions and reactions beginning with the takeover of cities in 1949 and followed by the First Five-Year Plan, the Great Leap Forward, downsizing during the early 1960s, the Four Cleanups, the sent-down youth movement, the Cultural Revolution, and the third front. Martin King Whyte is therefore correct in stating that the relationship between the Mao period and reform era should not be viewed as socialist-style equality followed by capitalist-style inequality, but that "the actual trend looks much more like descent into serfdom for rural residents in the Mao era, with only partial liberation from those

urban deputies (in 1995, the ratio changed from 8:1 to 4:1), leading some to say that "four peasants equal one city person." See RMRB, March 15, 2010, 16.

[3] Timothy Cheek, *Living with Reform: China Since 1989* (New York: Zed Books, 2006), 32–73; Elizabeth J. Perry, "Studying Chinese Politics: Farewell to Revolution?" *China Journal* 57 (January 2007): 1–22; Sebastian Heilmann and Elizabeth J. Perry, "Embracing Uncertainty: Guerrilla Policy Style and Adaptive Governance," in *Mao's Invisible Hand: The Political Foundations of Adaptive Governance in China*, ed. Sebastian Heilmann and Elizabeth J. Perry (Cambridge, MA: Harvard University Press, 2011), 1–29.

bonds in the reform era." In fact, as Whyte writes, anti-rural discrimination and inequality during the reform period can be directly attributed to the "two-caste system" built under Mao.[4]

The *hukou* system established in the 1950s is still in place. In spite of periodic challenges and piecemeal reforms, it appears that household registration will remain in force for the foreseeable future.[5] When the Mao-era food rationing regime was dismantled in the 1980s, however, it became much easier for rural migrants to survive in cities, even if they lacked non-agricultural *hukou*. Millions of villagers moved to China's urban centers.[6] But it is incorrect to assume that the massive migrations of the reform period meant that rural and urban people were meeting for the first time in thirty years. City-dwellers and villagers interacted regularly during the Mao period for work and family reasons and also during political campaigns. These interactions left a mixed legacy.

Under Mao, pro-rural rhetoric about transforming the countryside and studying advanced model villages obscured the systemic inequalities that shaped interactions between peasants and urbanites. When revolution was abandoned in favor of all-out modernization after 1978, pro-peasant paeans became unnecessary and even embarrassing. Many urban intellectuals blamed the excesses of the Mao period on "feudal thought" and "peasant consciousness" emanating from the countryside.[7] This antirural backlash made it perfectly acceptable to openly insult "backward" peasants. Because city dwellers had become accustomed to seeing the countryside as a source of guaranteed grain rations, a dumping ground for political enemies, or simply a "problem," it seemed natural that rural China should remain subordinate and that villagers should not enjoy

[4] Whyte, "The Paradoxes of Rural-Urban Inequality in Contemporary China," 5. On anti-rural discrimination in the reform period, see John Myers Flower, "Portraits of Belief: Constructions of Chinese Cultural Identity in the Two Worlds of City and Countryside in Modern Sichuan Province" (PhD diss., University of Virginia, 1997); and Lei Guang and Fanmin Kong, "Rural Prejudice and Gender Discrimination in China's Urban Job Market," in Whyte, *One Country, Two Societies*, 241–64.

[5] On the continuing relevance of household registration, see Kam Wing Chan and Will Buckingham, "Is China Abolishing the *Hukou* System?" *China Quarterly* 195 (2008): 582–606; and Wang, "Renovating the Great Floodgate."

[6] Two of the best works about the challenges facing rural migrants are Leslie T. Chang, *Factory Girls: From Village to City in a Changing China* (New York: Spiegel & Grau, 2008); and Tiantian Zheng, *Red Lights: The Lives of Sex Workers in Postsocialist China* (Minneapolis: University of Minnesota Press, 2009).

[7] John Myers Flower, "Peasant Consciousness," in *Post-Socialist Peasant? Rural and Urban Constructions of Identity in Eastern Europe, East Asia, and the Former Soviet Union*, ed. Pamela Leonard and Deema Kaneff (New York: Palgrave, 2002), 44–72.

equal rights. Since the state had treated peasants as second-class citizens before 1978, it made sense to continue to treat them as inferiors when some moved to cities in the reform period.

Not all interactions between urban and rural people since 1949, however, have been characterized by discrimination or negativity. There were plenty of opportunities for peasants and city people to cooperate or to become friends in the Mao period. Wei Rongchun, who migrated from his village to Tianjin in the 1950s before being downsized in the early 1960s, is a good example. Back in the village, Wei's city experience served him well before and after 1978 as he used his connections to urban friends to obtain scarce materials for rural industry.

Positive exchanges went in both directions. After 1978, some city people who had interacted with villagers during the Mao period also drew on their experiences in positive ways. Sent-down youth gather for reunions, travel to the countryside to visit old friends, and even offer gifts or development assistance to villages.[8] Many urbanites who spent time in villages as sent-down youth or even as deportees in the 1960s or 1970s have retained an awareness of village life and a sympathy for rural issues.[9] Their memories of rural China are often bittersweet and sometimes condescending. But when it comes to addressing rural-urban inequality today, former sent-down youths' previous interactions with rural people could be an important resource, especially compared with younger generations who have never set foot in a village or spoken with a peasant.

China's next leader Xi Jinping, for example, has made no secret of how his six years as a sent-down youth in a Shaanxi village during the Cultural Revolution shaped his "pragmatic thinking" and gave him the "courage to take on any challenge."[10] Xi has drawn on his rural experience to bolster his political capital while ascending the Communist Party's

[8] For an example of reunions and friendship, see Naihua Zhang, "In a World Together Yet Apart: Urban and Rural Women Coming of Age in the Seventies," in Zhong, Wang, and Bai, *Some of Us: Chinese Women Growing Up in the Mao Era*, 1–26. In 1999, an internally published book commemorating the experiences of sent-down Tianjin youth in Inner Mongolia included an "Inner Mongolia Investment Guide" for former sent-down youth who hoped to give back to the region in the reform period; Yuan fu Neimenggu Tianjin zhiqing lianyihui, *Tianjin zhiqing fu Neimenggu sanshi zhou nian jishi* [Record of the thirty-year anniversary of Tianjin educated youth who went to Inner Mongolia] (N.p., 1999), 251–56.

[9] Interviewee 14, interviewee 15, interviewee 37.

[10] Edward Wong and Jonathan Ansfield, "China Grooming Deft Politician as Next Leader," *New York Times*, January 23, 2011, A1; Edward Wong, "Tracing the Myth of a Chinese Leader to Its Roots," *New York Times*, February 17, 2011, A8.

leadership ladder,[11] but it remains to be seen whether his governing and developmental priorities will be affected by his time in the countryside.

The rural-urban gap under Mao has had a profound effect on economic development since 1978. This legacy is also mixed. Urban industrial development, consistently emphasized under Mao, has remained a priority in the reform period. The repudiation of revolutionary class struggle meant the end of policies intended to shrink the gap between city and countryside.[12] By 1978, the chasm was already quite wide: urban per capita incomes were 2.6 times higher than rural incomes (and this number does not include the non-monetary benefits of urban residency, including free or subsidized housing, food, health care, and education). In the new millennium, according to economist Barry Naughton, the rural-urban divide has ballooned. By 2002, urban residents were earning more than three times what rural people made.[13]

While economic development after 1978 expanded and exacerbated the inequalities of the Mao years, China's rapid growth in the reform era would have been impossible were it not for the foundation built during the 1950s, 1960s, and 1970s. Mao and his colleagues would have been aghast to learn that their policies laid the groundwork for China's capitalist takeoff. But in fact, as Naughton has pointed out, after three decades of state investments in rural education and health care, "Chinese people were healthier and better educated at the end of the Socialist era." This healthy, literate "human capital base" that had acquired "basic industrial skills" under Mao would become a huge economic asset during the reform period.[14]

[11] In 2008, Xi wrote a letter to the party branch in the village where he had lived as a sent-down youth, urging cadres to lead the "masses to achieve success through self-reliance, cooperation, and hard work." See "Xi Jinping gei Shaanxi Yanchuan Liangjiahe cun fu xin, guli yindizhiyi gaohao kaifa xiangmu" [Xi Jinping writes back to Liangjiahe village in Shaanxi's Yanchuan region, encouraging a development program that is suited to local conditions], *Zhongguo gongchandang xinwen wang*, July 31, 2008, http://cpc.people.com.cn/GB/64093/64387/7592059.html.

[12] It is an oversimplification to assume that policies have been consistent or that rural-urban inequality has followed a linear trend during the more than three decades of reform. In fact, the rural-urban income gap actually shrunk during the early and mid-1980s before growing rapidly after 1990. Terry Sicular, Yue Ximing, Björn A. Gustaffson, and Li Shi, "How Large Is China's Rural-Urban Income Gap?" in Whyte, *One Country, Two Societies*, 109. See also Yasheng Huang, *Capitalism with Chinese Characteristics: Entrepreneurship and the State* (New York: Cambridge University Press, 2008).

[13] Naughton, *The Chinese Economy*, 133.

[14] Ibid., 82.

Another unintended consequence of the Mao era was that more than two decades of privation in communes taught peasants to expect no help from the city. To survive during the collective era, villagers had to rely on themselves, be resourceful, and bend rules, as evidenced by rural cadres who refused to accept deportees during the Cultural Revolution and by farmers in Gengle who grabbed what they could from the Tianjin Ironworks. Such survival skills served villagers well after restraints on migration and private business were lifted in the 1980s and 1990s. Even though the countryside is still at the bottom of China's political and economic hierarchy today, it should come as no surprise when rural people find ways to successfully negotiate the rural-urban divide in years to come.

Appendix

List of Interviewees

Unless otherwise indicated, all interviews were conducted in person in 2004 and 2005. When available, I have indicated individuals' birthplaces and official class backgrounds. In the main text, all but two of the interviewees' names have been changed.

Interviewee 1. Male, born in 1934 in Baodi county, lower-middle peasant, interviewed in Baodi.

Interviewee 2. Male, born in 1932 in Wuqiao county (Hebei), upper-middle peasant, interviewed in Tianjin.

Interviewee 3. Female, born in 1934 in Raoyang county (Hebei), interviewed in Tianjin.

Interviewee 4. Male, born in 1938 in Baodi county, interviewed in Baodi.

Interviewee 5. Female, born in 1928, interviewed in Baodi.

Interviewee 6. Male, born in 1933, worker, interviewed in Tianjin.

Interviewee 7. Male, born in 1928, poor peasant, interviewed in Jinghai county.

Interviewee 8. Male, born in 1930, interviewed in Jinghai county.

Interviewee 9. Female, born in the 1940s, interviewed in Jinghai county.

Interviewee 10. Male, born in the 1930s, interviewed in Jinghai county.

Interviewee 11. Male, born in 1930 in Tianjin, underground party member, interviewed in Tianjin.

Interviewee 12. Male, born in 1936, born in Tianjin's south suburbs, urban poor (*chengshi pinmin*), interviewed in Tianjin.

Interviewee 13. Male, born in 1946 in Tianjin, urban staff (*chengshi zhiyuan*), interviewed in Baodi.

Interviewee 14. Male, born in the 1940s in Tianjin, interviewed in Tianjin.

Interviewee 15. Male, born in 1954 in Tianjin, capitalist, interviewed in Tianjin.

Interviewee 16. Male, born in 1946 in Tianjin, worker, interviewed at the Worker-Peasant Alliance State Farm.

Interviewee 17. Male, born in 1938 in a village near Baoding (Hebei), middle peasant, interviewed in Tianjin.

Interviewee 18. Male, born in 1929, middle peasant, interviewed in Gengle.

Interviewee 19. Male, born around 1952, interviewed in Tianjin.

Interviewee 20. Male, born in 1954, worker, interviewed in Tianjin.

Interviewee 21. Male, born in the 1940s, interviewed at the Tianjin Ironworks.

Interviewee 22. Female, born around 1952, interviewed in Tianjin.

Interviewee 23. Male, born in 1965 in Shexian (Hebei), lower-middle peasant, interviewed in Shexian.

Interviewee 24. Male, born in 1961, poor peasant, interviewed in Gengle.

Interviewee 25. Male, born in 1944 in Yangwuzhuang, lower-middle peasant, interviewed in Tianjin.

Interviewee 26. Male, born in 1945, self-employed (*ziyou zhiyezhe*), interviewed in Tianjin.

Interviewee 27. Male, born around 1960 in Dachang county (Hebei), interviewed at the Tianjin Ironworks.

Interviewee 28. Male, born in the 1960s in Baodi county, interviewed in Baodi in 2002.

Interviewee 29. Male, interviewed in Baodi in 2002.

Interviewee 30. Male, born in the 1950s in Baodi county, poor peasant, interviewed in Baodi in 2002 and 2003.

Interviewee 31. Male, born in 1945 in Baodi county, poor peasant, interviewed in Baodi.

Interviewee 32. Male, born in the 1930s in Baodi county, poor peasant, interviewed in Baodi in 2002 and 2003.

Interviewee 33. Female, born in the 1950s in Tianjin, interviewed in Beijing in 2003.

Interviewee 34. Male, born in 1935, interviewed in Laguna Woods, California, in 2003.

Interviewee 35. Male, born around 1960 in Tianjin, interviewed in Tianjin in 2002.

Interviewee 36. Male, interviewed via telephone in 2003.

Interviewee 37. Male, born in Tianjin in 1965, landlord, interviewed in Tianjin.

Selected Bibliography

Alexopoulos, Golfo. *Stalin's Outcasts: Aliens, Citizens, and the Soviet State, 1926–1936*. Ithaca, NY: Cornell University Press, 2003.

Ash, Robert. "Squeezing the Peasants: Grain Extraction, Food Consumption and Rural Living Standards in Mao's China." *China Quarterly* 188 (2006): 959–98.

Baodi xian zhi bianxiu weiyuanhui, ed. *Baodi xian zhi* [Baodi county gazetteer]. Tianjin: Tianjin shehui kexueyuan chubanshe, 1995.

Baum, Richard. *Prelude to Revolution: Mao, the Party, and the Peasant Question, 1962–66*. New York: Columbia University Press, 1975.

Baum, Richard, and Frederick C. Teiwes. *Ssu-Ch'ing: The Socialist Education Movement of 1962–1966*. Berkeley: Center for Chinese Studies, University of California, 1968.

Bernstein, Thomas P. "Mao Zedong and the Famine of 1959–1960: A Study in Wilfulness." *China Quarterly* 186 (2006): 421–45.

———. *Up to the Mountains and Down to the Villages: The Transfer of Youth from Urban to Rural China*. New Haven: Yale University Press, 1977.

Bo Yibo. *Ruogan zhongda juece yu shijian de huigu* [Reflections on certain major decisions and events]. 2 vols. Beijing: Zhonggong zhongyang dangxiao chubanshe, 1993.

Bowker, Geoffrey C., and Susan Leigh Star. *Sorting Things Out: Classification and Its Consequences*. Cambridge, MA: MIT Press, 1999.

Brady, Anne-Marie. *Making the Foreign Serve China: Managing Foreigners in the People's Republic*. Lanham, MD: Rowman & Littlefield, 2003.

Bramall, Chris. *In Praise of Maoist Economic Planning: Living Standards and Economic Development in Sichuan since 1931*. New York: Oxford University Press, 1993.

Cao Shuji. *Da jihuang* [Great famine]. Hong Kong: Time International, 2005.

Chan, Anita, Richard Madsen, and Jonathan Unger. *Chen Village: Revolution to Globalization*. 3rd ed. Berkeley: University of California Press, 2009.

Chan, Kam Wing. *Cities with Invisible Walls*. New York: Oxford University Press, 1994.

Chan, Kam Wing, and Will Buckingham. "Is China Abolishing the *Hukou* System?" *China Quarterly* 195 (2008): 582–606.

Chang, Jung and Jon Halliday. *Mao: The Unknown Story*. New York: Knopf, 2005.

Chang, Leslie T. *Factory Girls: From Village to City in a Changing China*. New York: Spiegel & Grau, 2008.

Cheek, Timothy. *Living with Reform: China Since 1989*. New York: Zed Books, 2006.

Chen Boda. *Chen Boda yigao: yuzhong zishu ji qita* [Manuscripts by the late Chen Boda: Accounts from prison and more]. [Hohhot]: Nei Menggu renmin chubanshe, 1999.

Chen Donglin. *Sanxian jianshe: beizhan shiqi de xibu kaifa* [Third front construction: The development of the west in the period of preparing for war]. Beijing: Zhonggong zhongyang dangxiao chubanshe, 2003.

Chen, Xiaomei. *Acting the Right Part: Political Theater and Popular Drama in Contemporary China*. Honolulu: University of Hawai'i Press, 2002.

Chen Xiaonong, comp. *Chen Boda zuihou koushu huiyi* [Chen Boda's final oral memoir]. Hong Kong: Yangguang huanqiu chuban Xianggang youxian gongsi, 2005.

Cheng, Tiejun. "The Dialectics of Control – The Household Registration (*Hukou*) System in Contemporary China." PhD diss., State University of New York at Binghamton, 1991.

Cheng, Tiejun, and Mark Selden. "The Origins and Consequences of China's Hukou System." *China Quarterly* 139 (1994): 644–68.

Cohen, Myron. "Cultural and Political Inventions in Modern China: The Case of the Chinese 'Peasant.'" *Daedalus* 122, no. 2 (1993): 151–70.

Cooper, Eleanor McCallie, and William Liu. *Grace: An American Woman in China*. New York: Soho Press, 2003.

Dangdai Zhongguo congshu bianjibu, ed. *Dangdai Zhongguo de Tianjin* [Contemporary China's Tianjin]. 2 vols. Beijing: Zhongguo shehui kexue chubanshe, 1999.

Dikötter, Frank. *Mao's Great Famine: The History of China's Most Devastating Catastrophe, 1958–1962*. New York: Walker, 2010.

Esherick, Joseph W. *Ancestral Leaves: A Family Journey through Chinese History*. Berkeley: University of California Press, 2010.

Eyferth, Jacob. *Eating Rice from Bamboo Roots: The Social History of a Community of Handicraft Papermakers in Rural Sichuan, 1920–2000*. Cambridge, MA: Harvard University Asia Center, 2009.

Feuerwerker, Yi-tsi Mei. *Ideology, Power, Text: Self-Representation and the Peasant "Other" in Modern Chinese Literature*. Stanford: Stanford University Press, 1998.

Flower, John Myers. "Peasant Consciousness." In *Post-Socialist Peasant? Rural and Urban Constructions of Identity in Eastern Europe, East Asia, and the Former Soviet Union*, edited by Pamela Leonard and Deema Kaneff, 44–72. New York: Palgrave, 2002.

______. "Portraits of Belief: Constructions of Chinese Cultural Identity in the Two Worlds of City and Countryside in Modern Sichuan Province." PhD diss., University of Virginia, 1997.

Friedman, Edward. "The Politics of Local Models, Social Transformation and State Power Struggles in the People's Republic of China: Tachai and Teng Hsiao-p'ing." *China Quarterly* 76 (1978): 873–90.

Friedman, Edward, Paul G. Pickowicz, and Mark Selden. *Chinese Village, Socialist State.* New Haven: Yale University Press, 1991.

———. *Revolution, Resistance, and Reform in Village China.* New Haven: Yale University Press, 2005.

Gao Jianguo. "Xiaojinzhuang de chenfu" [The rise and fall of Xiaojinzhuang]. Pts. 1 and 2. *Sanyue feng* 15 (February 1986): 3–17; 16 (March 1986): 6–20.

Gao, James Zheng. *The Communist Takeover of Hangzhou: The Transformation of City and Cadre, 1949–1954.* Honolulu: University of Hawai'i Press, 2004.

Gao Wangling. *Renmin gongshe shiqi Zhongguo nongmin "fan xingwei" diaocha* [An investigation into Chinese peasants' "counteraction" during the commune period]. Beijing: Zhongguo dangshi chubanshe, 2006.

Geng Chen. "Liushi niandai chuqi Tianjin shi kaifang tanfan shichang de qianqian houhou" [The whole story of opening peddlers' markets in Tianjin in the early 1960s]. *Tianjin wenshi ziliao xuanji* 79 (October 1998): 118–26, 110.

Gengle zhen zhi bianzuan weiyuanhui, ed. *Gengle zhen zhi* [Gengle town gazetteer]. Beijing: Xinhua chubanshe, 2001.

Gilley, Bruce. *Model Rebels: The Rise and Fall of China's Richest Village.* Berkeley: University of California Press, 2001.

Goodman, Byrna. *Native Place, City, and Nation: Regional Networks and Identities in Shanghai, 1853–1937.* Berkeley: University of California Press, 1995.

Guo Fengqi, ed. *Tianjin tong zhi: minzheng zhi* [Tianjin gazetteer: Civil affairs gazetteer]. Tianjin: Tianjin shehui kexueyuan, 2001.

———, ed. *Tianjin tong zhi: gongan zhi* [Tianjin gazetteer: Public security gazetteer]. Tianjin: Tianjin renmin chubanshe, 2001.

———, ed. *Tianjin tong zhi: shangye zhi, liangshi juan* [Tianjin gazetteer: Commerce gazetteer, grain volume] Tianjin: Tianjin shehui kexueyuan, 1994.

Guo Wenyu. *Guoying nongchang* [State farms]. Beijing: Chaohua meishu chubanshe, 1957.

Han, Xiaorong. *Chinese Discourses on the Peasant, 1900–1949.* Albany: State University of New York Press, 2005.

He, Jiangsui. "The Death of a Landlord: Moral Predicament in Rural China, 1968–1969." In *The Chinese Cultural Revolution as History*, edited by Joseph W. Esherick, Paul G. Pickowicz, and Andrew Walder, 124–52. Stanford: Stanford University Press, 2006.

Hebei sheng laodong ju, ed. *Jingjian zhigong daiyu wenjian huibian (1961–1966)* [Collected documents on the treatment of downsized employees, 1961–1966]. N.p., 1966.

Hebei sheng minzheng ting. *Hebei sheng xingzheng quhua biangeng ziliao, 1949–1984* [Changes in the administrative divisions of Hebei province, 1949–1984]. N.p., 1985.

Heilmann, Sebastian, and Elizabeth J. Perry. "Embracing Uncertainty: Guerrilla Policy Style and Adaptive Governance." In *Mao's Invisible Hand: The Political Foundations of Adaptive Governance in China*, edited by Sebastian Heilmann and Elizabeth J. Perry, 1–29. Cambridge, MA: Harvard University Press, 2011.

Hershatter, Gail. *The Workers of Tianjin, 1900–1949*. Stanford: Stanford University Press, 1986.

Hinton, William. *Through a Glass Darkly: U.S. Views of the Chinese Revolution*. New York: Monthly Review Press, 2006.

Huang, Yasheng. *Capitalism with Chinese Characteristics: Entrepreneurship and the State*. New York: Cambridge University Press, 2008.

Jianguo yilai Mao Zedong wengao [Mao Zedong's manuscripts since the founding of the People's Republic of China]. 13 vols. Beijing: Zhongyang wenxian chubanshe, 1987–1998.

Jin Qiu. *The Culture of Power: The Lin Biao Incident in the Cultural Revolution*. Stanford: Stanford University Press, 1999.

Jin Chongji and Chen Qun, eds. *Chen Yun zhuan* [Biography of Chen Yun]. 2 vols. Beijing: Zhongyang wenxian chubanshe, 2005.

Jinghai xian zhi bianxiu weiyuanhui, ed. *Jinghai xian zhi* [Jinghai county gazetteer]. Tianjin: Tianjin shehui kexueyuan chubanshe, 1995.

Kirkby, R. J. R. *Urbanization in China: Town and Country in a Developing Economy, 1949–2000 A.D.* New York: Columbia University Press, 1985.

Kwan, Man Bun. *The Salt Merchants of Tianjin: State-Making and Civil Society in Late Imperial China*. Honolulu: University of Hawai'i Press, 2001.

Lary, Diana. "Hidden Migrations: Movements of Shandong People, 1949–1978." *Chinese Environment and Development* 7 (1996): 56–72.

Lee, Ching Kwan and Mark Selden. "Durable Inequality: The Legacies of China's Revolutions and the Pitfalls of Reform." In *Revolution in the Making of the Modern World: Social Identities, Globalization, and Modernity*, edited by John Foran, David Lane and Andreja Zivkovic, 81–95. New York: Routledge, 2007.

Lee, Hong Yung. *From Revolutionary Cadres to Party Technocrats in Socialist China*. Berkeley: University of California Press, 1991.

Li Jingneng, ed. *Zhongguo renkou, Tianjin fence* [China's population, Tianjin volume]. Beijing: Zhongguo caizheng jingji chubanshe, 1987.

Li Xiannian zhuan bianxie zu, ed. *Li Xiannian zhuan, 1949–1992* [Biography of Li Xiannian, 1949–1992]. 2 vols. Beijing: Zhongyang wenxian chubanshe, 2009.

Li Zhisui. *The Private Life of Chairman Mao: The Memoirs of Mao's Personal Physician*. New York: Random House, 1994.

Li Zhongyuan. *Bashi shuwang* [Narrating the past at age eighty]. Tianjin: Tianjin renmin chubanshe, 1998.

Lieberthal, Kenneth. *Revolution and Tradition in Tientsin, 1949–1952*. Stanford: Stanford University Press, 1980.

Link, Perry, and Kate Zhou. "*Shunkouliu*: Popular Satirical Sayings and Popular Thought." In *Popular China: Unofficial Culture in a Globalizing Society*, edited by Perry Link, Richard P. Madsen, and Paul G. Pickowicz, 89–109. Lanham, MD: Rowman & Littlefield, 2002.

Liu Bingrong. "Wo suo zhidao de Xiaojinzhuang" [What I know about Xiaojinzhuang]. *Dangshi bolan* 6 (2002): 40–42.

Liu, Grace D. "Behind US-Made 'Bamboo Curtain': New Tientsin as Seen by an American." *China Digest* 6, no. 5 (June 14, 1949): 5–7, 19.

Liu Haiyan. *Kongjian yu shehui: jindai Tianjin chengshi de yanbian* [Space and society: The evolution of modern Tianjin]. Tianjin: Tianjin shehui kexueyuan chubanshe, 2003.

Liu Jinfeng. *Zhengrong suiyue: Liu Jinfeng huiyilu* [Extraordinary years: Liu Jinfeng's memoirs]. Tianjin: Tianjin renmin chubanshe, 2000.

Liu Pichang. "Chentong de huiyi" [Painful memories]. *Tianjin wenshi ziliao xuanji* 79 (1998): 112–17, 80.

Liu Xiaomeng et al. *Zhongguo zhiqing shidian* [Chinese educated youth encyclopedia]. Chengdu: Sichuan renmin chubanshe, 1995.

Lu, Hanchao. *Beyond the Neon Lights: Everyday Shanghai in the Early Twentieth Century*. Berkeley: University of California Press, 1999.

Lu Jinjun, Yu Xianbiao, and Zhao Jie. "Pijing zhanji dandang tiecheng weishi" [Hacking our way through difficulties, bodyguards of the iron city]. *Tansuo yu yanjiu* 3 (August 5, 1999): 204–7.

Luo Pinghan. *Da qianxi: 1961–1963 nian de chengzhen renkou jingjian* [Great migration: The downsizing of urban population, 1961–1963]. Nanning: Guangxi renmin chubanshe, 2003.

Lüthi, Lorenz. "The Vietnam War and China's Third-Line Defense Planning before the Cultural Revolution, 1964–1966." *Journal of Cold War Studies* 10, no. 1 (2008): 26–51.

MacFarquhar, Roderick. *The Origins of the Cultural Revolution: Vol. 2: The Great Leap Forward, 1958–1960*. New York: Columbia University Press, 1983.

———. *The Origins of the Cultural Revolution: Vol. 3: The Coming of the Cataclysm, 1961–1966*. New York: Columbia University Press, 1997.

MacFarquhar, Roderick, and Michael Schoenhals. *Mao's Last Revolution*. Cambridge, MA: The Belknap Press of Harvard University Press, 2006.

Mann, Susan. "Urbanization and Historical Change in China." *Modern China* 10, no. 1 (1984): 79–113.

Meisner, Maurice. *Mao's China and After: A History of the People's Republic*. 3rd ed. New York: Free Press, 1999.

Milton, David, and Nancy Milton. *The Wind Will Not Subside: Years in Revolutionary China, 1964–1969*. New York: Pantheon Books, 1976.

Naughton, Barry. *The Chinese Economy: Transitions and Growth*. Cambridge, MA: MIT Press, 2007.

———. "The Third Front: Defence Industrialization in the Chinese Interior." *China Quarterly* 115 (1988): 351–86.

Perry, Elizabeth J. "Studying Chinese Politics: Farewell to Revolution?" *China Journal* 57 (2007): 1–22.

Potter, Sulamith Heins, and Jack M. Potter. *China's Peasants: The Anthropology of a Revolution*. New York: Cambridge University Press, 1990.

Quan Yanchi. *Tianjin shizhang* [Tianjin mayor]. Beijing: Zhonggong zhongyang dangxiao chubanshe, 1993.

Ran Huaizhou. *Jianshezhe* [Builders]. Tianjin: Tianjin renmin chubanshe, 1974.

Ren Xizeng. "Jiang Qing shu Xiaojinzhuang de qianqian houhou" [The whole story of Jiang Qing establishing Xiaojinzhuang]. *Guoshi yanjiu cankao ziliao* 1 (1996): 18–20.

Renmin chubanshe ziliao shi. *Pipan ziliao: Zhongguo Heluxiaofu Liu Shaoqi fangeming xiuzhengzhuyi yanlun ji* [Materials for criticism: Collection of counterrevolutionary revisionist utterances by China's Khruschev Liu Shaoqi, June 1958–July 1967]. Beijing: Renmin chubanshe ziliao shi, 1967.

Rittenberg, Sidney, and Amanda Bennett. *The Man Who Stayed Behind*. Durham, NC: Duke University Press, 2001.

Rogaski, Ruth. *Hygienic Modernity: Meanings of Health and Disease in Treaty-Port China*. Berkeley: University of California Press, 2004.

Rowe, William T. *Hankow: Commerce and Society in a Chinese City, 1796–1889*. Stanford: Stanford University Press, 1984.

Schmalzer, Sigrid. *The People's Peking Man: Popular Science and Human Identity in Twentieth-Century China*. Chicago: The University of Chicago Press, 2008.

Schoenhals, Michael. "Consuming Fragments of Mao Zedong: The Chairman's Final Two Decades at the Helm." In *A Critical Introduction to Mao*, edited by Timothy Cheek, 110–28. New York: Cambridge University Press, 2010.

______. "Cultural Revolution on the Border: Yunnan's 'Political Frontier Defence' (1969–1971)." *Copenhagen Journal of Asian Studies* 19 (2004): 27–54.

______. "The Global War On Terrorism as Meta-Narrative: An Alternative Reading of Recent Chinese History." *Sungkyun Journal of East Asian Studies* 8, no. 2 (2008): 179–201.

Scott, James C. *Seeing Like a State: How Certain Schemes to Improve the Human Condition Have Failed*. New Haven: Yale University Press, 1998.

Shapiro, Judith. *Mao's War against Nature: Politics and the Environment in Revolutionary China*. New York: Cambridge University Press, 2001.

Sheehan, Brett. *Trust in Troubled Times: Money, Banks, and State-Society Relations in Republican Tianjin*. Cambridge, MA: Harvard University Press, 2003.

Shi Zhirui. "Tiantie jianchang zhichu de huiyi" [Memories of establishing the Tianjin Ironworks]. *Tansuo yu yanjiu*, no. 3 (August 5, 1999): 302–4.

Smith, S. A. "Fear and Rumour in the People's Republic of China in the 1950s." *Cultural and Social History* 5 (2008): 269–88.

______. *Revolution and the People in Russia and China: A Comparative History*. New York: Cambridge University Press, 2008.

______. "Talking Toads and Chinless Ghosts: The Politics of Rumor in the People's Republic of China, 1961–65." *American Historical Review* 111, no. 2 (2006): 405–27.

Solinger, Dorothy J. *Contesting Citizenship in Urban China: Peasant Migrants, the State, and the Logic of the Market*. Berkeley: University of California Press, 1999.

Song Yongyi, ed. *Zhongguo wenhua da geming wenku* [Chinese Cultural Revolution database]. Hong Kong: Xianggang Zhongwen daxue Zhongguo yanjiu fuwu zhongxin, 2002. CD-ROM.

Su, Yang. "Mass Killing in the Cultural Revolution: A Study of Three Provinces." In *The Chinese Cultural Revolution as History*, edited by Joseph W. Esherick, Paul G. Pickowicz, and Andrew Walder, 96–123. Stanford: Stanford University Press, 2006.

Sulian de guoying nongchang [Soviet state farms]. Beijing: Shidai chubanshe, 1956 [1953].

Terrill, Ross. *Madame Mao: The White Boned Demon*. Rev. ed. Stanford: Stanford University Press, 1999.

Thaxton, Ralph A. *Catastrophe and Contention in Rural China: Mao's Great Leap Forward Famine and the Origins of Righteous Resistance in Da Fo Village*. New York: Cambridge University Press, 2008.

Thurston, Anne F. *Enemies of the People*. New York: Alfred A. Knopf, 1987.

Tianjin gongnong lianmeng nongmuchang shizhi bangongshi. *Gongnong lianmeng nongchang shi* [History of the worker-peasant alliance farm]. N.p., Tianjin, 1992.

Tianjin renmin chubanshe, ed. *Xiaojinzhuang shige xuan* [Xiaojinzhuang poetry anthology]. Tianjin: Tianjin renmin chubanshe, 1974.

Tianjin shi dang'anguan, ed. *Jiefang chuqi Tianjin chengshi jingji hongguan guanli* [Tianjin city macroeconomic management in the initial stage after liberation]. Tianjin: Tianjin shi dang'an chubanshe, 1995.

———, ed. *Jindai yilai Tianjin chengshihua jincheng shilu* [Record of the process of urbanization in modern Tianjin]. Tianjin: Tianjin renmin chubanshe, 2005.

———, ed. *Tianjin diqu zhongda ziran zaihai shilu* [Record of major natural disasters in the Tianjin region]. Tianjin: Tianjin renmin chubanshe, 2005.

Tianjin shi Jinnan qu difang zhi bianxiu weihuanhui, ed. *Jinnan qu zhi* [Jinnan district gazetteer]. Tianjin: Tianjin shehui kexueyuan chubanshe, 1999.

Tianjin shi nongcun hezuo zhi fazhan shi bianji bangongshi, ed. *Tianjin shi nongcun hezuo zhi dashiji: 1949–1987* [Chronology of the Tianjin village cooperative system, 1949–1987]. Tianjin: Tianjin shi nongye hezuo zhi fazhan shi bianji bangongshi, 1988.

———, ed. *Tianjin shi nongcun hezuo zhi dianxing shiliao xuanbian: 1949–1987* [Selected representative historical materials on the Tianjin village cooperative system, 1949–1987]. Tianjin: Tianjin shi nongye hezuo zhi fazhan shi bianji bangongshi, 1988.

———, ed. *Tianjin shi nongcun hezuo zhi fazhan jianshi, 1949–1987* [Concise history of the Tianjin village cooperative system, 1949–1987]. Tianjin: Tianjin shi nongye hezuo zhi fazhan shi bianji bangongshi, 1989.

Tianjin shi renkou pucha bangongshi, ed. *Tianjin shi renkou tongji ziliao huibian, 1949–1983* [Collected materials on Tianjin population statistics, 1949–1983]. Tianjin: Nankai daxue chubanshe, 1986.

Tianjin shi renmin zhengfu yanjiu shi, ed. *Minzheng shehui shizheng ziliao* [Municipal government materials on civil affairs and society]. [Tianjin]: 1950.

Tianjin shi xumu ju, ed. *Tianjin shi gongnong lianmeng xumuchang chuangban "zhu shitang" de jingyan* [The Tianjin Worker-Peasant Alliance Stock Farm's experience in setting up a "pig cafeteria"]. Beijing: Nongye chubanshe, 1960.

Tianjin tiantie yejin jituan youxian gongsi. *'35 licheng* [35 year course]. N.p., 2004.

———. *Tiantie jingshen tiantie ren* [Tiantie spirit, Tiantie people]. N.p., 2004.

Tsou, Tang, Marc Blecher, and Mitch Meisner. "National Agricultural Policy: The Dazhai Model and Local Change in the Post-Mao Era." In *The Transition to Socialism in China*, edited by Mark Selden and Victor Lippit, 266–99. Armonk, NY: M. E. Sharpe, 1982.

Viola, Lynne. *Peasant Rebels under Stalin: Collectivization and the Culture of Peasant Resistance*. New York: Oxford University Press, 1996.
Vogel, Ezra F. *Canton under Communism: Programs and Politics in a Provincial Capital, 1949–1968*. Cambridge, MA: Harvard University Press, 1969.
Walder, Andrew G. *Communist Neo-Traditionalism: Work and Authority in Chinese Industry*. Berkeley: University of California Press, 1986.
Walker, Kenneth R. *Food Grain Procurement and Consumption in China*. New York: Cambridge University Press, 1984.
Wan Xiaotang jinian wenji bianjizu, ed. *Wan Xiaotang jinian wenji* [Collected writings commemorating Wan Xiaotang]. Tianjin: Tianjin renmin chubanshe, 2001.
Wang, Fei-Ling. *Organizing through Division and Exclusion: China's Hukou System*. Stanford: Stanford University Press, 2005.
Wang Haiguang. "Dangdai Zhongguo huji zhidu xingcheng yu yange de hongguan fenxi" [A macroscopic analysis of the formation and evolution of contemporary China's household registration system]. *Zhonggong dangshi yanjiu* 4 (2003): 22–29.
Wang Hui. "Wo suo zhidao de 'Xiaozhan siqing.'" [What I know about 'Xiaozhan's four cleanups']. *Tianjin wenshi ziliao xuanji* 102 (2004): 197–218.
Wang Kangzhi jinian wenji bianjizu, ed. *Wang Kangzhi jinian wenji* [Collected writings commemorating Wang Kangzhi]. Tianjin: Tianjin renmin chubanshe, 2001.
Wang Nianyi. *Da dongluan de niandai* [A decade of great upheaval]. Zhengzhou: Henan renmin chubanshe, 1988.
Wang Wei and Zhao Jihua, eds. *Wuqing xian zhi* [Wuqing county gazetteer]. Tianjin: Tianjin shehui kexueyuan, 1991.
Wang Yan. "Xiaojinzhuang yishi" [Xiaojinzhuang anecdote]. *Lingdao kexue* (October 2002): 14–15.
Wang Youqin. *Wenge shounanzhe* [Victims of the Cultural Revolution]. Hong Kong: Kaifang zazhi chubanshe, 2004.
Wemheuer, Felix. "'The Grain Problem Is an Ideological Problem': Discourses of Hunger in the 1957 Socialist Education Campaign." In *Eating Bitterness: New Perspectives on China's Great Leap Forward and Famine*, edited by Kimberley Ens Manning and Felix Wemheuer, 107–29. Vancouver: University of British Columbia Press, 2011.
White, Lynn T., III. *Careers in Shanghai: The Social Guidance of Personal Energies in a Developing Chinese City, 1949–1966*. Berkeley: University of California Press, 1978.
______. "The Road to Urumchi: Approved Institutions in Search of Attainable Goals during Pre-1968 Rustication from Shanghai." *China Quarterly* 79 (1979): 481–510.
Whyte, Martin King, ed. *One Country, Two Societies: Rural-Urban Inequality in Contemporary China*. Cambridge, MA: Harvard University Press: 2010.
Whyte, Martin King and William L. Parish. *Urban Life in Contemporary China*. Chicago: University of Chicago Press, 1984.
Witke, Roxane. *Comrade Chiang Ch'ing*. Boston: Little, Brown and Company, 1977.

Wu Li and Zheng Yougui, eds. *Jiejue "san nong" wenti zhi lu – Zhongguo gongchandang "san nong" sixiang zhengce shi* [The path of solving the problem of agriculture, villages, and farmers – a history of the Chinese Communist Party's ideology and policy on agriculture, villages, and farmers]. Beijing: Zhongguo jingji chubanshe, 2004.

Xiaojinzhuang de shenke biange [Xiaojinzhuang's profound change]. Changsha: Hunan renmin chubanshe, 1975.

Xiaojinzhuang zhengzhi yexiao ban de hao [Xiaojinzhuang's political night school is good]. Beijing: Renmin chubanshe, 1974.

Xie Yan. "Chen Boda zuo'e zai Xiaozhan" [Chen Boda does evil in Xiaozhan]. *Tianjin shi zhi* 6 (2004): 15–23.

Yang, Dali L. *Calamity and Reform in China: State, Rural Society, and Institutional Change since the Great Leap Famine*. Stanford: Stanford University Press, 1996.

Yang Jisheng. "*Neican* yinfa de jundui da banjia" [The great military move triggered by *Internal Reference*]. *Yanhuang chunqiu* 3 (2011): 62–64.

Yang Kuisong. "The Sino-Soviet Border Clash of 1969." *Cold War History* 1, no. 1 (2000): 21–52.

Yang, Rae. *Spider Eaters: A Memoir*. Berkeley: University of California Press, 1997.

Yick, Joseph K. S. *Making Urban Revolution in China: The CCP-GMD Struggle for Beiping-Tianjin, 1945–1949*. Armonk, NY: M. E. Sharpe, 1995.

Yue Daiyun, and Carolyn Wakeman. *To the Storm: The Odyssey of a Revolutionary Chinese Woman*. Berkeley: University of California Press, 1985.

Zhang Huaisan jinian wenji bianjizu, ed. *Zhang Huaisan jinian wenji* [Collected writings commemorating Zhang Huaisan]. Tianjin: Tianjin renmin chubanshe, 1999.

Zhang Qingwu. "Basic Facts on the Household Registration System in China." *Chinese Economic Studies* 22, no. 1 (1988): 22–106.

Zheng, Tiantian. *Red Lights: The Lives of Sex Workers in Postsocialist China*. Minneapolis: University of Minnesota Press, 2009.

Zheng Zhiying, ed. *Tianjin shi sishiwu nian dashiji* [Forty-five year chronology of Tianjin]. Tianjin: Tianjin renmin chubanshe, 1995.

Zhong, Xueping, Wang Zheng, and Bai Di, eds. *Some of Us: Chinese Women Growing Up in the Mao Era*. New Brunswick, NJ: Rutgers University Press, 2001.

Zhonggong Hebei shengwei *Hebei siqing tongxun* bianjibu, ed. *Hebei nongcun jieji douzheng dianxing cailiao* [Representative materials on class struggle in Hebei villages]. 2 vols. N.p., February-April 1966.

Zhonggong Tianjin shiwei dangshi yanjiu shi, ed. *Chengshi de jieguan yu shehui gaizao (Tianjin juan)* [Urban takeover and social reform (Tianjin volume)]. Tianjin: Tianjin renmin chubanshe, 1998.

Zhonggong Tianjin shiwei dangshi ziliao zhengji weiyuanhui, ed. *Mao Zedong he Tianjin renmin zai yiqi* [Mao Zedong together with the people of Tianjin]. Tianjin: Tianjin renmin chubanshe, 1993.

Zhonggong Tianjin shiwei dangshi ziliao zhengji weiyuanhui, Tianjin shi dang'anguan, eds. *Tianjin jieguan shilu* [History of the takeover of Tianjin]. 2 vols. Beijing: Zhonggong dangshi chubanshe, 1991, 1994.

Zhonggong Tianjin shiwei jiaoqu siqing gongzuo zongtuan. *Shehuizhuyi jiaoyu xuexi wenjian* [Socialist education study documents]. Tianjin, January 1966.

Zhonggong Tianjin shiwei zuzhibu, Zhonggong Tianjin shiwei dangshi ziliao zhengji weiyuanhui, Tianjin shi dang'anguan, eds. *Zhongguo gongchandang Tianjin shi zuzhi shi ziliao, 1920–1987* [Materials on the history of the Tianjin CCP organization, 1920–1987]. Beijing: Zhongguo chengshi chubanshe, 1991.

Zhonggong zhongyang dangxiao dangshi jiaoyan er shi. *Zhongguo gongchandang shehuizhuyi shiqi wenxian ziliao xuanbian* [Selected documentary materials from the Chinese Communist Party's socialist period]. N.p., 1987.

———, ed. *Jianguo yilai zhongyao wenxian xuanbian* [Selected important documents since the founding of the People's Republic of China]. 20 vols. Beijing: Zhongyang wenxian chubanshe, 1992–1998.

Zhou Licheng and Li Keyi. "Liu Qingshan, Zhang Zishan tanwu an jishi" [Record of the Liu Qingshan, Zhang Zishan corruption case]. Pts. 1, 2, 3, and 5. *Tianjin shi zhi* 2 (April 2001): 37–39; 3 (June 2001): 37–38; 4 (August 2001): 38–41; 6 (December 2001): 41–42.

Zweig, David. *Agrarian Radicalism in China, 1968–1981*. Cambridge, MA: Harvard University Press, 1989.

Index

CPSIA information can be obtained
at www.ICGtesting.com
Printed in the USA
LVOW13s0917220717
542234LV00015B/309/P